100 THINGS
THE SIMPSONS
FANS
SHOULD KNOW & DO
BEFORE THEY DIE

Allie Goertz and Julia Prescott

TRIUMPH
B O O K S

Library of Congress Cataloging-in-Publication Data

Names: Goertz, Allie, author. | Prescott, Julia, author.
Title: 100 things the Simpsons fans should know & do before they die / Allie Goertz and Julia Prescott.
Other titles: One hundred things the Simpsons fans should know & do before they die | One hundred things the Simpsons fans should know and do before they die
Description: Chicago, Illinois : Triumph Books LLC, [2018]
Identifiers: LCCN 2018009771 | ISBN 9781629375311
Subjects: LCSH: Simpsons (Television program)—Miscellanea.
Classification: LCC PN1992.77.S58 G64 2018 | DDC 791.45/72—dc23
LC record available at https://lccn.loc.gov/2018009771

This book is available in quantity at special discounts for your group or organization. For further information, contact:
Triumph Books LLC
814 North Franklin Street
Chicago, Illinois 60610
(312) 337-0747
www.triumphbooks.com

Printed in U.S.A.
ISBN: 978-1-62937-531-1
Design by Patricia Frey

*This book is dedicated to Poochie,
who died on his way to his home planet.*

Contents

Foreword *by Bill Oakley and Josh Weinstein* ix

Introduction xiii

1 Homer Simpson 1

2 Read *Life In Hell* 3

3 *The Tracey Ullman Show* 6

4 Watch *The Simpsons* 8

5 Family Tree 10

6 Marge Simpson 14

7 Homer and Marge: "The Way They Was" 16

8 The Voices 18

9 Bart Simpson 22

10 Make a Prank Phone Call 24

11 Bartmania 28

12 Couch Gags 33

13 Sam Simon: Unsung Hero 35

14 Impact on Television 38

15 Go to *Simpsons* Trivia 41

16 50 Trivia Nuggets 43

17 Chalkboard Gags 49

18 First Episode: "Simpsons Roasting on an Open Fire" 51

19 Lisa Simpson 53

20 Mr. Burns 55

21 Pop Culture References 57

22 *Simpsons* Words and How to Use Them 59

23 *Simpsons* Quotes for Every Day 62

24 Itchy and Scratchy. 65

25 Treehouse of Horror 67

26 Merch 70

27 Maggie Simpson 73

28 Writers You Must Know. 75

29 Future Timelines. 77

30 How a Script Becomes an Episode 80

31 Make a Costume 83

32 The Thursday Time Slot. 86

33 Homer's Jobs. 88

34 Network Notes 94

35 Internet Message Boards 97

36 "Deep Space Homer" Controversy 98

37 Write a Song. 101

38 Watch Other Shows Created by *The Simpsons* Writers 104

39 Milestones. 107

40 Accomplishments and Awards. 109

41 Ned Flanders. 111

42 Make *Simpsons* Food 115

43 Springfield Elementary 118

44 Showrunners. 121

45 Principal Skinner. 124

46 The Controversy Over Armin Tamzarian 126

47 Milhouse Van Houten 129

48 Sign Gags 131

49 Nerds 132

50 Get a Tattoo 135

51 Ralph Wiggum 137

52 Bullies 139

53 Visit Knoxville's World's Fair 141

54 Learn "Classical Gas" 143

55 Who Shot Mr. Burns? 144

56 The Economic Value of *The Simpsons* 146

57 Smithers 148

58 *Mr. Burns, a Post-Electric Play* 151

59 The Fox Studios Lot 153

60 *The Simpsons* House 155

61 Krusty the Clown 158

62 Sideshow Bob 160

63 Predicting the Future 161

64 The Golden Years 164

65 Start a Lisa Simpson Book Club 167

66 Troy McClure 169

67 Springfield's Entertainers 174

68 The Legend of John Swartzwelder 176

69 Moe 179

70 Mix *Simpsons* Drinks 181

71 Barney 184

72 Make Art from *The Simpsons* 187

73 The Town of Springfield 189

74 Celebrity Cameos 191

75 Watch *The Problem with Apu* 193

76 The Doctors of Springfield 195

77 Play *Simpsons* Games. 197

78 Bad Guys. 201

79 Frank Grimes' Death. 202

80 Love Affairs. 204

81 Go to Simpson Land at Universal Studios. 206

82 Visit All the Springfields 209

83 Losers 211

84 Rivals 215

85 Nameless Characters 217

86 Lenny and Carl 219

87 Animation Evolution. 221

88 One-Time Characters 223

89 The Many Loves of Selma Bouvier 226

90 *Simpsons* Pets. 228

91 Directors and What They Do 230

92 *The Simpsons Movie*. 232

93 Musical Guests 235

94 Crossover Episodes 237

95 Meme'd Hams. 239

96 Controversial Moments. 241

97 Product Tie-Ins. 244

98 Explore the DVDs. 248

99 Music 250

100 Follow the Writers on Twitter. 252

Acknowledgments 255

Foreword

If you're reading this foreword, you are exactly the type of obsessive fan this book was written for. We should know because we were huge fans of *The Simpsons* before we ever worked on the show. And we still have the VHS tapes of every episode we recorded on Sunday night (if we weren't taping *Mad About You* because, you know, who could resist it?) There's a lot of stuff we saved in boxes, and whenever we go through an old first draft or design packet, we discover something new, something we forgot, or something we can't believe we cut from the show. This book is a similar treasure trove of things even the most die-hard *Simpsons* fan might not know. We'd say it's exhaustive—except it won't put you to sleep like Homer at his workstation. You'll find yourself going "Sweet merciful crap! I didn't know that!" or "So Swartzwelder really does exist!" or "Aurora Borealis? At this time of year?"

Authors Allie Goertz and Julia Prescott are also fellow obsessive-to-the-point-of-being-able-to-have-an-entire-conversation-just-using-*Simpsons*-quotes-fans. And here's a *Simpsons* quotes fact: did you know that a lot of writers would fall in love with certain lines from scripts, and we'd end up quoting them nonstop in the office *before the episode even aired*? (We constantly quoted things like: "That's really more of a weekend thing, Ray" and "I certainly hope someone got fired for that blunder.") So in a way, the biggest *Simpsons* nerds were the writers themselves—though in another, more accurate way, you're a bigger nerd since you purchased this book. And this book is the ultimate glorious nerdfest (bigger even than the legendary StacyCon '94 at the San Diego Airport Hilton).

With this esteemed volume, Allie and Julia have taken advantage of a rare opportunity to show both hard work and stick-to-itiveness and have truly become the Indiana Joneseseses of *Simpsons* treasures. We've been pals with them for years since we first appeared on their awesome *Everything's Coming Up Simpsons* podcast and attended Stonecutters trivia nights at (the now sadly defunct) Meltdown Comics shop in Los Angeles. By reading this book, you are joining the community of obscure-*Simpsons*-reference-lovers, and there's no Homer around to say, "What the hell are you talking about?" (Unless, of course, you're referencing episode 4F12.)

It's a worldwide community these days, thanks to the otherwise-useless Internet (with the sole exception of Frinkiac.com—glayvin!) You can easily connect with other fans around the globe and even writers and producers of the show—as well as the two of us via @thatbilloakley and @joshstrangehill—on Twitter anytime. That's something we couldn't really do while working on the show in the mid-1990s. We were mainly writing to amuse ourselves, especially 'cause it seemed like anyone over 35 hated the show or had no idea it existed. A lot of times, we got a celebrity to guest star only because they'd say, "Oh, my grandkids like that show." Or if they had no grandkids and rudely rejected us like a certain Academy Award winner, we'd honor them by making them the co-star of *Honk If You're Horny.*

We had almost no contact with the outside world back then—except when the Northridge earthquake caused us to have to leave the office for one day, thereby delaying the first draft of "Sideshow Bob Roberts" by 24 agonizing hours. Our exposure to fandom was limited to our 9600 baud modem through which we dialed up alt. tv.simpsons to see almost every now-supposedly-classic episode derided as the "Worst Episode Ever." (We had Fox remove the modem shortly after demanding they install it.) So we really had no idea there were people out there like you who really loved the show, who were growing up on it, having it influence your sense of humor, maybe even inspiring you to write or speak out for something like Lisa, or drink a lot of alcohol—the cause of and, solution to, all of life's problems. And so, this book is for you. For us. For the real *Simpsons* fans. For everybody but Frank Grimes.

—Bill Oakley and Josh Weinstein
Former executive producers and writers of *The Simpsons*

Introduction

Hi, I'm Allie Goertz.

And I'm Julia Prescott.

And everything we do, we do because of *The Simpsons*.

If you're flipping through this book, then chances are your Sunday nights were spent camped around the TV, VHS mix tapes have been worn out from constant re-watches, and you engage in incoherent conversations that are 80 percent quotes from *The Simpsons*.

The Simpsons taught us everything: how to craft a joke; tell a compelling story; and love our imperfect brothers and sisters, mothers, and fathers, and evil twins named Hugo we keep locked in the attic. Its impact is manifold. For writers, it's comedy college; for artists, it's a front-row seat to David Silverman's master class; and for humans the world over, it's a how-to guide for maintaining a delicate balance of silly/serious sophistication that can get you through any day in your life.

The Simpsons taught us how to laugh with life's many punches, to persevere with the ambition of a thousand Lisas, and to always know that at the end of the day it's all about the family. *The Simpsons* is the great unifier that calls us all, and its lessons will live on long after the last Squishee is sold and last Snowball is crowned. It's the greatest television show ever created because it never tried being a television show. Even in 1988 its fate was fixated on so much more.

But none of this matters. I mean, don't get us wrong, of course, *The Simpsons* matters. Its standing in television history matters. Because of the writers who helped craft it, the fans who helped support it, the generations of kids and creatives who've been inspired by it for decades, it totally matters.

But this ranking of 100 things? Determining the importance of what's No. 1 or No. 42? Yeah, we can't.

We wrote this book because we saw ourselves in the show. Its references run deep within our veins like a lifetime supply of Duff beer. We wrote this book because we've experienced the unadulterated joy of shouting "Boo-urns" in the back of a high school classroom and finding our new best friends based on how many people chuckled under their breath.

We wrote this book because we'd willingly eat a jagged metal Krusty-O if it gave us just five seconds in Euro Itchy & Scratchy Land. We wrote this book because no other bit of pop culture or work of fiction has better prepared us for the world, inspired us to be better people, or taught us how to write a proper joke. We wrote this book because of Horny Marge. We wrote this book for you. This 100 things list is not so much a pyramid of dominance but rather a roundup of essential facts and fan favorites. So don't sweat the numbers and just surrender to it like it was a sweet, sweet can (or a plate of steamed hams). We're all Springfieldians here.

Author's Note

This book was not written by a thousand monkeys typing on a thousand typewriters.

1 Homer Simpson

In 2010 *Entertainment Weekly* named Homer Simpson, "the greatest character of the last 20 years," upping him into the echelon of iconic fictional fathers. It's easy to see why Homer's achieved such a strong status—there's really something for Homer in everyone. Homer can be silly, but also heartfelt; dumb, but also capable of forming a barbershop quartet; and his daily wants may ebb and flow, but his moral compass remains constant, much like the show itself.

If you're reading this book, you probably know the basics of who Homer Jay Simpson is, but given the show's decades-spanning run, how well do you know the man behind a "No Fat Chicks" T-shirt?

Let's start with the softballs and amp up to the incredibly deep cuts. Homer works as a safety inspector at the nuclear power plant in Springfield. He'll stop traffic for a pink sprinkled donut, a cold beer at Moe's, or a line of baby ducks walking across the street. He's the husband to Marge Simpson, whose love for him—despite his dopey behavior—redeems his otherwise ridiculous qualities. He's the father of Bart, Lisa, and Maggie Simpson. Despite his shortcomings and selfishness, his tenderness has always been untouchable. Over the years he's played father to a lobster named Pinchy, a pet pig named Spider-Pig, and a giant submarine sandwich he didn't have the heart to throw out despite its graying and moldy state.

He attends church, though often snoozes through sermons, and migrates to Moe's Tavern in such a predictable pattern that he takes doctor calls from its dusty landline. He's the American

Despite his proclamations in the Season 16 episode "Thank God It's Doomsday," Homer Simpson is an enduring TV character. (Fox Television Network/Photofest © Fox Television Network)

standard of a typical male in his 30s: he loves sports (one of his all-time dreams is to own the Dallas Cowboys, *not* the Denver Broncos—as he's later gifted in "You Only Move Twice"), dislikes ballet (once he discovers it doesn't include bears), and treats television with a tenderness he often withholds from most humans.

Homer's inner circle are his power plant co-workers—mainly Lenny and Carl, though a running a joke has been made on how he can't tell them apart. (He writes down "Lenny = white; Carl = black.") His best friend is Barney Gumble, who he's known since childhood and may or may not have coerced him into becoming a fall-down drunk.

Homer was named after *Simpsons* creator Matt Groening's father, Homer Groening, who himself had been named after the ancient Greek poet. "Homer originated with my goal to both amuse my real father and just annoy him a little bit," Groening said. "The only thing he had in common with Homer was a love of donuts." Homer's voiced by Dan Castellaneta and has undergone three significant design changes since his original debut in the short "Good Night" on *The Tracey Ullman Show* in 1987.

At the beginning of *The Simpsons* inception, Homer was a stern voice of reason, as Castellaneta's style was vaguely based on the actor Walter Matthau. As the show evolved, so too did the family's patriarch. Fans often dissect Homer's evolution within the show's run itself, relegating early seasons (Season 1–2) with Homer being a fatherly voice of reason. The following seasons (3-6) fixated on his foibles, and the seasons after that (7–10) transformed him into a man whose id is firmly behind the wheel, crashing into whatever chaos will provide the most pleasure.

2 Read *Life in Hell*

Long ago, in a time before the sacred word "boo-urns" had meaning, a young, brooding artist by the name of—you guessed it—Matt Groening left behind his humble Portland, Oregon, beginnings to pursue a career in the magical land of La La Land's backdrop: Hollywood, California. Like most people trying to make it in showbiz, the young Groening tried his best, failed miserably, and fell into obscurity forever. We hope you have enjoyed our book.

The End.

Well, we were possibly a little hasty earlier and would like to reaffirm our allegiance to this chapter and its human subject, Matt Groening. It may not be perfect, but it's still the best chapter on Matt Groening we have...for now. Although Groening obviously went on to create the most successful (and objectively hilarious) animated show in history, his early days weren't all sunshine and glory. The 23-year-old Groening found himself in a self-described series of "lousy jobs," ranging from dishwashing at a nursing home to clerking at the now-defunct punk record store chain, Hollywood Licorice Pizza. While working there (most likely alongside a team of squeaky voiced teens), Groening channeled his angst and disdain into his self-published comic strip *Life in Hell*, which starred the nihilistic but relatable one eared rabbit, Binky, who makes many small cameos in backdrops and short films of *The Simpsons*. *Life in Hell* broached topics of sex, angst, and rebellion and entertainingly mirrored Groening's contempt for authority and frustrations with everyday life. Although the comic would famously land him the opportunity to pitch his earliest version of *The Simpsons* to James L. Brooks, it should be celebrated independently from what doors it opened for Groening and immediately find its way onto your bookshelf.

So how do you do that? Well, if it was 1977 and you had $2, you could have bought the photocopied version outside Licorice Pizza from Groening himself. Had you purchased the first issue, you would have found Binky on the cover in a cloud of smoke saying, "What you see is what you breathe." *Too true, Binky. Too true.* Inside you would have found comic strips featuring not only Binky, Binky's estranged girlfriend Sheba, or Binky's illegitimate son Bongo—but the always funny yet sometimes painfully relatable Akbar and Jeff. Groening describes them as being "brothers or lovers...and possibly both."

The two characters were added to the strip when Groening's then-girlfriend accused him of always making the female character in an argument come across as worse. By making both characters male, it was no longer charged by gender and he got off scot-free. (Well, sorta. The couple isn't still together.) If these two Charlie Brown-looking characters look familiar to you, you may remember their cameo in the form of finger puppets aka tiny aorta fairies in "Homer's Triple Bypass." If this seems like a stretch to you, take it up with Al Jean, who explained this on the Season 4 DVD commentary.

If you're looking for a place to find *Life in Hell* in the modern era, consider starting with the compendium *Big Book of Hell*, which features a decade's worth of Groening's best work. From 1986 to 2007, there have been 14 books of hell, including *Love is Hell*, *School is Hell*, *Box Full of Hell*, and *How to Go to Hell*. That's a lotta hell! Yet inside each book are commentaries so insightful, you'd think you are in…heaven? (Sorry.) In a 1992 chapter of *Binky's Guide to Love*, we observe "The Weird World of Ambivalence," in which Binky and Sheba share the simple exchange, "I'll call you" "Whatever" surrounded by a page of thought bubbles full of both doubt and desire: "Ambivalence is that brain-in-taffy-pulling-machine sensation you get when seized by simultaneous and contradictory feelings [such as attraction and repulsion] toward a person [who is probably gripped by the same desire to say or do two opposite things]. It's part of the fun of being human, and if you're really lucky, you can find someone to share your mutual ambivalence with for the rest of your life."

Boy, it wasn't enough for the guy to create *The Simpsons*, he had to be a poet, too? It's no surprise that someone who could come up with one brilliant thing could have come up with something brilliant before it—and after it. (Looking at you, *Futurama*.) Across all Groening's work are similarities that make them a cohesive collection—not the least of which is his almost poetic love for bad characters, the Eddie Haskells of the world. As a child who was disappointed yet deeply enthralled by the bland family-oriented television he grew up on, Groening fantasized. In the BBC documentary, *My Wasted Life*, he explained, "that's what *The Simpsons* is. Bart Simpson is the son of Eddie Haskell!" Although this may be true, in many ways Bart is more the human son of Binky. That same rebellious charm that lives in Bart runs deep in *Life in Hell*, which we hope will be a part of your life, too.

3 The Tracey Ullman Show

On April 19, 1987, the Simpson family made their national television debut with a one-minute episode titled "Good Night." Long before White Walkers, the Kardashians, and fake news, variety shows were the kings of the TV landscape. Returning from movies and back to television with his brave tail between his heroic legs, executive producer James L. Brooks took triple-threat Tracey Ullman (actor/dancer/singer) under his wing and created the longest-running scripted show of all time. Technically, that last sentence is correct since *The Simpsons* is a spin-off *of The Tracey Ullman Show*.

Upon arrival, Brooks immediately hired a young Matt Groening to write a series of animated shorts about a dysfunctional American family, which were animated by Klasky Csupo. The shorts would serve as bumpers between sketches and commercial breaks in Seasons 1 and 2 and were subsequently expanded to full segments for Season 3. What resulted were 48 mini-episodes that quickly became the most popular segment on *The Tracey Ullman Show*. (The rest, as they say, is history, but we're still supposed to write another 500 words for this chapter.)

Groening was in luck when he arrived with the talents of cast members Dan Castellaneta and Julie Kavner at his immediate disposal. Castellaneta initially based his voice for Homer on Walter Matthau, which carried all the way into the first season of the full half-hour series. As the character of Homer Simpson evolved from classic sitcom father to king of the morons, so did the voice. After initially being brought in to audition for Lisa, Nancy Cartwright was hired on the spot when she decided to audition for Bart. Yeardley Smith, a 22-year-old B-movie actress at the time, was then hired to voice Lisa. Early recordings were reportedly done with a tape deck in the bleachers on *The Tracey Ullman Show* set. The lesson, as always: no matter what, take the audition.

Most *Simpsons* fans only know the shorts that were featured in "The Simpsons 138th Episode Spectacular," the Season 7 episode where Troy McClure takes us on a self-deprecating stroll down memory lane. The shorts showcased were "Good Night," "Space Patrol," "World War III," "The Perfect Crime," and "Bathtime." The stories were simplistic and the characters relatively shallow, but they gradually became the lovable family we know and love today. If only our families had such a positive trajectory (author notes while sobbing).

Much like the television series that followed, *The Simpsons* had a distinct evolution of animation style as the shorts progressed. Initially, the animators would simply trace over Groening's storyboards like a lazy college student copying answers off the student next to him. But as the series developed so did the designs, layouts, and animation quality of the characters like a hardworking college student who pays good money for those answers.

Tracey Ullman would eventually sue FOX for restitution, claiming that her show was the source of *The Simpsons'* success in what we dub "The Most Sadly Predictable Lawsuit in United States History." FOX would go on to win in what we dub "The Most Sadly Predictable Lawsuit Result in United States History."

The comedy may be dated, but if you truly want to call yourself a fan, we highly recommend watching all 48 shorts on a loop until they're as committed to memory as the monorail song.

4 Watch *The Simpsons*

Okay, so this seems obvious. Maybe even a little insulting. You bought this book about *The Simpsons*, and the first thing we're doing is telling you to watch *The Simpsons*. Duh. But there are very good reasons why we're saying this. Bottom line: no information or amusement you derive from this book will ever compare to the enriching experience of watching an episode of the show. I mean, still read this thing but remember that it is merely a companion piece to the show itself!

It is possible that you, the person reading this, have never seen an episode of *The Simpsons*. Unlikely, for sure, but maybe you're using this book as a primer of sorts to get into the show. That's great. We're happy to start you off on your journey by recommending some episodes to watch. Unlike many sitcoms that have come out in the past decade or so, you don't need to start from the beginning. In fact, we suggest that you don't. The show has no serialized elements, and by the end of each episode, everything is resolved and back to normal. For the most part, each episode mostly exists in a vacuum unaware of the events of previous episodes. Although the format is not en vogue anymore, the DVD sets are a great way to watch the show and overall a great purchase. We'll get more into those in another chapter. However you wish to watch the show (DVD, simpsonsworld.com, illegal downloading), we'd recommend starting with an episode produced somewhere between the fourth season and the eighth season. Generally speaking, this is what fans will dub "the classic era," when the show was firing on all cylinders. The stories were compelling, the jokes were hilarious, and the series was past its growing pains but not yet tired. Any episode you pick will be a good choice. Although if you choose a "Treehouse of Horror" episode, just know these are non-canonical anthology stories created specifically for Halloween.

The episodes are so densely layered with so many jokes and references and moments that re-watching is an extremely rewarding experience. Maybe there's an episode you haven't seen in a while. You'll be surprised by how much you don't remember. Even if you're a mega-fan who's seen the episodes over and over, you should consider this: were you watching them in syndicated reruns? If you were, those episodes were chopped up to fit in more commercials. There are likely jokes in the full versions that you've never seen. What are you waiting for? Watch those babies again!

There are different ways to watch the show, too. Do you have a friend who's never really seen *The Simpsons*? Show them one of your favorites and experience the joy of someone watching it for the first time with fresh eyes or get together with a friend who is a fan! Watching *The Simpsons* communally can be a very different and fun endeavor. Get a whole bunch of friends together. Throw a dang party! And if you don't want to do the organizing, look into what your city might have to offer. Across the globe, there are meetups, fan clubs, and other gatherings that screen episodes, among other things like hosting trivia and generally providing a place for *Simpsons* nerds to meet and have fun. Look it up online to see if there's one of these near you. They're nearly all called "Stonecutters" for obvious reasons.

5 Family Tree

Even though the show has gone everywhere from space to Spain, Australia to Egypt, and all dark dimensions in between (looking at you, "Treehouse of Horror"), the show at its core has been and always will be about the Simpsons family themselves. Over its run, we've seen the Simpsons clan expand and take shape from long-lost uncles to long lost mothers to cousins, kids, and kooky Clancy Bouvier, but before we get too bogged down by bonus brothers and sisters, it's time we got to know our core nuclear family.

Jacqueline Bouvier
Wife to Clancy Bouvier
Mother of Patty, Selma, and Marge

What to Know: Julie Kavner voices her, doing a raspier, harder-edged version of Marge. She's curt and to the point—not unkind but just impatient. Every molecule of her movements hangs with the self-awareness that this day could be her last, and you get a sense that she's okay with that.

Fun Facts: She was engaged in a love triangle with Abe Simpson and Mr. Burns ("Lady Bouvier's Lover," Season 5, Episode 21) and resides in the Hal Roach Apartments in the cemetery district. That apartment name blatantly riffs on the writer/producer of *Laurel and Hardy*. According to producers of *The Simpsons*, her design was created by "taking Marge's model and squashing it."

Patty Bouvier

Daughter of Clancy Bouvier and Jacqueline Bouvier
Sister to Selma Bouvier and Marge Simpson

What to Know: Julie Kavner voices her, and she's one part of the cynical chain-smoking sisters who make DMV lines longer, devour *MacGyver* episodes, and make shaving your legs a thing of the past. For several seasons the world knew the romantic wants of sister Selma as it drove several episodes. The the world discovered precisely why she never participated in the romantic rat race. As she confessed to Marge, "Did you actually think I was straight?" And later, "you could see it from space!" She's softened quite a bit in later seasons but maintains her undying distaste for Homer.

Fun Facts: She dated Principal Skinner in "Principal Charming," Season 2, Episode 14). Her hair is actually red (not gray as it appears), but the dark hues she's accrued are attributed to a near lifetime of cigarette smoke and ash.

Selma Bouvier

Daughter of Clancy Bouvier and Jacqueline Bouvier
Sister to Patty Bouvier and Marge Simpson
Mother to adopted daughter Ling Bouvier

What to Know: Julie Kavner voices her, and she's often referred to as the slightly sweeter twin of the "gruesome twosome" (as Homer would put it). This is mostly due to her deep-seeded desire to be a mother, something that has never quite come easy for the salty sister. But her maternal goals eventually reached that sweet conclusion in the episode "Goo Goo Gai Pan" where Selma travels to China to adopt a baby girl named Ling.

Fun Facts: She's been married a total of five times. Her husbands were Sideshow Bob, Lionel Hutz, Troy McClure, Disco Stu, and even an ethically ambiguous union with Abraham "Grampa" Simpson in "Rome-old and Juli-Eh," Season 18, Episode 15).

Clancy Bouvier
Husband to Jacqueline Bouvier
Father to Patty Bouvier, Selma Bouvier, and Marge Simpson

What to Know: Existing mostly in flashbacks (from Marge's perspective), his hobbies include chain-smoking, swearing, and singing the Springfield city anthem. He's best known as being one of the earliest male flight attendants, which caused him great grief and embarrassment as revealed in the episode "Fear of Flying" (Season 6, Episode 11).

Fun Facts: He's one of the few Bouviers who was actually pleasant to Homer as depicted in "The Way We Was," (Season 2, Episode 12), though it's been argued that's partially due to him mistaking Homer for Artie Ziff, Marge's intended (and more impressive) prom date.

Abraham Simpson
Husband to Mona Simpson, Selma Bouvier
Father to Homer Simpson

What to Know: Dan Castellaneta voices the often out-of-sorts character. His catchphrase (as listed in several proper-looking spots on the Internet) is simply, "Ahhhhh." He's the stereotypical disoriented geriatric, oscillating between bargaining for his family's affection and concocting harebrained schemes in a fight to remain relevant. Despite all of this, he's probably the most present of the Simpsons extended family. As we dive deeper into awkward Abe, we learn that his standoffishness when Homer was a boy was probably a projection of his own insecurities about fatherhood and manhood, his desire to love and be loved the same as any other, and his longing for a stronger relationship with his son is an undercurrent that surfaces whenever his senility isn't fully in the driver's seat, which it is 99.9 percent of the time.

Fun Facts: He was part of a secret society with Monty Burns called The Flying Hellfish, he once told a bank teller that his name was King Olaf of Sweden so he could get some money (and then later went back and apologized), and he co-founded a love tonic company with Homer called Simpson and Son's Revitalizing Tonic as seen in "Grampa vs. Sexual Inadequacy," (Season 6, Episode 10).

Mona Simpson
Wife of Abraham Simpson
Mother of Homer Simpson

What to Know: Maggie Roswell (1991–94), Glenn Close (1995–97), and Tress MacNeille (only for the episode "D'oh-in' in the Wind") each have provided the voice for her. She's Homer's 1960s radical activist mother who skipped out on most of his life— only to return when Homer was fully grown (and full of questions).

Fun Facts: Though she appeared in brief glimpses throughout *The Simpsons'* early run, her first fully-developed character arc was introduced in the episode "Mother Simpson" (Season 7, Episode 8). Named after Richard Appel's wife (who also wrote the episode), her character was based off of Bernardine Dohrn of the far-left revolutionary group Weather Underground.

Herb Powell
Son of Abraham Simpson and "Gaby"
Half Brother to Homer Simpson

What to Know: Voiced by Danny DeVito and the product of a brief affair between Abe Simpson and "Gaby" (a prostitute and carnival worker) while Abe was trying to court Mona Simpson, he exists as the opposing counterpart to Homer and in some ways can be seen as "what could have been" if Homer spent less time listening to Queen and more time cranking through his studies. When we first meet him, he's an accomplished businessman on the hunt for a new idea in the car market, but when he hands the hypothetical keys to Homer for his next design, it turns out to be a bust that bankrupts him and bursts the once rosy relationship he had with his estranged half brother.

Fun Facts: He's the inventor of a "toddler translator" (with Maggie as inspiration) that restores his success.

Marge Simpson

It's easy to see why superfans have deemed Marge "the most underrated Simpsons family member." She's relegated to the backseat by design. Marge can never keep up with the fun and fancy-free foibles of Homer, the hell-yeah-hell-raiser antics of Bart, or the poetic precociousness of Lisa. Her role in this comedy chaos is to ground it, to keep the kids fed, to keep the house intact, and serve as the moral compass always pointing true north, but because *The Simpsons* strives to give every character full dimensions (yes, even Duff Man has been known to have nuance) we know there's so much more to the Simpsons matriarch, which is why we celebrate her.

Marge was actually originally voiced by Tracey Ullman when the Simpsons first appeared on *The Tracey Ullman Show* in 1987. Julie Kavner took the reins once the show had been picked up by FOX and has been carrying the torch ever since. Similar to Homer's origin story, creator Matt Groening based Marge on his own mother, Margaret Groening.

Marge's trademark blue hair is allegedly based partly on The Bride in *Bride of Frankenstein* and partly on Groening's mother's hairstyle in the 1960s. It is almost always in a perfect bouffant that defies gravity, though it has been known to (given the time period or the sexy sexiness of whatever she and Homer are up to) melt into cascading locks.

Marge was born and raised in Springfield and takes a great deal of civic pride for her hometown, protecting it from outside forces and protesting the discovery of a burlesque house within its city limits. Her naysaying is frequently noted in almost every Town Hall meeting. She's the youngest daughter to parents Jacqueline and Clancy Bouvier, a bright ray of light to her joyless older sisters Patty and Selma. When Marge first met Homer in high school, she was wary at first that the two would get along but was eventually won over by his goofy earnestness.

Marge is fluent in French and surprisingly athletic, has gambling addiction issues, and, unlike her chain-smoking sisters, has tried cigarettes just *twice*. She's sweet and sympathetic to even the most despicable Springfield citizens. Her personality is so perfectly suited for celebrating others that she once volunteered as the Listen Lady at the Springfield church (and was quickly exhausted by all of the selfless self-help).

It's notable to mention Marge's favorite Beatle is Ringo Starr—proof that she prefers pop culture's many underdogs. When faced with anything that's a shred above simple and plain, Marge goes wild. Deviled ham, buttered noodles, even a Top 40 pop song can send her mind spinning. "Music is none of my business," she exclaims in "Homerpalooza."

Marge's most constant role in Springfield is homemaker. "The only thing I'm high on is love. Love for my sons and daughters. Yes, a little LSD is all I need," she say is Season 7's "Sweet Homediddly-Dum-Doodily." But Marge has picked up quite a few side gigs over the seasons, including notable ones as a police officer, portrait painter for Mr. Burns, Pretzel Wagon saleswoman, realtor, and baker for an erotic bakery. She's crafty and creative with a needle and thread, as she is with a can of Cheeze Whiz and pimento slices. But the most important thing to know about Marge Simpson is that she doesn't give up.

Anything but passive, Marge takes an incredible responsibility toward her family. Though she's not often the one sparking the locomotive that takes them off the tracks, she's often the one who guides them home.

Given all this, it's no surprise that some of the show's most tender moments have come from Marge's mind. When Lisa's depressed in the Season 1 episode "Moaning Lisa," Marge gives one of the most honest pep talks the show has ever crafted. She tells Lisa, "Always be yourself. You want to be sad? Be sad. We'll ride it out with you. When you get finished feeling sad, we'll still be there." This line alone speaks volumes to the resilient dynamic of the Simpsons family and why Homer going to space, Bart becoming famous, Lisa designing a Malibu Stacy Doll, and all of the other outlandish hijinks in between don't feel too out there. We know we'll always nestle back into the heart.

Homer and Marge: "The Way They Was"

Few plot lines on *The Simpsons* are quite as sentimental as the origin story of Homer and Marge. After having spent all of Season 1 and most of Season 2 getting to know our favorite TV couple in their roles as tired parents and members of lower-middle-class suburbia, an episode gave us the opportunity to see them as wide-eyed teenagers falling in love is a particularly moving experience.

In the 1991 episode "The Way We Was," the family TV breaks, and Homer and Marge attempt to entertain the kids by sharing the story of how they first met. Suddenly, we are trans-ported to 1974, where high school Marge and Homer have their meet-cute in detention. It's clear that although their fashion and hair have changed over the years—isn't there something so endear-ing about Marge with her hair down and Homer with any hair at all?—the two characters have virtually identical spirits to their present day selves. Marge is a straight-A student on the debate team who finds herself attracted to the highly smart and articulate Artie Ziff, the near opposite of Homer, who's in detention with Barney for smoking cigarettes in the boy's bathroom. Marge and Homer far from hit it off during their initial encounter, but Homer is so taken by Marge that he works to be with her by pretending to be a French student who needs tutoring. Although Homer's ploy to get Marge to spend time with him was manipulative and dishonest, his intention was not mean-spirited nor intentionally selfish, as he knew they were "meant to be together." So rarely does Homer ever work for anything that him putting in the effort to win Marge over shows how special she is to him.

The episode takes a crushing turn when Marge confronts him, asking why he can't accept that she's at the prom with someone else. He explains, "Because I'm sure we were meant to be together. Usually when I have a thought, there's a lot of other thoughts in there…something says yes, something says no. But this time, there's only yes! How can the only thing I've ever been sure about in my life be wrong?" She answers him, "Hmmm…don't know…But it is."

It's a heart-wrenching scene in the middle of an episode jam-packed with laughs. Homer, who had always been the main source of laughs, was now exuding peak vulnerability, leaving many of us worried that he and Marge would not end up together, even though we clearly know they would. After Artie ruins his chance with Marge with his "busy hands," Marge picks up Homer on the side of the road and admits that she should have gone to the prom with him instead. The episode ends with Homer telling her he knows he'll never be able to let her go after their first embrace ("I've got a problem. As soon as you stop this car, I'm gonna hug you and kiss you and then I'll never be able to let you go") and cuts to them present day, arm in arm. It's an incredibly moving episode that's beloved by many writers and fans alike.

In the 2008 episode "That 90s Show," Homer and Marge are still dating in the '90s, thus changing the timeline of when Homer and Marge met to accommodate for the current year. The decision to change the timeline was extremely controversial to fans, and many compared the effect to "The Principal and the Pauper," which undid the history of the characters that the show had spent so many years developing. Matt Selman, who wrote the episode and has won five Emmys working on *The Simpsons*, said that he's proud of the episode even if it "irritated some of [the] more hardcore fans because they felt we were deliberately ret-conning the classic flashbacks of how Homer and Marge met and how the kids were born." Whether that episode is one of your favorites or it ruined your childhood, "The Way We Was" still exists and is ready to leave you feeling warm and nostalgic for the vintage early Homer and Marge years whenever you want.

The Voices

Dan Castellaneta and Julie Kavner were the show's first major hirings and have stayed on through its entire tenure. Originally, the two performers were regular cast members on *The Tracey Ullman Show* and thus voiced the first iteration of the Simpsons family when they were just animated shorts.

Though Homer's voice has changed over time, going from a deep growl to a lighter, more whimsical dopiness, the magic touch from Castellaneta has remained the same. Dan's most notable voices are Homer and Abraham "Grampa" Simpson. However, his side character roster is long and varied. It includes Groundskeeper Willie, Sideshow Mel, Mayor Quimby, Squeaky Voiced Teen, Krusty the Clown, Barney Gumble, Hans Moleman, and Gil Gunderson—and that's just scratching the surface.

From left to right, voice actors Nancy Cartwright, Hank Azaria, Yeardley Smith, and Dan Castellaneta pose with creator Matt Groening, who is in between Smith and Castellaneta, and director David Silverman (far right) at the premiere of The Simpsons Movie. (AP Images)

Kavner's most well-known for voicing Marge Simpson, as well as various other members of the Bouvier family, including Patty and Selma, as well as Bouvier matriarch, Jacqueline Bouvier. But her talent lies in her versatility She can expertly switch from a frustrated sigh to an upbeat declaration about potatoes—"I just think they're neat!" Kavner's performance as Marge is unwavering in its conviction, as she reads lines both silly and serious with the same committed inflection.

The additional core cast includes Nancy Cartwright (voice of Bart) and Yeardley Smith (voice of Lisa). Though Hank Azaria and Harry Shearer don't voice a member of the core Simpsons family, their rich contributions to the show have elevated their status as part of the main six. Azaria's characters include Moe Szyslak, Chief Wiggum, Apu Nahasapeemapetilon, Frank Grimes, and many more. Shearer has Springfield stars like Mr. Burns, Ned Flanders, Principal Skinner, Waylon Smithers, Kent Brockman, and heaps more within his arsenal.

Get to Know Your Springfield Voice Regulars

Pamela Hayden: Milhouse Van Houten, Rod Flanders, Jimbo Jones, Malibu Stacy

Tress MacNeille: Agnes Skinner, Bernice Hibbert, Brandine Spuckler (Cletus' wife)

Karl Wiedgergott: Jimmy Carter, Bill Clinton, Happy Little Elf

Maggie Roswell: Helen Lovejoy, Maude Flanders, LuAnn Van Houten, Elizabeth Hoover

Russi Taylor: Martin Prince, Sherri, Terri, Wendell

Chris Edgerly: Leroy Jethro Gibbs, Marv Szyslak

Doris Grau: Lunch Lady Doris, Lurleen Lumpkin

Marcia Mitzman Gaven: Maude Flanders (after Maggie Roswell's departure on the show), Helen Lovejoy, Elizabeth Hoover

The Simpsons regularly features outside talent as guest voices. During the Bill Oakley/Josh Weinstein Years, these would often be lesser known character actors that the showrunners were fans of. The best example of this occurs in the Season 7 episode, "Marge Be Not Proud," where Bart shoplifts the popular new video game *Bonestorm*, and the menacing store manager, who catches him, is voiced by the equally menacing actor Lawrence Tierney. Tierney was famous for playing mobsters and tough guys throughout the 1940s and '50s and was the perfect fit to strike terror into the heart of Bart as he faced down the law. Other voice highlights of Oakley/Weinstein's tenure include *The Godfather*'s own Alex Rocco, Donald Sutherland, Tom Kite (as himself), and R. Lee Ermey (as Colonel Leslie Hapablap).

In the seasons that followed, it became more commonplace to have celebrities voice themselves or to include the celebrity's voice appearance as part of a promotion for the show itself. In the show's 10th season opener, "Lard of the Dance," Lisa Kudrow voices a new girl arriving in Lisa's class, whose adult-like sophistication sends Lisa into a tailspin. At the time of its airing, *Friends* was at the peak of its popularity, and the synchronicity between the two shows was no doubt making both NBC and FOX as happy as Rainier Wolfcastle sleeping on a big pile of money.

What's great about *The Simpsons* is how loyal and receptive they are to their voice talents and to the fans. If a character particularly resonates with their audience, they'll often find ways to spring them back into Springfield again and again and again. One of the strongest examples of this zero to hero rise is Sideshow Bob. Since 1990 *Cheers* and *Frasier* star Kelsey Grammer has voiced Sideshow Bob, the menacing, bloodthirsty former star of *The Krusty the Clown Show* Over the seasons Bob's been given a pretty hefty character arc, taking him from bloodthirsty menacing murderer to reformed and docile dreamer of a simpler life.

Other honorable mentions for recurring guests stars are Joe Mantegna as Fat Tony, Jon Lovitz as Artie Ziff, Llewellyn Sinclair, and, most notably, Jay Sherman. But before you toss this book into the depths of the Cracker Factory, rest assured, we'll be covering the granddaddy of all *Simpsons* guest stars, Troy McClure chapter, later in the book.

Bart Simpson

In the early '90s, it was all about Bart. "Bartmania" soon swept through the nation, leading to unprecedented merchandise sales, pop songs, and more. His "underachiever and proud of it" attitude resonated with legions of kids, infuriated adults, and birthed an underground market dubbed "Bootleg Bart." In those days it was Bart on all the merchandise—T-shirts, dolls, posters, and more—that was flying off of the shelves. Simply put, Bart was cool.

But what do you absolutely need to know about Bart Simpson? He's the oldest child of Homer and Marge and their only son. He's in Edna Krabappel's fourth-grade class at Springfield Elementary. He wears the same outfit—a reddish-orange T-shirt, blue shorts, and blue shoes—every day. At any angle there are always nine spikes atop his head. His best friend is Milhouse van Houten, and he's Krusty the Clown's biggest fan.

Whereas many members of the Simpsons family are all named after creator Matt Groening's own siblings and parents, Bart is simply just an anagram for "brat." Originally, Groening envisioned Bart as somewhat more angst-y than mischievous, but this apparently changed to fit Nancy Cartwright's performance of the character. Cartwright has been the actress behind the voice of Bart since the very beginning. Legend has it that she actually came to the audition with the intention to read for the part of Lisa but became more interested in Bart upon hearing the character description. Good move.

Bart is a crucial part to many of the show's hallmark moments. It's Bart writing the chalkboard gags in the opening sequence of each episode. It's Bart making prank phone calls to Moe's Tavern. It's Bart whom Sideshow Bob is always trying to kill. It's Bart who's uttered many of the show's early catchphrases like: "Ay caramba," "Don't have a cow, man," or "Eat my shorts!" It's Bart who officially responded to president George H.W. Bush's infamous put-down of the show. At the time of this writing, Bart's name has been in the titles of 45 episodes. And although it may be a somewhat embarrassing part of the show's legacy, "Do the Bartman," the hit novelty song from 1990 that topped the charts in five countries, features Bart on lead vocals and Michael Jackson on backup.

As of the publication of this book, Bart Simpson continues to be a global sensation. *Time* magazine listed him as one of the top 100 influential people of the 20th century, and he was the only fictional character to make the list. It's been widely reported that "Bart Simpson" is among the most popular write-in votes during any major political election. It's hard to escape him. I mean, he's Bart Simpson. Who the hell are you?

ALLIE GOERTZ AND JULIA PRESCOTT

10 Make a Prank Phone Call

If there's one thing *The Simpsons* loves, it's series-spanning running jokes. It tickles us to know that Mr. Burns can't be bothered to remember who Homer is, or whenever Moe calls Marge "Midge," we die. But nothing could be a more warm and fuzzy runner than Bart's prank phone calls to Moe. Appearing as early as Season 1, it's one of the show's more classic set-up/punch-line bits that consistently satisfies.

Fans are so in love with the prank calls to Moe that there's even fan conspiracy theories about them. Maybe Moe doesn't recognize Bart's voice is because he's been hit in the head so many times due to his past boxing career. Another story offers a sweet and simple solution: Moe actually *does* recognize Bart's voice, but he's so hungry for human connection he doesn't mind getting pranked.

However, the real reason for Moe and Bart's back and forth may exist outside of the show. Many fans speculate that this bit is actually based on The Tube Bar tapes made in the 1970s, which was then distributed widely on an underground cassette network. The Tube Bar was a bar in New Jersey that became the constant target of mockery from John Elmo and Jim Davidson (later known as "The Bum Bar Bastards"), and—you guessed it—they kept bugging the barkeep, asking for fake patrons over and over and over and over and...you know where this is going.

So in the spirit of the show's scampiest so-and-so, it's time to fire up that phonebook! Gather your grimiest gal pals or morally ambiguous bros and let this list inspire you to play some funny phone tomfoolery.

24

"Homer's Odyssey"—Season 1, Episode 3

Bart: "Is Mister Freely there?"

Moe: "Who?"

Bart: "Freely, first initials I. P."

Moe: "Hold on, I'll check. Uh, is I. P. Freely here? Hey everybody, I.P. Freely! *(The customers laugh.)* Wait a minute...Listen to me, you lousy bum. When I get a hold of you, you're dead. I swear I'm gonna slice your heart in half."

"New Kid on the Block"—Season 4, Episode 8

Moe: "Yeah, just a sec, I'll check. Amanda Hugginkiss? Hey, I'm lookin' fer Amanda Hugginkiss. Why can't I find Amanda Hugginkiss?"

Barney: "Maybe your standards are too high!"

Moe: "You little S.O.B. Why, when I find out who you are, I'm going to shove a sausage down your throat and stick starving dogs in your butt!"

Bart: "My name is Jimbo Jones, and I live at 1094 Evergreen Terrace."

Moe: "I knew he'd slip up sooner or later!" *(He unsheathes a rusty knife and heads out of the tavern.)*

"One Fish, Two Fish, Blowfish, Blue Fish"—Season 2, Episode 11

Moe: "Hello, Moe's Tavern. Birthplace of the Rob Roy."

Bart: "Is Seymour there? Last name Butz."

Moe: "Just a sec. Hey, is there a Butz here? A Seymour Butz? Hey, everybody, I wanna Seymour Butz...Wait a minute...Listen, you little scum-sucking pus-bucket! When I get my hands on you, I'm gonna pull out your eyeballs with a corkscrew!"

"Treehouse of Horror II"—Season 3, Episode 7

Moe: "Moe's Tavern...Hold on, I'll check. Uh, hey, everybody! I'm a stupid moron with an ugly face and big butt, and my butt smells and I like to kiss my own butt."

Barney: "Ho ho, that's a good one."

Moe: "Wait a minute..."

Bart: *(hangs up and laughs)*

"Flaming Moes"—Season 3, Episode 10

Moe: "Flaming Moe's."

Bart: "Uh, yes, I'm looking for a friend of mine. Last name Jass. First name Hugh."

Moe: "Uh, hold on, I'll check...Hugh Jass! Somebody check the men's room for a Hugh Jass!"

Man: "Uh, I'm Hugh Jass."

Moe: "Telephone." *(hands over the receiver)*

Hugh: "Hello, this is Hugh Jass."

Bart: "Uh...hi."

Hugh: "Who's this?"

Bart: "Bart Simpson."

Hugh: "Well, what can I do for you, Bart?"

Bart: "Uh, look, I'll level with you, Mister. This is a crank call that sort of backfired, and I'd like to bail out right now."

Hugh: "All right. Better luck next time. *(He hangs up.)* What a nice young man."

"Burns Verkaufen der Kraftwerk"—Season 3, Episode 11

Moe: "Moe's Tavern, Moe speaking."

Bart: "Uh, yes, I'm looking for a Mrs. O'Problem? First name, Bea."

Moe: "Uh, yeah, just a minute, I'll check. Uh, Bea O'Problem? Bea O'Problem! Come on guys, do I have a Bea O'Problem here?"

Barney: "You sure do!"

Moe: "Oh…It's you, isn't it! Listen, you. When I get a hold of you, I'm going to use your head for a bucket and paint my house with your brains!"

"The PTA Disbands"—Season 6, Episode 21

(This takes place when Moe is taking over as the substitute teacher for Mrs. Krabappel's class during the strike.)

Moe: "Okay, when I call your name, uh, you say 'present' or 'here.' Er, no, say 'present.' Ahem, Anita Bath?"

Moe: "All right, settle down. Anita Bath here?"

Moe: "All right, fine, fine. Maya Buttreeks!"

Moe: "Hey, what are you laughing at? What? Oh, oh, I get it, I get it. It's my big ears, isn't it, kids? Isn't it? Well, children, I can't help that!"

(Moe runs out of the classroom crying.)

"Homer the Moe"—Season 13, Episode 3

(Homer is looking after Moe's Tavern.)

Bart: "I'd like to speak to a Mr. Tabooger, first name Ollie."

Homer: "Ooh! My first prank call! What do I do?"

Bart: "Just ask if anyone knows Ollie Tabooger."

Homer: "I don't get it."

Bart: "Yell out, 'I'll eat a booger.'"

Homer: "What's the gag?"

Bart: "Oh, forget it…"

11 Bartmania

When *The Simpsons* first debuted on FOX, the family as a whole was the intended focal point of the show's weekly stories. Each member had an equal share in contributing to the chaos of every episode, and no singular Simpson was the star. Then 1990 hit, and "Bartmania" soon took over. Somehow, inexplicably, Bart Simpson was in high demand. Fans clambered for T-shirts with his signature catchphrases or just anything that depicted his likeness, and just like that, an unexpected craze was sparked.

In the early 1990s, millions of Bart T-shirts were sold. (Some sold one million *in just one day*.) However, not everyone was buying into the Bart craze. Soon, protests across public schools erupted, banning the merchandise—most notably shirts that said, "Underachiever and Proud of It" and "I'm Bart Simpson, Who the Hell Are You?" This only ignited the craze higher, catapulting *The Simpsons* into such strong viewership that FOX decided to switch its time slot to compete with NBC's *The Cosby Show*, the highest rated comedy series at the time.

In 1990 *Entertainment Weekly* crowned Bart as "Entertainer of the Year," following other news outlets that dubbed him, "television's king," "television's brightest new star," and "an undiminished smash." In various elections throughout 1990, Bart became the most frequent write-in candidate. In that year's Macy's Thanksgiving Day Parade, Bart made his hot air balloon debut and has been a part of the festivities ever since.

Around that time *The Simpsons* got into the music game with their debut album, "The Simpsons Sing the Blues." Unsurprisingly, the first single released was titled "Do the Bartman," a pop rap song that features Bart slyly acknowledging his own surprising shot

In the early 1990s, T-shirts of Bart Simpson and his signature catchphrases were a very popular item. (Joe Kwaczala)

to fame. The song came about after Michael Jackson called the show personally, offering to write Bart a No. 1 single in exchange for Jackson appearing on the show. Though Jackson later commissioned his friend, Bryan Loren, to compose the music, *The Simpsons* held up their part of the deal when they featured Jackson as a guest voice in the episode, "Stark Raving Dad."

The proliferation of parents and public figures dubbing Bart a bad influence continued to carry on throughout the early 1990s. He was labeled a threat to learning in public schools, a threat to polite behavior for growing children. *The Simpsons* creators were quick in their defense, explaining that Bart had a vulnerable side that allowed for remorse for his rebellion and that his ability to be multidimensional was not dissimilar to the next American kid.

In *Entertainment Weekly*'s 1990 "Entertainer of the Year" article, they described Bart as "a rebel who's also a good kid, a terror who's easily terrorized, and a flake who astonishes us, and himself, with serious displays of fortitude." In regards to the "Bart as poor role model" criticism, *Simpsons* producer James L. Brooks quickly retorted, "I'm very wary of television where everybody is supposed to be a role model. You don't run across that many role models in real life. Why should television be full of them?"

Bartmania soon reached its peak when its influence reached the White House. On January 27, 1992, then-president George H. W. Bush said in a speech, "We are going to keep on trying to strengthen the American family to make American families a lot more like the Waltons and a lot less like the Simpsons." Bush unknowingly opened the door for what would be the most bizarre and beautiful pop cultural moment in television history.

Not long after, first lady Barbara Bush echoed her husband's criticism, describing the show as, "the dumbest thing she had ever seen." It seemed as though a now-political campaign against the show was rallying. The show's writers took this as an invitation, soon writing her a note (on *Simpsons* stationery) from the perspective of Marge. The letter read:

```
THE SIMPSONS™
September 28, 1990
Mrs. Barbara Bush
The First Lady
The White House
1600 Pennsylvania Avenue
Washington, D.C.
Dear First Lady:
    I recently read your criticism of my family.
I was deeply hurt. Heaven knows we're far from
perfect and, if truth be known, maybe just a
wee bit short of normal; but as Dr. Seuss says,
"a person is a person."
    I try to teach my children Bart, Lisa, and
even little Maggie, always to give somebody
the benefit of the doubt and not talk badly
about them, even if they're rich. It's hard to
get them to understand this advice when the
very First Lady in the country calls us not
only dumb, but "the dumbest thing" she ever
saw. Ma'am, if we're the dumbest thing you
ever saw, Washington must be a good deal dif-
ferent than what they teach me at the current
events group at the church.
    I always believed in my heart that we had
a great deal in common. Each of us living
our lives to serve an exceptional man. I hope
there is some way out of this controversy. I
thought, perhaps, it would be a good start to
just speak my mind.
    With great respect,
    (Signed)
    Marge Simpson
```

One would think the interaction was over, but *The Simpsons* received a new message in their inboxes. This time it was on presidential stationery:

> Dear Marge,
> How kind of you to write. I'm glad you spoke your mind; I foolishly didn't know you had one.
> I am looking at a picture of you depicted on a plastic cup with your blue hair filled with pink birds peeking out all over. Evidently, you and your charming family—Lisa, Homer, Bart, and Maggie—are camping out. It is a nice family scene. Clearly, you are setting a good example for the rest of the country.
> Please forgive a loose tongue.
> Warmly,
> Barbara Bush
> P.S. Homer looks like a handsome fella!

This interaction symbolically shut the door for the "Bartmania" craze, and the public soon shifted their focus. Schools still had a disdain for the hell-raiser, but bans waned, and merchandise sales steadied. Bart would continue to be one of the most popular characters in television, but soon he would exist in the shadow of the Simpsons patriarch and the "d'oh!" heard 'round the world.

12 Couch Gags

Every episode of *The Simpsons* starts with the main characters zipping around Springfield, eventually culminating in a hastened meetup in front of the TV. All of the steps leading up to this moment play out more or less the same: Homer's car rushes into the driveway, he parks, he sprints, he pushes his way into the house, and then calamity ensues.

What would later be dubbed "the couch gag" refers to the visual joke placed here, which is different in each episode. Most often, the Simpsons family rushes into the living room and discovers some kind of abnormality with the couch that prevents them from watching television; sometimes this could be the couch mysteriously missing; other times, the entire living room is suddenly under water.

The world of the couch gag is detached from the canon of the Simpsons family reality. A couch gag may see characters like aliens, wizards, ghosts, or skeletons; other times, we may see our Simpsons family transformed into stretched out versions of themselves, balloon-shaped human shells, and other absurdities.

In the beginning of the show's run, couch gags hinged on the relatively normal. The first appearance of the couch gag came in the Season 1 episode, "Bart the Genius." In this gag the family accidentally squashes Bart in their rush to the couch, hurling him up in the air, and then catching him as he lands six seconds later. In Season 2 we saw slightly more creativity: the Simpsons do an Egyptian dance, the Simpsons barge in on Grampa fast asleep, the couch tips backward, exposing its seams as if it were a true to life prop.

It wouldn't be until Season 3 in the episode "Homer Defined" that the couch gags would break into the brink of lunacy. In this opening the Simpsons family rushes in to find a space alien on the couch with drink in hand; the alien panics for a second before opening a trapdoor and escaping through it.

Similar to *The Simpsons* opening chalkboard gag, the couch gag would become its own means of artistic expression for the show's creators. *The Simpsons'* signature meta-commentary would come to fruition when the family stumbles into their living room and finds the Flintstones already occupying it, a sly nod to the baton of "biggest primetime animated show" being passed from show to show.

In later seasons the show began offering the opportunity of writing and animating the couch gag to guest directors. Fans were soon treated to an onslaught of different styles. In one opening couch gag, viewers saw *The Simpsons* world twisted and tortured into an all-encompassing apocalypse where zombies, mystical behemoths, and other fantastical threats from the mind of Guillermo del Toro ran rampant. In another opening the sequence plays fairly straightforward until the couch gag rips into the iconic loopy animation style of *The Ren & Stimpy Show* creator John Kricfalusi; it soon became apparent that these guest-directed openings were not so much an opportunity for a zag on a couch gag but for a short film of sorts.

One of the most notable examples of this occurred in the episode "MoneyBART," where the entire opening credit sequence has been designed by the graffiti artist Banksy. The episode begins fairly normal: the camera transitions smoothly from the iconic "Simpsons" text in the clouds, drifting throughout Springfield where Banksy's name has been spray-painted on a billboard of a sullen Krusty the Clown.

From there the Simpsons happily sit in silent stillness on the couch. It lingers for a beat until a sweatshop-type animation studio is revealed where every frame is painstakingly hand-drawn. Dramatic, somber music plays as an orphan boy grabs a single animation cell from a worker and dips it in radioactive sludge, pinning it to dry over hordes of feral rats and human skeletons.

And then it dives deeper, revealing the bleak circumstances that plague the factory's production of *Simpsons* merchandise (with furry adorable creatures being blatantly sacrificed for their fluffy fur in order to make Bart plush dolls). The short culminates in the gratuitously gruesome image of a severed dolphin head being used as a box adhesive through its droopy, lifeless tongue, drifting directly into a malnourished unicorn's horn implemented as a stabbing device for *Simpsons* DVD holes.

Needless to say, Banksy took some creative liberties.

The transition from simple visual joke to absurdist gag to complete short film is an indication that *The Simpsons* has no hesitation with exploring and reinventing itself in how it tells jokes, explores visual styles, or collaborates with its contemporaries.

Sam Simon: Unsung Hero

Matt Groening
James L. Brooks
Sam Simon

As a fan of *The Simpsons*, you've seen these names more times than you can count (and you can count really, really high). Although most people know and love the extended works of James L. Brooks and Matt Groening, fewer recognize the third name, Sam Simon, whom Brad Bird described as the "unsung hero" of *The Simpsons*. Whether their names are known across households or reserved for devoted trivia fans, these three producers are as crucial to *The Simpsons'* success as each eye is to Blinky.

Groening, Brooks, and Simon are like members of a band, and each bringing their unique strengths together to form one cohesive sound. Inarguably, the band could not have existed without Matt Groening, who created *The Simpsons* characters after James L. Brooks asked him to pitch animated short ideas for *The Tracey Ullman Show*, of which he and Sam Simon were producers. In this way Groening acts as the band's front man. But it was largely Simon and Brooks who developed the characters and world as we know them today. Simon is often credited as giving the two-dimensional characters their three-dimensional depth and was described by *The Simpsons* writer Ken Levine in a Vox.com article as the "the real creative force behind *The Simpsons*." Simon designed the models for such beloved characters as Mr. Burns, Chief Wiggum, and Dr. Hibbert and placed the importance of each episode on the heart of the family as opposed to the string of gags on which other Saturday morning cartoons relied. In addition to being one of the three executive producers, he assembled and led the initial team of writers and acted as creative supervisor for the first four seasons. If Groening is the band's front man who gets all the credit, Simon is the underappreciated guitarist who quietly writes some of their best songs. Like many creative partnerships, the two developed a contentious relationship, struggling over the direction of the show in addition to credit for the show's success.

Homer and Moe share a similar dynamic in the episode "Flaming Moe's," in which Homer invents a cocktail called the Flaming Homer and gives it to Moe, who mass-produces the drink and renames it after himself. Vox's TV critic, Todd VanDerWerff, once explored the rumor (first published on the infamous No Homer's Club) that the parallel to Groening and Simon was far from happenstance. "The rumor is this: 'Flaming Moe's' is an elaborate, barely veiled story of the massive success of *The Simpsons* creator Matt Groening, which came at the expense of Simon, the series' original showrunner and a producer and writer in Seasons 3 and 4," VanDerWerff wrote. "Simon is Homer, closed out of the origin story of the program, even though he and James L. Brooks were the ones to help turn Groening's characters into an actual TV series. Groening is Moe—a good person, maybe, but someone who gets too much credit." When Simon was asked about the rumor by podcaster Guy Evans, Simon slyly replied, "That may be true."

The episode ends with Homer becoming so overcome with resentment that he sabotages them both by revealing the secret ingredient is cough syrup. Although there was never such an extreme falling out, Simon left *The Simpsons* in 1993, stating his unhappiness with the direction of the show. (He sounds like the people on the Internet message boards.) Although this episode may have captured Simon's feelings of bitterness toward Groening, it also had a self-awareness regarding how difficult Simon was to work with. He was described by Groening in a piece of *The New York Times Magazine* as "brilliantly funny and one of the smartest writers I've ever worked with, although unpleasant and mentally unbalanced." Simon's assistant Daria Paris said he was "an asshole—whom I adore." It would seem this is a perfect summation of Simon and other artists like him.

Despite the contentious relationship between the pair, Simon will always be remembered for his amazing contributions to the show. In the episode that aired the day after his funeral, the show gave him a touching tribute after the credits with two stills that read, "One of the greatest comic minds ever. Thank you, Sam." The funeral was described by his charitable foundation as a "a perfect mix of laughter and tears." Actress Holly Marie Combs wrote, "You will be happy to know you had a room full of writers competing for the most poignant/hysterical eulogy of all time. And as your fellow [animal rights activist] Bob Barker put it, 'I have never before been to such an unusual funeral. It's like nobody died.'"

14 Impact on Television

In the beginning primetime animation was off to a shaky start. Adult audiences weren't ready for what so many deemed as "children's entertainment" co-existing next to their big-time beloveds like *Andy Griffith* and *Gilligan's Island*. Heck, even *The Addams Family* and its stupefyingly silly set-up was still deemed more sophisticated than saddling up in front of the idiot box and watching cartoons. But when *The Flintstones* hit the airwaves, everything changed.

To talk about *The Simpsons* and its historical impact would be impossible without first citing *The Flintstones*. That show is often credited as the first primetime animated comedy, and when it took its final bow in 1966, another show would struggle to slip into its shoes for a very, very, very long time. There were of course other attempts through the years; the Hanna-Barbera era would surface and offer *Wait Till Your Father Comes Home*, but its run was a paltry tenure of two years.

To say that transitioning *The Simpsons* into a fully fledged show was a gamble is a vast understatement, but FOX was in the business of busting through barricades. This new attempt at adult animation needed to work or else the very concept might be put to pasture. We, of course, know what happened next. *The Simpsons* shocked the system through high ratings and windfall viewerships, startling critics into submission. Not only was *The Simpsons* the return of the primetime animated comedy, but it also made *The Flintstones* look flimsy by comparison, a risk-averse kiddie attempt, where this new show was unafraid of asking the hard questions running the gamut of religion, marriage, and more. *The Simpsons* was not only paving the way, but it was also exploring territory that had never even been touched, and the world quickly caught on.

The early 1990s saw an explosion of new animation post-*Simpsons* shows like *Dr. Katz, Duckman,* and *Space Ghost Coast to Coast.* Unfortunately, each show failed to really take off; while *The Simpsons* paved the way for such shows, it also set the impossibly high bar for them to measure up. Audiences unfairly compared each new offering to the FOX family. The only thing that worked was to carve out another path that broke the boundary so completely, something that offered a completely different cast of characters and style of storytelling, something that was specifically...*Beavis and Butt-head.*

Much in the way that *The Simpsons* established a new edgy show style, so too did *Beavis and Butt-head.* Mike Judge created a show that blew the Bart hell-raiser era out of the water. Soon the world was wrapped up in the dawn of a new dumb comedy chapter, where butts and boners, innuendos and anarchy were front and center and freaking out the establishment.

After *Beavis,* all was fair game, and it was open season for green-lighting new animated adult comedies. Around this time came *The Critic* in 1994 from *The Simpsons'* own James L. Brooks, which saw Jon Lovitz playing Jay Sherman, a film critic in New York. Though this show evoked the general style and feel of an episode of *The Simpsons,* including some of the show's very own writers, it failed to pick up steam with viewers and was abruptly cancelled after just one season.

Another primetime animated hit wouldn't occur until 1997, when *King of the Hill* and *South Park* debuted. The latter unexpectedly gave *The Simpsons* tenure a run for its money while outlasting many of its other animated peers. What was significant about these shows and their hit-making formula was the very style that made *The Simpsons* such a disruption to the primetime landscape in the first place: the simple act of approaching their shows as if being an animated world was a secondary concept.

Certainly, *The Simpsons* had its zippier, cartoonier moments. Former showrunner Mike Scully has commented that a mandate within the show's writers' room was made to "justify the animation," which is why we're often treated to the innerworkings of Homer's head, the daydreams that haunt Bart when he's failing history class, and classic moments like The Land of Chocolate.

But more importantly, and part of the reason why the later 1990s hit animated shows struck such a chord and have endured, is that they never talked down to their format. *King of the Hill* could exist as a live action show without changing nearly anything, acting as a straight primetime sitcom. *South Park's* mature premises and unabashed skewering of political and pop culture topics have allowed it to level-up in a way never before seen. Even in the year 2018, news outlets cite the "South Park style" as a bona-fide satirical hot take to be taken seriously.

The Simpsons tree has branches that span wide and far, giving way to the creation of shows like *Family Guy* and *Bob's Burgers* while also opening the door for whole networks like Adult Swim. Whether or not they intended this from the start, their approach to storytelling has been a creative game of chicken. By striving far beyond what was required, by basking in the premise of being better than they needed to be, they've inadvertently inspired whole generations of other creatives to keep pushing the bar.

15 Go to *Simpsons* Trivia

Sure, there are a ton of places where you can cup your sweaty palm around a gold pencil in a fight for cerebral supremacy, but we're not talking 'bout your local dive's Trivia Tuesday; we're digging deep into the cromulent decathlon that is *Simpsons* trivia! Where else can you bond with your fellow older, balder, fatter sons over what Homer's middle name is? What real life animation legend was Dr. Nick based on? Why the hell was Smithers brown and blue in the first season? You'll soon feel like a damn hell ass king laying down the law when you shout, "It was a mistake from the animators! A mistake! IT WAS A MISTAKE FROM THE ANIMATORS! A MISTAKE!" Correct! But also you really shouldn't shout your answers.

Simpsons trivia is the best way to meet fellow Springfieldians like yourself who transform from dead-eyed suburbanites into white-hot grease fires of pure entertainment...over the course of two to three hours. Depending on which trivia night you attend, there may be bonus elements such as costume contests, themed treats, and other things that'll keep you up until 2:00 AM prepping the night before.

Most often *Simpsons* trivia nights operate as pub style where the game's divided into three rounds with each team comprising one to five superfans. They range from easy (What's the color of Marge's hair?), medium (a visual round where you're forced to name *The Simpsons* snack), and hard, or as the Los Angeles chapter calls it, "The Lil' Bastard Round" (How old is Hans Moleman? But like... really?)

Before playing trivia the first step is to create an awesome team name. Sometimes they'll be kind to the capdabblers and

Chazwazer's for not being as strong as the super friends clutching first place. That's when you bust out your best team name, and the room finally acknowledges your geode. The anatomy of a great team name is one part *Simpsons* reference, one part creativity, and all parts fun. Note to avoid using Team Discovery Channel. Here are some better examples:

- Our Team Name is AGNES! You know it's Agnes. It means lamb, Lamb of God!
- From Team Pan-A to Team Pan-Z
- That's Not a Team Name, That's Just a Waffle That Bart Tossed Up There
- Stupid Sexy Flanders
- The Editors of *Gigantic Asses* Magazine
- Nude Photos of Whoopi Goldberg

Trivia Locations

Sure, you may be thinking, *But I don't live in Springfield. Where on Earth can I possibly locate my local weirdos as I take a bow?* Well, as of fall of 2018, here are some of the biggest *Simpsons* trivia nights around.

Stonecutters LA (Hollywood, California)
Go to Lyric Hyperion Theater on the first Saturday of every month at 5:00 PM.

90s Simpsons Trivia SF (San Francisco, California)
Go to The Knockout on the fourth Sunday of every month at 6:00 PM.

Woo Hoo! Classic Simpsons Trivia (Brooklyn, New York)
Go to Berry Park on the first Thursday of every month at 7:30 PM.

The Ultimate Simpsons Pub Quiz (London, England)
Go to Sebright Arms on the first Sunday of the month at 7:30 PM.

So let's say you're sitting in the back of Lyric Hyperion in Hollywood, and the hosts have just asked a particularly hard question. Do you bail? Do you quit? Do you do another word that means give up? No, this is where you're a Viking. Whenever you don't know the answer to *Simpsons* trivia (and this can't be said of all trivia games), just make something up. Be funny, be creative, be clever. Write a haiku on the back of your paper, so that the hosts can revel in it onstage. Draw Mr. Stinky from answer two to answer seven. Your stick-to-itiveness will be appreciated—even if it doesn't get you the coveted first place.

And lastly, but not least-ly: don't cheat. People who cheat at *Simpsons* trivia belong in a circle of hell where a botched karaoke version of Homer singing "Convoy" plays for eternity. Besides, if you cheat, you'll probably be strapped to the stone of shame and forced to do donuts in the parking lot—and that's never a good look.

16 50 Trivia Nuggets

Q: Who is the Simpsons' family doctor?
A: Dr. Hibbert

Q: Why can't you make Üter run?
A: He is full of chocolate

Q: When Homer asks Mr. Burns for money to start a bowling team, he hallucinates and sees Homer as whom?
A: Poppin' Fresh/Pillsbury Dough Boy

Q: Finish the line: "Yeah____sucks."
A: Stuff

Q: What did Homer give up so Marge could afford a nanny?
A: His civil war recreation society

Q: Homer beats what statue in a game of foosball?
A: Michelangelo's David

Q: True or false: in "Homer The Great," the Stonecutters honor the momentous occasion of their society's 1,500th anniversary with an all-night poker game.
A: False, they have ribs

Q: The Capital City Hotel has been free of what disease since 1990?
A: Legionnaire's Disease

Q: What was the name of the Simpsons' musical housekeeper?
A: Shary Bobbins

Q: What is the name of Mr. Burns' teddy bear?
A: Bobo

Q: Which rock band performed at Krusty the Clown's comeback special?
A: The Red Hot Chili Peppers

Q: In "King Size Homer," which movie does Homer come to see in peace?
A: *Honk If You're Horny*

Q: What is Capital City's nickname?
A: The Windy Apple

Q: Bart used a photo of this late NHL great when writing love letters to Ms. Krabappel.

A: Gordie Howe

Q: Mr. Burns has a robotic what?

A: Richard Simmons

Q: In "Lemon of Troy," what did the Shelbyvillians drink in celebration of banishing the haunted lemon tree?

A: Turnip Juice

Q: According to a newspaper sight gag, the Springfield Isotopes forfeited the pennant because Homer lived out what dream?

A: Running out on a baseball field during a game

Q: According to Grampa Simpson, what word was used in place of the No. 20?

A: Dickety

Q: What is the name of Lisa's late jazz mentor?

A: Bleeding Gums Murphy

Q: Who stayed up all night dyeing their underwear?

A: The Human Fly

Q: Where is the entrance to Apu's secret rooftop garden?

A: Non-Alcoholic Beer Freezer

Q: In "Bart the Fink" after Krusty runs into some financial trouble, Krusty Burger becomes what?

A: IRS Burger

Q: Which Springfield character went to Gudger College?
A: Kirk Van Houten

Q: Who are Eastern Europe's equivalent to Itchy and Scratchy?
A: Worker and Parasite

Q: What is the name of Apu's film submission in the Springfield Film Festival?
A: *Bright Lights, Beef Jerky*

Q: Why doesn't Mr. Burns eat donuts?
A: He doesn't like ethnic food

Q: Why is Homer sent to a mental institution?
A: For wearing a pink shirt to work

Q: Marge's mother lives in what retirement community?
A: Hal Roach Apartments

Q: The doorbell to the Flanders' house plays the theme song from what Christian TV show?
A: *Davey and Goliath*

Q: In what part of the nuclear power plant does Homer work?
A: Sector 7G

Q: Homer has a tattoo of what sucky folk-pop band?
A: Starland Vocal Band

Q: After searching the entire army base looking for Sideshow Bob, Colonel Leslie "Hap" Hapablap was said to find only what?
A: Porno

Q: Homer ran a fake news website under what alias?
A: Mr. X

Q: Reverend Lovejoy once saved Ned Flanders from what kind of primate?
A: Baboon

Q: Why did NASA hire an average man to go into space?
A: Low TV ratings

Q: Who is the star player for the Springfield Atoms?
A: Stan "The Boy" Taylor

Q: In "The Homer They Fall," Moe says all angels wear what?
A: Farah Slacks

Q: According to Martin Prince, the common box kite was originally use for what?
A: Drying wet string

Q: In "Homer to the Max," which tree is said to be the only one that can defend itself?
A: The Mexican Fighting Tree

Q: What song does Mr. Burns play as he descends upon the Simpsons' home in a battle tank?
A: "Waterloo" by ABBA

Q: Who sleeps on top of a pile of money with many beautiful ladies?
A: Rainier Wolfcastle

Q: What fake holiday did Principal Skinner (with the help of Groundskeeper Willie) make up in a sting operation on Bart?
A: Scotchtoberfest

Q: In "Brick Hithouse," what is Homer's other boxing nickname?
A: The Southern Dandy

Q: What was Professor Frink's first patented invention?
A: The AT-5000 Auto-dialer

Q: Name one of the two gifts Bart gets Marge when he commits credit card fraud.
A: A frying pan radio or 15 pounds of Vancouver smoked salmon

Q: What was the name of Ned Flanders' bowling team?
A: The Holy Rollers

Q: What is the name of Homer's half brother's company?
A: Powell Motors

Q: Who sang to Homer and his NASA crew while they were in space?
A: James Taylor

Q: What club from Springfield Elementary got stranded on an island?
A: The UN Club

Q: Where did Bart say he went to the National Grammar Rodeo?
A: Canada

17 Chalkboard Gags

Every episode of *The Simpsons* starts nearly the same: a heavenly shot floats through the clouds, dissolves into an aerial gaze of the town of Springfield, and then shoots like a rocket through the city streets, zipping past various members of the Simpsons family. If the episode is particularly long, we'll get an abbreviated version that sees us hopping from the sky to the Simpsons' driveway in record time, but when the episode is timed just right, we'll be treated to a chalkboard gag.

A chalkboard gag, sometimes called a blackboard gag, is a running visual joke that has Bart Simpson writing as a punishment for something that has happened outside of the episode's story. The first gag appeared in the episode "Bart the Genius" in Season 1, Episode 2 and had Bart simply writing, "I will not waste chalk." From there the gags seemed within a similar simple realm. (Episode 3 had "I will not skateboard in the halls," and Episode 4 had "I will not burp in class.") It's easy to spot the writers dipping their toes into this idea, realizing a potential opportunity for comedy while being unsure if it'll track with audiences.

In the episode "Moaning Lisa" (Season 1, Episode 6), Bart writes, "I will not instigate revolution," and behold, the chalkboard gag joke runner officially took flight. Over time, the chalkboard gags ranged from a meta-commentary on the show itself ("I will not defame New Orleans") to social commentary ("I did not see Elvis") to jokes that poked fun at the very style in which the chalkboard gag appeared ("I will not finish what I sta" and "I will not squeak chalk" as Bart squeaks chalk while writing).

The production required for the chalkboard gags was fairly simple and thus could be turned over quickly as compared to the production of the episode itself. Because of this the gags could be fitted more specifically to topical events that were occurring. For example, the chalkboard gag, "South Park, We'd Stand Beside You if We Weren't So Scared" is in direct reference to the death threats *South Park* creators Trey Parker and Matt Stone received two weeks prior to their airing of two episodes that depicted the Muslim prophet Muhammad. Another gag reads, "I Will Not Leak the Plot of the Movie" after *The Simpsons Movie* had been officially announced.

As you may imagine, over *The Simpsons'* decades-long run, the chalkboard gag itself has gone through many iterations and unconventional styles. In "The Simpsons Halloween Special IX" (Season 10, Episode 4), we see the first time a Treehouse of Horror episode has used a chalkboard gag, and Bart uses a bucket of blood to paint.

In the episode "Bonfire of the Manatees" (Season 17, Episode 1), Bart writes, "Does Any Kid Still Do This Anymore?" This commentary not only refers to the somewhat archaic school punishment, but also on the show's much less frequent use of the chalkboard gag in the episodes around that time. (The previous two seasons only featured five chalkboard gags over 43 episodes.) Lastly, one could also read this as speaking to the viewers of the show itself, a self-deprecating tact that *The Simpsons* writers have often used.

One of the most famous and tender chalkboard gags appeared in the episode "Four Regrettings and a Funeral" (Season 25, Episode 3). Bart sadly writes, "We'll Really Miss You Mrs. K." This episode aired just nine days after the death of longtime voice actor Marcia Wallace, who famously voiced Mrs. Krabappel during the show's run.

First Episode: "Simpsons Roasting on an Open Fire"

The first episode of *The Simpsons* was a mistake. Usually, TV shows debut with their pilot episode. In most cases this episode introduces the characters and world, conveys the inciting incident that got us here in the first place, and shows viewers what to expect week by week. But *The Simpsons* had a different approach. For starters, they already made their TV debut through *The Tracey Ullman Show* and thus didn't need to spend much time introducing themselves to the world. Yet, the FOX network was still nervous. Sure, people were fans of *Ullman*, and Matt Groening's *Life in Hell* comics had a cult following, but would half an hour of animation in primetime be enough to sustain the public's wandering eye?

So the network proposed this: cut the regular 22-minute sitcom format into a segmented style of three seven-minute shorts. The plan was to ease fans into seeing them shine on their own platform while still evoking the flow and style of what pulled them in the first place. *The Simpsons* producers wouldn't stand for it. By breaking up the episodes in this way, they would be inadvertently presenting the show as no different than a children's cartoon, in which 11-minute half-episodes are commonplace. In order to compete with the likes of *The Cosby Show* and other ratings juggernauts, they would have to be taken seriously. More importantly, in order to completely carve their path away from being nothing more than an expansion of their original vignettes on FOX, they would have to not only be a full 22 minutes every episode, but they also would have to have a series order as well. The producers pushed FOX for an initial 13-episodes, and the network eventually obliged.

Though the show's creators got what they wanted, the road to air was anything but easy. Animation mishaps, production hiccups, rewrites, and redevelopment of the look and style of the show took longer than anyone anticipated, and soon the original premiere date was pushed back further and further.

Originally, *The Simpsons'* first episode was destined to be "Some Enchanted Evening," in which Homer and Marge spend a night on the town and leave the kids with a masochistic babysitter named Ms. Boltz. When the premiere date was pushed back and the animation quality for this episode was not up to snuff, the producers quickly brainstormed when and how the world would get to know Springfield.

A confluence of perfect elements quickly assembled by chance. The premiere date soon became mid-December, a roundup of eight or so episodes were hastily being animated, and the strongest episode they had in their arsenal happened to be…their Christmas special. It was almost too perfect.

"Simpsons Roasting on an Open Fire" centers around Homer discovering he won't be getting a Christmas bonus and thus unable to provide presents for his family that year. In order to save face and keep the embarrassing secret, he gets a job as a mall Santa, but even this pursuit becomes fruitless. As a last ditch effort to win back the holidays, Homer and Bart bond on the dog racing track, where they find the Simpsons family's future pet, Santa's Little Helper.

"Simpsons Roasting on an Open Fire" was nominated for two Emmy Awards in 1990, an unusual feat for a pilot episode. The gamble to make the show's introduction a special episode soon paid off. The concept about it being family-oriented read loud and clear, and the ludicrous antics (Bart getting a tattoo at age nine and then promptly getting it removed) promised a loopy future that has kept viewers watching well beyond what the network could have ever projected.

19 Lisa Simpson

Lisa Simpson, the singing dorkette who married a carrot (she admitted it), is the voice of a generation. Her gift of intelligence and passion for justice has gotten her far in life and even if she doesn't control the birds (she will one day), she's accomplished more in her eight years of life than most people have in a lifetime. An inspiration for feminists young and old, the precious middle child stands up to government corruption, promotes animal rights, and rejects gender norms so strongly that she helped create the first (and last) feminist Malibu Stacy doll.

Lisa isn't always Miss Perfect, but her deeply human desire to be popular has led her to trade in aspects of her identity for friendship, popularity—and in "Lisa's Rival"—a winning score on her diorama. In the emotionally charged Season 6 episode "Summer of 4 Ft. 2," Lisa ditches her old look and tries to copy Bart's behavior to win her points with the cool kids on vacation. In her famous "like ya know, whatever" transformation, she eventually learns the only way to make true friends is to be yourself (since you don't make friends with salad). Like most of us, Lisa is flawed and makes the same mistake more than once. In a momentary lapse of judgment in the Season 10 episode "Lard of the Dance," she succumbs to the pressure of the popular new girl Phoebe and ditches her "we're still kids" look for a grown-up costume of lipstick, high heels, and pierced ears. When she can't even get a date with Milhouse—"There's plenty of Milhouse to go around"—she realizes once more the importance of being yourself.

Being yourself when you're a Simpson can be a gamble depending on your gender. For the hyper intelligent straight-A student, the threat of the Simpsons gene hindering her intelligence threw

Lisa through the wringer. Thanks to the discovery that the gene only affects males, Lisa thankfully didn't have to worry for long. However, in the heart-wrenching episode "HOMR," it's revealed that Homer's dim nature can be attributed to a childhood instance in which he jammed a crayon up his nose and into his brain. Once the crayon was removed, Homer's IQ skyrocketed, and he and Lisa were able to connect on a new level, which allowed him to truly appreciate Lisa. In the sitcom's typical reset ending, Homer put the crayon back in his nose, explaining in a letter she found after the surgery. "I'm taking the coward's way out. But before I do, I just wanted to say being smart made me appreciate just how amazing you really are," he wrote. This was one of the many sweet father/daughter moments on the show.

In a prediction of Lisa's future in "Lisa's Wedding," the two share a touching exchange.

Homer: "Since you've been able to pin your own diapers, you've been smarter than me."
Lisa: "Oh, Dad."
Homer: "No, no, let me finish. I just want you to know I've always been proud of you. You're my greatest accomplishment and you did it all yourself."

Amongst all of the amazing Lisa moments in the show, some of the most often overlooked are the ones in which she gets to just be a kid. We get a glimpse of this with her poem about Snowball 1:

> *"I had a cat named Snowball. She died! She died!*
> *Mom said she was sleeping. She lied! She lied!*
> *Why, oh, why is my cat dead? Couldn't that Chrysler hit me instead?*
> *I had a hamster named Snuffy. He died."*

Whether you love Lisa because of her relatability or you simply find her a real character, there's no denying that she is an emotional backbone to the show. Homer and Bart may get all the big laughs, but the humor of Lisa is in some ways greater because it's grounded by her earnest character. Lisa provides insight, heart, and also some of the best jokes. Yes, sometimes they are at her expense—"I can see through time"—but other times it's Lisa just being Lisa like when she says: "Science has already proven the dangers of smoking, alcohol, and Chinese food, but I can still ruin soft drinks for everyone!"

20 Mr. Burns

There was a time in the recent past when an openly greedy, scheming, ruthlessly self-interested billionaire with a flair for the cruel and unusual was, well, a fun joke. Right now it hits a little too close to reality, but he's still a great character. In fact, in a 2007 *Vanity Fair* interview, Conan O'Brien called Mr. Burns the most fun character to write for. "He had two qualities that are perfect if you're a comedy writer and want to have fun: he's infinitely old and he has unlimited wealth. And he's evil. So, three. Those three qualities are great because they allow you to create anything. A scene can open with him coming out of a hyperbaric chamber where he sleeps at night. He can have sinister robots. He can have a cavernous basement under his mansion. He can have a bat cave. There is literally nothing you can't do with Mr. Burns."

Charles Montgomery Burns, the billionaire owner of the nuclear power plant and the boss of Homer (and Lenny and Carl) is certainly evil. He's a villain's villain. He's literally stolen candy from a baby, has released vicious attack dogs on Bart, and used a giant net to turn millions of ocean creatures into a seafood paste called Lil' Lisa's Seafood Slurry. Mr. Burns even hired Homer to throw pudding in Lenny's eye, and you're not supposed to get pudding in it!

Mr. Burns is also wildly and opulently wealthy. A vessel for jokes and ideas about America's history of greed, Mr. Burns was modeled after famous rich American men like John D. Rockefeller, Howard Hughes, the fictional Charles Foster Kaine, and Matt Groening's high school teacher Mr. Bailey, the last of whom is probably not a billionaire unless the state of Oregon has really started paying teachers more. (If that's the case, congrats Oregon school teachers, ya rich bastards!)

Mr. Burns acquired his wealth initially by inheriting a fortune from his cold and heartless billionaire grandfather Colonial Wainwright Montgomery Burns, whom he was sent to live with when his parents couldn't afford all of their 12 children. Burns went on to steal a trillion-dollar bill from the U.S. treasury in 1941 (which he later lost to Fidel Castro) and now seems to make an endless amount of money from his properties in Springfield, among which include the nuclear power plant, Isotope Stadium, Springsonian Museum, and the Spellympic Village.

And finally, Monty Burns is ancient. At different points in the three decades of *Simpsons* episodes, Burns is 81, 104, and old enough to fight in the Civil War. Mr. Burns' superior age allows for some of the best jokes and most obscure references in the entire series. Burns uses antiquated phrases like "Count Ferdinand used the Zepplin." Some of Burns' phrases include, but are not limited to: referring to gasoline as "petroleum distillate," the brake pedal as the "deceleratrix," and a TV as a "jumping box" and "picto-tube." Burns also answers the phone by saying "Ahoy hoy," a reference to Alexander Graham Bell's original idea for the proper way to answer a phone.

Burns, like all key *Simpsons* characters, has a softer side. He loved his teddy bear Bobo, which held a Rosebud-like significance. He tries to bond with both Bart and Lisa. And, of course, he has someone who loves him, and that is his deeply closeted right-hand man, Waylon Smithers

Oh yeah, and he steeples his fingers and says, "Excellent." But if you didn't know that already, we've got some international hay you can invest in.

21 Pop Culture References

Read any article about *The Simpsons*, and no doubt the show's encyclopedic and often esoteric cache of references will be mentioned. Although it might not seem so strange today, a television show making references to literature, film, and many other aspects of culture was a pretty rare thing for a sitcom to do in the '90s, especially for a cartoon. Consider that the show's fourth season aired when programs like *Home Improvement* and *Full House* were in the top 10 most watched shows of that year, according to the Nielsen ratings. If you really want a stark comparison, watch an episode of one of those shows after watching an episode like "Last Exit to Springfield." Yikes. *The Simpsons* was clearly ahead of its time in terms of treating the audience as though they're smart enough to keep up.

Any given episode of *The Simpsons* (especially after the first few seasons) is jam-packed with all sorts of references, which might explain why the show gained so much popularity with early adopters of the Internet. Nerds (for lack of a better term) love to obsess over things, and *The Simpsons* is so densely layered with references that it practically requires multiple viewings in order to catch them all. If you want the most complete list of references for an episode, you're not going to do better than what you can find online at sites like simpsons.wikia or most notably simpsonsarchive.com, which features new posts and archives from the newsgroup alt.simpsons.tv.

The Simpsons is such a reference-heavy show that you could write endlessly about the allusions in the episode titles alone. And before DVDs and the Internet, the titles were rarely seen by anyone! In the first two seasons alone, titles reference a Christmas carol from the '40s, a Jack London novel, an Edgar Allan Poe short story, a John Steinbeck novel, the Old Testament, a Herbert Hoover quote, a Dr. Seuss book, and a Barbra Streisand movie. And that's not even a complete list. The title references run the gamut of high-brow to lowbrow. Third season episode "When Flanders Failed" is a reference to "In Flanders Field," a poem written by a Canadian physician during World War I. Fourteenth season episode "Dude, Where's My Ranch?" is a reference to the 2000 Ashton Kutcher movie *Dude, Where's My Car?* As of the writing of this book, there are four separate episode titles that reference Alfred Hitchcock's film *The Man Who Knew Too Much.*

Although it might not technically be the most referenced film in the history of the show, Orson Welles' 1941 masterpiece *Citizen Kane* appears to be a favorite of the writers. The fifth season episode "Rosebud" contains the most direct allusions—from the episode's title to its *Kane*-inspired plot of a powerfully wealthy mogul (Mr. Burns) longing for a lost toy from his youth. Generally, the character of Mr. Burns seems to be modeled after Charles Foster Kane. Much like the title character in *Citizen Kane*, Burns uses his extreme wealth to fund his own gubernatorial campaign that culminates in a speech where he stands in front of a massive self-portrait. His mansion and estate have a striking resemblance to Kane's, including the front gate and the layout of his bedroom. We've seen Burns be the recipient of a song-and-dance number paying tribute to him, much like the one in the film. Heck, even Burns' first name of Charles is an homage to Kane, according to Matt Groening himself. Be sure to check out the great side-by-side comparison video uploaded by YouTube account "Moon Film" that showcases just how visually meticulous the show has been when referencing the film. You can find that video by searching "Citizen Kane 75th Anniversary—A Simpsons Tribute."

If you're the type of person who likes reading about all of *The Simpsons'* references in one convenient place episode by episode, check out the official episode guides released by HarperCollins. The most recent edition, *Simpsons World: The Ultimate Episode Guide*, covers the first 20 season and includes thorough break-downs of just about every allusion and homage. It will no doubt be the thickest book on your shelf, so don't say we didn't warn you.

Simpsons Words and How to Use Them

The linguistic contributions *The Simpsons* have made to the English language are legitimately impressive. Most successful TV shows will get one, *maybe* two catchphrases or jokes that break out into the general lexicon, but *The Simpsons* has dozens if not hundreds. *D'oh* was even added to the *Oxford English Dictionary*. It's British, so you know it's fancy.

The Simpsons uses language like actual people do, which is perhaps why it's permeated the lexicon in such a deep way. Everybody has, whether consciously or not, their own equivalent to "Yoink!" or has mispronounced a word in a funny way that became the standard pronunciation in their lives. The language on the show is a perfect companion to modern American English. It's loose, it's simple, and it also can be kinda dumb. Below is a perfectly cromulent—yet incomplete—list, which includes the word followed by the definition:

- **Cromulent**—The best of the best, a sterling example of quality and craftsmanship, which embiggens the soul of all who hear it. See also: embiggen.
- **Embiggen**—To expand patriotically. See also: cromulent.
- **Yoink**—The sound made when trying to discreetly steal an item from someone who can clearly see you. It is almost always followed by the speaker running away.
- **Jebus**—An invocation toward a higher power in one's moment of need and proof you didn't really pay that much attention in church. (And who can blame you? That Lovejoy guy is a real drag.)
- **Boo-Urns**—This is what Hans Moleman was saying.
- **Okily Dokily**—This is a super duper useful wordiddly-durddily for all you Flanderinos.
- **Dollareydoos**—Australian currency often won in high stakes games of Knifey Spooney.
- **Rageahol**—A substance consumed by rageaholics.
- **Doctorb**—The "B" stands for "bargain!" The rest stands for "Doctor!" (Under no circumstances should you visit a Doctorb.)
- **Fer it/Agin it**—If you ain't one, yer t'other.
- **D'oh**—The accepted shortening of "Annoyed Grunt," which is literally how it reads in the dictionary.
- **Cheese-Eating Surrender Monkey**—They know who they are.
- **Glavin**—An all-purpose exclamation for the yelling, the flailing, and the falling (mmmHEY) of Professor Frink.

- **Dealie**—Ya' know, one of those…things…with the, um… lemme get back to you on that…
- **America Junior**—This refers to those lousy moochers up north.
- **Jiminy Jillikers**—A comic book-style exclamation used by Radioactive Man's young sidekick, Fallout Boy. It's the phrase that gave Milhouse van Houten a nervous breakdown.
- **Rastafy**—A mathematical value that can be heightened to enhance the attitude of a cartoon dog.
- **Sacrilicious**—The delicious taste of sin.
- **Saxamaphone**—The sound one must make to power a brass instrument.
- **Tramampoline/Trabopoline**: There's a *what* in the backyard! Yeah, it refers to that apparatus.
- **Steamed Ham**—An Albany expression that is completely real and used by real people who exist.
- **Unpossible**—The chance that one might fail English.
- **Traumedey**—When you injure yourself in a hilarious manner.
- **Don't Have A Cow Man**—A long forgotten relic of a phrase now seen only on bootleg Rasta Bart T-shirts from 1992.
- **Meh**—It's like, you know, whatever.

Simpsons Quotes for Every Day

Sometimes original thought escapes us. Us fail English? Totally possible. That's why we turn to the words of the wise, wonderful, weird writers who keep our favorite show afloat. Here's a breakdown of some of our favorite finds that not only serve as a superfan litmus test, but also help communicate what you truly mean in any real-life situation:

When You've Seen Something You Can Never Unsee:
"The goggles do nothing."
—"Radioactive Man" (Season 7, Episode 2)

When Someone Cuts You Off in Traffic
"Enjoy your death trap, ladies."
—"Fear of Flying" (Season 6, Episode 11)

When You're Protesting
"Where's my burrito? Where's my burrito?"
—"Last Exit to Springfield" (Season 4, Episode 17)

When Someone Asks For Your Political Views
"I just came here to see *Honk If You're Horny* in peace!"
—"King-Size Homer" (Season 7, Episode 7)

When You're Too Cool to Say "I Love You"
"Sticking together is what good waffles do!"
—"Marge on the Lam" (Season 5, Episode 6)

When Karen from HR Mispronounces Your Name for the 12ᵗʰ Time
"My son's name is also named Bort."
—"Itchy & Scratchy Land" (Season 6, Episode 4)

When You Meet Your Soulmate
"So this is what it feels like when doves cry."
—"Lemon of Troy" (Season 6, Episode 24)

When Your Best Friend Refuses to Admit Horny Marge is the Actual Best Character
"Hey, you, let's fight. Them's fightin' words."
—"Colonel Homer" (Season 3, Episode 20)

When All Other Words Escape You
"Woozle wazzle?"
—"Bart Gets Famous" (Season 5, Episode 12)

When You're Three Seconds from Blowing Up
"I see you've played knifey spoony before."
—"Bart vs. Australia" (Season 6, Episode 16)

When Someone Asks You for Career Advice
"In America first you get the sugar, then you get the power, then you get the women."
—"Lisa's Rival" (Season 6, Episode 2)

When You Open Twitter
"Marge, my friend, I haven't learned a thing."
—"Homer Badman" (Season 6, Episode 9)

When You're Saying Yes to the Dress
"I really like the vest."
—"All Singing, All Dancing" (Season 9, Episode 11)

When You Find Out There's a Sale
"What time and how burnt?"
—"Scenes from a Class Struggle in Springfield" (Season 7, Episode 14)

When Your Bridesmaids/Groomsmen Have Moved On
"Sorry Mom, the mob has spoken."
—"All Singing, All Dancing" (Season 9, Episode 11)

When You're Wine Tasting
"Wow. It's like there's a party in my mouth, and everyone's invited."
—"Homer at the Bat" (Season 3, Episode 17)

When You See a Bad Play
"Boo-urns."
—"A Star is Burns" (Season 6, Episode 18)

24 Itchy and Scratchy

Itchy and Scratchy, the beloved anthropomorphic cat and mouse who star in the cartoon within a cartoon, *The Itchy & Scratchy Show*, are a stand-out feature of the show's early years into its mid-1990s renaissance period. A grotesque, hyper-violent parody of wholesome *Tom and Jerry* cartoons, the shorts feature the psychotic blue mouse Itchy finding equally creative and disturbing ways to torture and kill the sweet, hapless black cat Scratchy. They're practically synonymous with the show they appear on.

Itchy and Scratchy made their first appearance in *The Tracey Ullman Show* short "The Bart Simpson Show" on November 20, 1988, and made their first appearance on the series in the first-season episode "There's No Disgrace Like Home." The shorts appear within *The Krusty the Clown Show*, and the creation of the characters has an impressively detailed backstory that borrows a lot from Walt Disney and early 1930s animation lore. (The first cartoon Itchy and Scratchy appeared in was called "Steamboat Itchy.") It's a testament to what makes *The Simpsons* such a uniquely ambitious show, willing to delve deeply into the fictional history and environment of a cartoon within a cartoon. This was explored in numerous episodes that centered on the production and fandom culture surrounding Itchy and Scratchy, which include "Itchy & Scratchy & Marge" (Season 2, 1990), "Itchy & Scratchy: The Movie" (Season 4, 1992), "Itchy & Scratchy Land" (Season 6, 1994), "The Day the Violence Died" (Season 7, 1996), and "The Itchy & Scratchy & Poochie Show" (Season 8, 1997).

The show is said to be based on many different cartoons beyond *Tom and Jerry*. The 1980s Italian comic strip *Squeak the Mouse* is considered a direct influence and arguably beat *Itchy & Scratchy* to the punch of doing violent send-ups of classic cartoons. Longtime *Simpsons* director David Silverman has said the characters are based on *Herman and Katnip*, a series of theatrical animated shorts from the '40s and '50s that he's called "hilarious because it's just bad." Matt Groening said as a kid that he and his friends fantasized about an ultra violent kids cartoon and how much fun it would be to work on a show like that. When he watched *101 Dalmatians* as a kid, he was particularly inspired by a scene where the puppies watch television, and the idea of having a cartoon within a cartoon thrilled the young Groening.

As *The Simpsons* progressed and the shorts became more popular, the show's writers and animators would often add them when an episode needed expanding. They were a favorite of John Swartzwelder's, who wrote many episodes that centered on them and often pitched the ideas for the shorts. David Silverman has called the *Itchy & Scratchy* cartoons "an ironic commentary on cartoon mayhem in the sense that it's taken to a more realistic level." And that level of mayhem often got the writers in trouble with the FOX network.

During Season 5 and 6, showrunner David Mirkin was asked by FOX to not do anymore *Itchy & Scratchy* cartoons due to the amount of violence. Instead of heeding that warning, the show produced "Itchy & Scratchy Land," arguably one of the series' most terrifying episodes. When the network threatened to cut Itchy and Scratchy out of episodes moving forward, Mirkin threatened to tell the media. As a compromise, the writers promised to not overdo the violence moving forward.

Perhaps the most acclaimed Itchy and Scratchy-centric episode of the entire series is Season 8's "The Itchy & Scratchy & Poochie Show," a self-reflective commentary on what it's like to work on a long-running show that's pressured by its fanbase and network to find ways to stay fresh and relevant. The episode was inspired by FOX executives suggesting that the writers add a new character to the show on a permanent basis. From there, they crafted a storyline where the obnoxious, inauthentic hip-hop surfing dog Poochie (voiced by Homer) is added to *Itchy & Scratchy* to help boost ratings. Endlessly hyped-up by the media and fan culture, Poochie lands with a thud in his debut episode and is swiftly killed off in his second appearance. It's a really smart examination of the process by which art is labored upon, twisted by executives, consumed by fans, and immediately disparaged. (There's a reason why this episode marks the debut of Comic Book Guy's catchphrase: "Worst episode ever!")

Itchy & Scratchy is more than just mindless, ultra-violent cartoons that add filler to an episode of *The Simpsons*. It is the inspiration behind some of the smartest and most satirical episodes that the series has ever produced. But most importantly, without them, we wouldn't have the Bort license plate gag from "Itchy & Scratchy Land."

25 Treehouse of Horror

"Hello everyone. You know, Halloween is a very strange holiday. Personally, I don't understand it. Kids worshiping ghosts, pretending to be devils, and things on TV that are completely inappropriate for younger viewers. Things like the following half hour. Nothing seems to bother my kids, but tonight's show, which I totally wash my hands of, is really scary. So if you have sensitive children, maybe you should tuck them into bed early tonight instead of writing us angry letters tomorrow. Thanks for your attention."

With the thoroughly judgmental words of the Simpsons matriarch, not to mention a fantastic hearkening back to the opening of the Universal classic *Frankenstein*, so begins the 29 consecutive years of *The Simpsons'* "Treehouse of Horror" episodes. These yearly installments, which began in Season 2, have three segments that each tell separate spooky short stories along with a wraparound segment to tie everything together...as much as one can in a 30-minute horror cartoon. This style was brought about by the anthology (or portmanteau) films popularized in the late 1960s and 1970s by Amicus productions with their films *Asylum* and *The House That Dripped Blood*. Portmanteau is a word whose meaning is derived from two or more distinct words like smog, which is of course made up of smoke and fog, or Los Angeles, which is of course being made up of smoke and smog. When used in the anthology horror film or "Treehouse of Horror," it reinforces the idea that the three different stories can create one cohesive piece of art. (You can read more in our next book: *100 Things Portmanteau Fans Should Know & Do Before They Die*.) Anyway, these, in turn, were inspired by the schlocky E.C. comics *Vault of Horror* and *Tales from the Crypt* from the 1940s and 1950s as well as Rod Serling properties, *The Twilight Zone* and *The Night Gallery*.

The Simpsons used different writers for different segments per episode until the 14th episode but used multiple directors on only the first. Since the 14th season, it has employed only one writer and one director per episode to handle said duties. This is very similar to the films on which they are based, which had different writers and directors handling the different segments of the film. The humor, characters, and setting in "Treehouse of Horror" episodes were outside of the main *Simpsons* universe so the writers could kill off any character with impunity in any of the segments. This was often the case with supporting characters (Groundskeeper Willie is a particular favorite), but this can include the main cast and even members of the titular family. The only rules seem to be including Kodos and Kang in every episode. Another strange, dare we say scary, thing is that only the first 10 episodes aired on or during the week of Halloween because of a frightening thing called Major League Baseball. After the FOX contract with MLB was changed, the episodes, while sometimes airing quite early in the month, were once again an October viewing staple. Over time these episodes became so popular that they garnered their own DVD releases. This was a collection of a collection of stories! We are talking Simpsonsception here!

The writers take great care to make these episodes special and horror-themed in everything from the hokey names on the tombstones in the cemetery to changing the opening credits, couch gag, and theme song. If an important movie or director hasn't been given a direct story, then they show up as a parody somewhere here. The first episode runs the gamut by doing parodies of the haunted house genre, an absolute classic *Twilight Zone* episode, and some jerk named Edgar Allan Poe. The wraparound is even where all classic scary stories originated from: people sitting around on a dark night telling them to each other. The other episodes have done everything from *A Nightmare on Elm Street* to *The Island of Doctor Moreau* to *Bram Stoker's Dracula* and anything in between. If you didn't like this chapter, don't blame us, we voted for Kodos!

 **Merch**

After "Bartmania" ignited the early 1990s, FOX knew it had something special on its hands and soon laid the groundwork for a multi-billion-dollar merchandising industry. Early items included simple dolls with big, hulking plastic heads, lunchboxes, hats, and bendable palm-sized figures. Demand for collectables of *The Simpsons* soon spiked higher than supply could keep up, giving way to bizarre and scattered creative choices. A trip to your local swap meet may treat you to coffee mugs with character catchphrases that have never actually been uttered. (One such mug depicts Marge holding up a plate of gray mush with the quote, "I made it myself!") Later the first series of action figures released by Mattel would depict Homer coupled with a speech bubble saying, "Do I smell cupcakes? Do I ever!"

But another merchandise sensation emerged in the early '90s. Around this time "Black Bart" made its way into society, wearing Air Jordans and dancing MC Hammer-style while touting political epithets. "Black Bart" no doubt baffled the show's creators. It's hard to decipher the cause for "Black Bart." Was it a symbol for a marginalized community that potentially sought to capitalize on the visibility and popularity of Bart as a platform for their politics? Or was it just an example of an off-model interpretation of the popular character? The writers of this book aren't quite sure but appreciate his creation nonetheless.

Similar to the explosion of *Star Wars* merchandise, there's a strong, "If you dream it, you can do it" sensibility to the onslaught of collectables from *The Simpsons*. Everything from candy, toys, watches, shoes, shampoo, you name it—nothing was sacred in its collectable conquering. Comic books became particularly big.

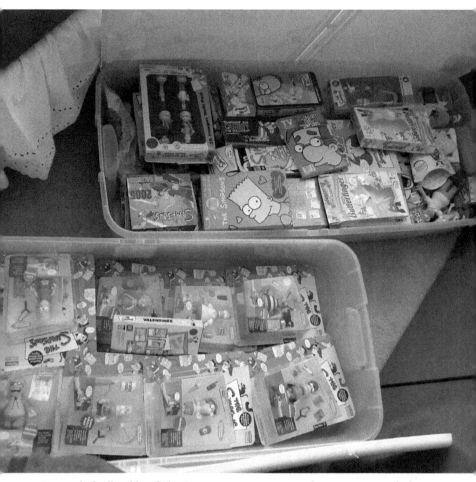

Demand of collectibles of The Simpsons *remains strong, but it was particularly high during the early 1990s.* (Joe Kwaczala)

Initially intended as a one-off comic book edition of the magazine *Simpsons Illustrated*, *Simpsons Comics and Stories* first debuted in 1992. On its cover Bart, masked as his super-alter-ego Bartman, glares with disdain, as other stories featuring Radioactive Man, Maggie, and Lisa are teased.

Perhaps due in part to Bart's presence being front and center, perhaps due to *The Simpsons* mania at large, there was no arguing with the comic's ravenous reception from superfans the world over. Plans were soon formed to make *The Simpsons* comics its own branch on the merchandise tree. In 1993 Matt Groening founded Bongo Comics with Steve and Cindy Vance and Bill Morrison as a platform for Springfield's graphic novel adventures, as well as a hub for other artistic pursuits. Today the company publishes comics for animation titans like *Futurama, SpongeBob SquarePants,* as well as other original material.

Another era of *Simpsons* merch was born when Universal Studios unveiled Simpsons Land in the Florida and California parks. Theme park-specific items were created such as Springfield sipper cups and Duffman baseball caps. Though not to be one-upped by their amusement park peers, *The Simpsons* added their personal touch, creating merchandise that catered to every Bort who needs a license plate or every Homer who needs a Triple-XL pink sprinkled donut.

Since 2010 *Simpsons* merch has shifted with social trends, expanding from standard fare to more artistic endeavors like inter-active toys with "voice activating platforms," as well as Mr. Sparkle vinyl figures whose elegant, sculpted form suggests it could take down your G.I. Joes. And "Simpsons as Art" is almost its own category on Etsy.com, giving way to heaps of DIY enamel pins, patches, purses, and more.

27 Maggie Simpson

Born May 12, 1988, Maggie "Margaret" Simpson is the youngest of the Simpsons family clan. She was named after creator Matt Groening's sister and borne out of the idea that he thought it'd be funny to have a non-verbal character who never aged. She's often seen sucking on her pacifier, a sound effect that was famously voiced by Gabor Ksupo, one part of the animation studio Klasky Csupo, which was the first animation home for the show in the early 1990s before transitioning over to Film Roman.

Due to the fact that Maggie's merely a one-year old and pre-verbal, most of her character turns come in the form of a careful eyeroll, a poke to her parents' attention, or a stumble down a staircase. Maggie is usually along for the ride in any given episode but occasionally is granted her own storytelling space to express her distinct character. Most often, this comes in the form of her demonstrating competence and organizational abilities. With a single wave, she can summon other babies to follow her; with a glare she can shoot death stares to her baby nemesis, Gerald; and in most other cases, she can express pure joy with a simple head pat or hug from Marge.

Despite the fact that Maggie's character isn't as prominent a presence as other members of the Simpsons family, her impact on the show has been tremendous. In the conclusion to the famous 1995 two-parter "Who Shot Mr. Burns?" we learn that the true culprit to the crime was an innocent Maggie in her stroller. In the Season 5 episode "Rosebud," it's a sweet-natured Maggie who melts the heart of Montgomery Burns when she gets attached to his beloved teddy bear Bobo. In the Season 6 episode "And Maggie Makes Three," we discover that Maggie's unplanned birth led to Homer re-strengthening his resolve for the 9–5 by littering his office space with her baby photos (and a simple reminder to "Do it for her").

Throughout the show's run, Maggie's moments of speaking have consistently been treated as a larger event. In the Season 4 episode, "Lisa's First Word," Maggie speaks for the first time, and though it's simply one word (Daddy), the show gave the honors to Elizabeth Taylor to voice it, and it is a moving moment. Within the non-canon episode specials ("Treehouse of Horror" mostly), the show's creators apply creative license by giving usually mute Maggie the darkest of character traits. Fans can hardly forget the image of the terrifying toddler spinning her head back in "Treehouse of Horror V." After hacking an ax into the back of Groundskeeper Willie, Maggie pulls out her pacifier to say in a deep voice, "This is indeed a disturbing universe."

Though it's hard to predict precisely how Maggie's role in the Simpsons family dynamic will play out as she gets older, many hints from the show's writers have tipped to the fact that she may be a kind of prodigy. Throughout the show's run, Maggie's spelled mathematic equations through her building blocks, steered a car, and served the intelligent voice box for her Uncle Herb's baby translator invention.

In the Season 6 episode "Lisa's Wedding," viewers witnessed what a grown-up Maggie may actually be. Snarky, sassy, and strapped into stereotypical teenage garb, the writers continually tease how "chatty" she is once she's gotten older, though the running joke of the episode is that other characters constantly interrupt her before she has a chance to truly express herself.

One of the greatest Maggie moments came not in the form of a regular episode, but in an Oscar-nominated short. In 2012 "The Longest Daycare" was an idea proposed by *The Simpsons* producer James L. Brooks as a potential short to screen before a feature, like how Pixar Animation creates isolated shorts before their films. True to that established style, "Longest Daycare" hinges on mostly visual storytelling and a heightened cinematic soundtrack.

In the plot Maggie stars as she's enrolled in the militaristic Ayn Rand School for Tots, where she battles her nemesis Baby Gerald, befriends a caterpillar, and strategizes a breakout before Marge swings back to pick her up. According to *The Simpsons* showrunner Al Jean, they created the short as a simple way of saying, "Thanks" to the fans who have stuck through the show's 25-plus season run.

28 Writers You Must Know

At the time of writing this book, *The Simpsons* will have had around 115 guest and staff writers since its inception in 1989. Of the 115 people who have written on the show, we're going to focus on the seven writers you *must* know. This is no discredit to the amazing writers we left out; we just don't expect you to memorize the names of all 45-odd individuals who only wrote one episode.

One quick exception to the "one-episode rule" is Mimi Pond, who is downright crucial to the history of *The Simpsons* as she penned "Simpsons Roasting on an Open Fire." Despite her episode being a huge hit that was nominated for two Emmys, Mimi was never asked to be a staff writer. According to an interview with Vulture, Pond didn't find out until much later that the late Sam Simon had wanted an all-male writing room at the time. Had Pond been invited to join as a staff writer, who knows how many more amazing episodes she would have helped create. All the same, she remains an important part of *The Simpsons* history. Now on to the rest of the tour!

The initial writing team was assembled by Simon and consisted of John Swartzwelder, Jon Vitti, George Meyer, Jeff Martin, Al

Jean, Mike Reiss, and the writing team of Jay Kogen and Wallace Wolodarsky. Remember these names and pull them out the next time you're at a party. Your crush will respect you for knowing this. Respect yourself by digesting and memorizing the following writers and their credits:

George Meyer

Have you ever wondered how *The Simpsons* is so funny? Of course you have, and there are many reasons—not least of which are the rewrite sessions led by Meyer.

Greg Daniels

Before Daniels went on to dominate the TV landscape by co-creating *King of the Hill*, adapting *The Office* for NBC, and creating *Parks and Recreation*, he was an instrumental member of *The Simpsons* writing staff. He wrote some of the classic episodes, including "Homer and Apu," "Homer Badman," "Secrets of a Successful Marriage," "Lisa's Wedding," and "Bart Sells His Soul."

Conan O'Brien

Despite his short tenure on the show, Conan is famously considered one of the show's most beloved writers. When you write "The Monorail," that's bound to be expected. More than penning the lyrics, "the ring came off my pudding can, take my pen knife, my good man," Conan was responsible for "New Kid on the Block," "Homer Goes to College," and the name of Patty and Selma's iguana, Jub Jub. He also went on to become the host of *Late Night* and *The Tonight Show*.

David X. Cohen

Futurama writer and executive producer Cohen wrote for *The Simpsons* from 1994 to 1998 and penned such notable episodes as

"Lisa the Vegetarian," "Itchy & Scratchy & Poochie Show," "Lisa the Skeptic," and "Das Bus."

Carolyn Omine

This hilarious writer and producer of *The Simpsons* happens to be one of the few women to ever write for the show. Omine previously worked on *Full House* before she started working on *The Simpsons* in Season 10.

Ian Maxtone-Graham

The inspiration for the "Very Tall Man in 22 Short Films About Springfield," Maxtone-Graham wrote 22 episodes between 1996 and 2014 (including the great "The City of New York vs. Homer Simpson") but is credited by some Internet commenters as being the person who "ruined" *The Simpsons*, citing him as an integral figure in *The Simpsons* becoming a "cartoon" when it was once a sitcom. That's a lot of credit to give one man, and we disagree entirely. If anyone "ruined" *The Simpsons*, it's likely one of the authors of the book who forced you to analyze the best show of all time for so long that we ran it into the ground.

Future Timelines

The Simpsons exists in a floating timeline typical of most animated shows. Due to the fact that the show's writers don't have to accommodate the aging of their actors, every episode of *The Simpsons* is under the assumption that no time has passed from the previous week. No matter how many decades the show's run endures, Bart will always be 10 years old, Lisa will be eight, and Maggie will be sucking on her pacifier.

The Simpsons escapist fantasies have often centered around the future of our favorite family: would Lisa finally become president? Will Bart bump his way through life? Will Maggie finally speak? Of course, the show can't formally advance forward in time, but the writers soon found creative ways of working around that. They introduced future episodes—part of a trope that the show would summon every couple of seasons to both satiate fan appetite and surrender to the inevitable.

The first glimpse of the future came as the coda of the Season 4 episode, "Itchy & Scratchy: the Movie." After Homer punishes Bart, banishing him from seeing *The Itchy & Scratchy: The Movie* "for the rest of his life," we see months and months pass with Homer's ruling staying resolute. Even after the other family members beg Homer to lighten up, he's focused and determined. Bart needs to learn his lesson, and for once Homer doesn't crumble into a hollowed-out softie. In the episode's final moments, we're transported 40 years into the future, amid flying cars and strolling robots. Now Chief Justice of the Supreme Court (a potentially sly nod at the sloppiness of politics), Bart and Homer, who withered and wavering from his signature spunky stroll down the street, see that a revival screening of *Itchy & Scratchy* is playing at a local theater. Believing Bart has finally learned his lesson, the two mosey inside. Though this is just a quick scene, the mere glimpse into the escapist fantasies appealed to many superfans, and it gave way to a world the writers were eager to explore.

In Season 6's "Lisa's Wedding," the show would lean in to their future fantasies for the bulk of the 22-minute episode. The story treats us to the year 2010, where Lisa is freshly post-college and pre-nuptials. Within this version of their world, Lisa's still high-achieving, Bart is contentedly working in construction (where he gleefully demolishes high-rises), and Maggie's mustering up the courage to finally make conversation. Her "incredible singing voice" is referenced and was a plant the show would follow up on in later seasons.

Later in Season 11's "Bart to the Future," we see the future through Bart's eyes. In the year 2030, Bart's a struggling musician with Ralph Wiggum and Lisa's the president of the United States. Though this episode is wrapped within the guise of it being a daydream, out of all of the future-focused episodes, this certainly feels the closest to reality right on down to former president Donald Trump vacating the government seat for Lisa to situate herself in the role. Yikes.

Season 16's "Future Drama" would be the first future-focused episode that would exist slightly within canon. Bart and Lisa accidentally stumble into Professor Frink's "future projector," a device that makes predictions through astrology. In this episode we see the Simpsons children at the tail end of high school, where both Bart and Lisa are prepped to graduate together, and Lisa finishes early to earn early acceptance to Yale.

Future episodes after Season 20 would take on another style. Following the format established in these structure-stretching years, bottle episodes became more standard and thus creative takes on the Simpsons siblings' future soon followed. In Season 27's "Barthood," we see Bart's past and future rewritten through the style of Richard Linklater's *Boyhood*. In this version escapist fantasies are less colored by gags and zags and hinge more on emotional developments between Bart and Lisa that later inform their successes and failures in life. In this version "Bart the dirtbag," as he's so often painted as an adult, is swapped for "Bart the businessman." In the end of the episode, Bart opens up a bike shop and even receives retribution from Nelson for "bullying him all those years" by being repaid for all the lunch money that was stolen from him.

What's interesting about *The Simpsons*' take on their own future is their lack of loyalty to a singular view. Of course there are certain consistent broad strokes—Lisa's success, Bart's failings,

Maggie's independence—but their Magic 8 Ball, scattered take on multiple outcomes makes the case that anything could be possible. Such is the very fabric of *The Simpsons'* own style of the floating timeline. It is a creative device to add new life season by season, allowing it to endure way beyond what any of us thought possible.

30 How a Script Becomes an Episode

When the writers of this here book first got into *The Simpsons*, we figured the writers of the greatest TV show of all time lived atop a Writers Guild of America-eligible Mount Olympus, where brilliance would never reach a standstill, and everyone glowed beneath perfect lighting. The actual reality is more of a studio lot, a bungalow, a creaky carpet, and a fridge full of free Red Bulls. Most shows flesh out their seasons by breaking story together as a room. Writers often come in with premise pitches (one to two sentences worth of an idea), and the group decides if they want to flesh it out more, or if they want to scrap it. *The Simpsons* does things slightly different.

Every season of *The Simpsons* begins with a writer's retreat, usually a weekend or so of off-site story breaking. There the writers are expected to not simply bring premises, but also fully fleshed out outlines. They present their stories to the group in an effort to win approval from the showrunners and other staff writers. After their stories are approved, writers then spend about two weeks on their first draft of the script. "Almost all of the writing is done here at the FOX [lot] in one of two rewrite rooms," showrunner Al Jean told theverge.com. The additional writers' room was a change-up that occurred around Season 9 of the show, when the writing staff had grown to a point where they could split up and increase productivity.

After that, a writer has four to six weeks to address any rewrites, reworking the script about six or seven times before it's presented to the table read. The table read is a big deal. The finished script is presented to not only the rest of the writing staff, but also to the voice actors. Friends and family of the core group are often invited to sit on the side and witness the future episode's evolution. A week after the table read, the voice actors finally get into the studio and record their parts. Then the episode's supervising director steps in.

The director will communicate with the storyboard artist, who will then interpret the script into sketches that more or less play out the beats of the episode. The animation begins with an on-site team at the Los Angeles studios that drafts, sketches, and polishes their storyboards before sending it off to South Korean animation studio Akom, who will then finish the job. Throughout this process several rounds of notes from not only *The Simpsons* creative staff, but also FOX executives will be provided. Once that process is completed, the show moves onto the layout phase.

The layout phase is when the character's performance really starts to shine. Animators take the storyboard elements and match the character drawings to their model sheer (a visual bible of sorts that includes the perfect ratio of character features, the ideal amount of hair spikes for Bart, etc.). This step ensures that there's a continuity between episodes of the look, design, and feel of the show. It also includes a great amount of creativity to inject visual jokes in the way of facial expressions and other elements of performance to amp up the story and jokes as much as possible. The layout stage is also when shots are properly framed. With the help of the supervising and episodic director (often two different roles), the episode is mapped out much like a live action script with close-ups, pans, wide shots, etc.

The animation production then goes to a stage called the timer. The timer works closely with Akom to make sure they know how to interpret all of the animation work done in Los Angeles. They're called timers because they break down the episode to the tiniest detail, ensuring that the episode flows and matches the required 22-minute run time, not allowing for any kind of error.

From there, the episode may be carried over to scene planning. This is a phase in the animation process that deals with particularly difficult scenes, such as angry mobs, dance numbers, train sequences, etc. Lastly, the episode is then received by the checkers, who pore over every element before shipping it off to Korea.

What comes back to FOX is a completed, full-color version of what will likely air. Editors on-site in California spruce it up a bit, show it to shareholders, and then any last-minute jokes or punch-ups will be added to make sure the episode's in great shape before it hits the airwaves. From there any retakes or revisions are done by Akom (depending on how intense the notes are) or on-site revisionists who work with Al Jean.

Surprisingly, it is only now that music is added with the exception of original songs that may have been present in the script since its early stages. Composer Alf Clausen would normally take this nearly-finished episode and compose whatever musical flourishes it required.

31 Make a Costume

Whether or not it's Halloween—or just a trek into your own Treehouse of Horror—any time's a good time to get weird with your own getup of *The Simpsons*. Don't let the premise intimidate you, though; we've all seen those flawless renditions of the family with yellow face paint and all. There are plenty of other easier Springfield options where you can still win the hearts of your co-workers, community, or corner of the Internet.

The State of Florida
Like in the Season 5 episode, "$pringfield (or, How I Learned to Stop Worrying and Love Legalized Gambling)," Homer's hasty mistake can be your saving grace in your next costume contest. All you need is a piece of foam you can get from a local craft or hard-ware store, a roll of duct tape, black paint, and a dangling orange, and voila! You're almost as good as a piece of paper with the words "IDAHO" written plainly across.

"Give Me Ride, or Everybody Dies"
This is a slow burn, but it's well worth it. From the Season 7 episode, "King-Size Homer," get your flowered muumuu, your newsboy cap, and make sure everyone knows you just, "came here to see *Honk If You're Horny* in peace." If your local Goodwill doesn't have the goods, simply hand paint giant flowers on a blue smock and don't forget your cardboard sign. Bonus points for a trash bag filled with popcorn as your prime accessory.

As demonstrated by co-author Allie Goertz, dressing as Fallout Boy is an excellent costume idea. (Allie Goertz)

Inanimate Carbon Rod

And for the laziest of the lazy…give everyone a chance to look at the rod. All you need for this head-turner is a cardboard paper towel roll, bright neon green paint, and a strong upper body to hold it up for hours upon hours for all to see. Bonus points if you dress up like a velvet-lined car seat befitting a hero's welcome.

A Mass of Marges

Get your best besties together and go shopping for matching green dresses because you're about to turn heads faster than Professor Frink injects unsettling truths. Though most of this costume could be easily assembled through items purchased online, the real trick will be coordination with a collection of other Springfieldians. The reward is not only a Slave Leia-type mass of other cool weirdos walking together (go to any Comic-Con, and you'll know what this means), but also the opportunity to quote Marge's best lines throughout the night. Keep pushing potatoes into the conversation because you "just think they're neat!"

"Like, You Know, Whatever" Lisa

Straight from the Season 7 finale, "Summer of 4 Ft. Two," take your best tie-dye and don your most disenchanted stare and you're well on your way to embodying one of the most heartbreaking episodes the show's ever crafted. The only requirement when getting into this get-up is ending the night gluing seashells to some unsuspecting stranger's car, but we all pay our cool dues somehow.

Satanic Ned Flanders

This one requires a little more hot glue gun and some go-go-getter attitude. Assemble the look from the neck down from your local thrift store or costume shop. Grab a maroon-colored cape with a heightened collar, snag some furry maroon pants straight from the 1970s, and craft together your own devil's tail by stuffing fluff into a nylon leg of a pair of tights. Not so fast with the yellow body paint. Instead, get a piece of cardboard and tap into your tender, more artistic side. Paint Ned's face into a mask and freak out your friends by negotiating their souls.

Stupid Sexy Flanders

Now that you've already got a Flanders mask in your arsenal, might as well use it for one of the most popular memes since "Old Man Yells at Cloud." This is for all the ladies in the crowd (and bootylicious gentlemen) who aren't afraid to strut around in a pair of spandex.

Ripped Ned Flanders

This is for the dudes who have been hitting the gym like they've been gobbling up PowerSauce bars. Grow out that mustache, slick back that hair, get your bible, and go shirtless, so all of Springfield can see what God gave you.

32 The Thursday Time Slot

In our current television landscape, a show's time slot on the prime-time schedule is not a concern for a lot of people. With streaming services, DVRs, and VOD, it's easy to watch nearly any episode of television whenever you want. However, when *The Simpsons* premiered in December of 1989, its place on the fledgling FOX network's schedule was extremely important, to the producers, the fans, and the executives at FOX. And those three didn't always agree on what time slot was best.

For its first season, *The Simpsons* aired at 8:00 PM on Sunday. Based on the numbers alone, this time slot must have been perfect. The premiere episode "Simpsons Roasting on an Open Fire" pulled in 26.7 million viewers, the second highest rating ever for the FOX network at that point, placing it at No. 30 of all shows that week. It should be mentioned that the network was so new at that point that not every television set even received its signal. The show's popularity grew during this season, and ratings peaked on March 18, 1990, for its ninth episode, which pulled in 33.5 million viewers. At this time *The Simpsons* was becoming such a cultural phenomenon that its reruns that summer would likely bring in new viewers, culminating in monster ratings numbers for its second-season premiere.

However, FOX saw the force that *The Simpsons* was becoming and recognized it as a powerful weapon in its arsenal. So they announced that summer that the show would be moving time slots. And not just anywhere. No, *The Simpsons* would be moved to the 8:00 PM slot on Thursdays. The significance of this hour was widely known to anyone with a television set at that time: this was when *The Cosby Show* was on, the same *Cosby Show* that had been the No. 1 show in the Nielsen ratings for the past five years. FOX saw *The Simpsons* as a show so popular that it could take down the once-thought-invincible *Cosby*. Or at the very least, it could take away a significant chunk of its audience.

The Simpsons' producers, on the other hand, were less thrilled about this move. James L. Brooks was particularly pissed. The show had been thriving in the Sunday night time slot and eventually was pulling in ratings healthy enough to put it in the top 10 of all shows. He saw this move as unfair, as it was taking a successful show and making it fight for its survival. This also stung Brooks on a personal level, as throughout his long career as a highly successful television writer and producer, he had only experienced two weeks of working on a No. 1 show. He felt that *The Simpsons* on Sunday could have had this distinction.

Regardless of how Brooks or the other producers felt, the time-slot change was happening, and the media ate it up. It was a television David and Goliath story, the likes of which hadn't been seen—maybe ever. It was Bill vs. Bart. TV's dad vs. TV's underachieving son. A show with a moral center vs. one that seemingly had none. (Okay, let's take a second to just acknowledge the irony here. The sexual assault allegations against Cosby were known by very few at this point, while *The Simpsons* was thought to be the ultimate bad influence. Go figure.) In a cover story for *Entertainment Weekly*, the headline: "Can Bill Beat Bart?" hung above Cosby's smug face on the front of the magazine, as he's wearing a Bart Simpson shirt. Even Johnny Carson joked about the situation in his monologue on *The Tonight Show*.

Many so-called television experts and prognosticators thought *The Simpsons* was doomed in this match-up and wouldn't even come close to Cosby's numbers. Yet, the second season premiere, "Bart Gets an F," aired on Thursday October 11, 1990, and pulled in an 18.4 Nielsen rating. And *The Cosby Show*? It recorded an 18.5. It was a narrow margin of defeat, but given expectations it was actually a win by many standards for *The Simpsons*. Plus, this Nielsen rating number is based on the number of household televisions that were tuned into the show. The estimated number of viewers is a different statistic, and *The Simpsons* was said to have reached 33.6 million viewers to *Cosby*'s 28.5. So, ultimately, they did win. The 33.6 million remains the all-time highest number of viewers for any episode of *The Simpsons* ever. But after the show failed to push past *Cosby*, the network returned *The Simpsons* back to its original Sunday home, and peace was restored.

Homer's Jobs

Throughout *The Simpsons*' run, we've most commonly known Homer to be the flunkiest eff-up of Sector 7-G. He snoozes, he spills Buzz Cola, and he sparks a nuclear shutdown. When it comes to working hard or hardly working, you know full well which way Homer Jay lies.

Though if you thought being safety inspector of the Springfield Nuclear Power Plant was the only profession our Simpsons patriarch had, you'd qualify for a paddlin'. According to an interview with Matt Groening, Homer held an astonishing 188 jobs in the first 400 episodes. Here are the highlights you should know.

Astronaut—"Deep Space Homer" (Season 5, Episode 15)

Job Interview: Due to declining Nielsen ratings, NASA decides to launch an average schmo into space. Cue Homer Jay, the Springfield schmo who just barely edges out Barney Gumble for the coveted seat.

Career Highlights: Homer sasses to "former President James Taylor" and saves the space men with the help of an inanimate carbon rod.

Clown Impersonator—"Homie the Clown" (Season 6, Episode 15)

Job Interview: Homer enrolls in clown college after being the victim of persuasive billboard marketing and soon finds himself filling in for Krusty at ribbon cuttings and rowdy birthday parties. When Krusty collides with the local mob, Homer's mistaken for the misanthropic clown, and they have to go toe-to-toe with Fat Tony.

Career Highlights: A gleeful mobster sees both Homer and Krusty's doppelganger-y sight and remarks: "I'm seeing double… Four Krustys!" Homer also beats a Hamburglar-type actor to a pulp at a Krusty Burger ribbon cutting.

Clerk at the Kwik-E-Mart—"Lisa's Pony" (Season 3, Episode 8)

Job Interview: After disappointing Lisa by forcing her to flop at her school's talent show, Homer becomes desperate to win back his daughter's love and decides to buy her a pony. When the pony upkeep's too pricy, he applies for a job at the Kwik-E-Mart.

Career Highlights: Homer falls asleep in between the automatic doors of the Kwik-E-Mart, and the doors open and close on his button nose.

Assistant to Mr. Burns—"Homer the Smithers" (Season 7, Episode 17)

Job Interview: After Waylon Smithers fails to protect Mr. Burns from a drunk, leering Lenny, Burns forces Smithers to take his first work vacation. Smithers spots Homer as being the ideal candidate for his substitute, as he'll not outshine him while away.

Career Highlights: Homer impersonates Mr. Burns' mother after accidentally hanging up on her, being coached by Smithers to "sound more desiccated" and that she doesn't call her son, "Mr. Burns."

Country Music Manager—"Colonel Homer" (Season 3, Episode 20)

Job Interview: After meeting aspiring country singer Lurleen Lumpkin (voiced by Beverly D'Angelo) at a dive bar outside of town, Homer decides to become her manager and raise her up from her downtrodden surroundings in a moment of inspired motivation.

Career Highlights: He picks out a recording booth where the sound engineer describes its steep history: "Buddy Holly stood on this spot in 1958 and said, 'There is no way in hell that I'm going to record in this dump.'"

Team Mascot—"Dancing Homer" (Season 2, Episode 5)

Job Interview: After firing up the crowd at a Springfield Isotopes game, he's chosen to be the team's new mascot. Due to his popularity, Homer sparks a winning streak with the Isotopes and is soon promoted to Capital City, where it all quickly burns out.

Career Highlights: His butt-swinging dance to "Baby Elephant Walk" shoots him to stardom. When he dances with Bart, you get a whiff of the tender father-son moments that would characterize this chapter of the show.

Monorail Conductor—"Marge vs. the Monorail" (Season 4, Episode 12)

Job Interview: After watching monorail salesman Lyle Lanley's commercial for the Institute of Monorail Conducting, Homer eagerly signs up. After the three-week course, Lanley chooses Homer at random to be the newest conductor.

Career Highlights: After prying the "M" in monorail off the side of the car, he fastens it like an anchor to the road below, and it eventually catches on the giant Lard Lad donut. Homer remarks, "Donuts…is there anything they can't do?"

Musician—"Homer's Barbershop Quartet" (Season 5, Episode 1)

Job Interview: Homer, Apu, Principal Skinner, and Chief Wiggum make a splash, performing at Moe's Tavern and are discovered by a music scout. On the scout's suggestion, they expel Wiggum from the group and add Barney for his tremendous tenor.

Career Highlights: He wins a Grammy, performs on Moe's rooftop, meets George Harrison, and appropriately freaks out.

Sideshow Freak— "Homerpalooza" (Season 7, Episode 24)

Job Interview: While attending Hullabalooza a stray cannonball shoots into the crowd and right into Homer's stomach. When Homer discovers his incredible ability to absorb pain, he goes on the road with the fest as part of their patented "freak show."

Career Highlights: He meets the other bands, including The Smashing Pumpkins' Billy Corgan.

Teacher—"Secrets of a Successful Marriage" (Season 5, Episode 22)

Job Interview: After fearing he may be "a little slow," Homer goes to the adult education center, where he discovers a need for a teacher to explain the success of the modern marriage.

Career Highlights: He runs through town excitedly before his first day and rolls through the Krusty Burger drive-through. When asked for his order, he says: "Nothing for me today. I've got a class to teach!" The drive-through operator responds: "Sir, it's a felony to tease the order box."

A List of All of Homer's Jobs (in Alphabetical Order)

Account Executive
Acrobat
Army Private
Agent
Ambulance Driver
Arm Wrestler
Asking Man at Products
  Demonstration
Astronaut
Assassin
Attack Dog Trainer
Baby Proofer
Bartender
Bass Player
Beef Jerky Manufacturer
Blackjack Dealer
Bodyguard for Mayor Quimby
Bootlegger
Bowling Alley Employee
Bounty Hunter
Boxer
Butler
Bum Wrestler
Candle Maker
Car Designer
Caricaturist of Open Coffins
Carny
CEO of the Springfield Nuclear Power
  Plant
Chauffeur for Classy Joe's
Chief of Police
Child Caretaker for Uncle Homer's
  Daycare Center
Choreographer for the Super Bowl
  Halftime Show
Chiropractor
Clerk at the Kwik-E-Mart

Coach of Bart's Little League Football
  Team
Cook at a Diner
Con Artist
Conceptual Artist
Curler
Detective
Drug Smuggler
Door-to-Door Knife Salesman for
  Slash Co.
Door-to-Door Sugar Salesman
Door-to-Door Spring Salesman
Duffman
Deacon of the Church
Employee at Gulp'n'Blow Drive-
  Through
Executive of Globex Corporation,
  Cypress Creek
Executive Vice President of Power
  Plant
Farmer
Film Critic
Film Producer
Fireman
Fish Gutter
Fisherman
Food Critic
Foot Locker Employee
Fortune Cookie Writer
Founder and Junior Vice President of
  Compu-Global-Hyper-Mega-Net
Garbage Commissioner
Grease Collector
Greek Restaurant Dishwasher
Greenhouse Manager
Grim Reaper
Guard of Springfield Juvenile
  Correctional Facility

Guard of Springfield Women's Prison
Hitman
Hairdresser
Ice Cream Truck Driver
Impotency Spokesman for Vlag Rogaine
Internet Service Provider
Inventor (multiple times)
Krusty Impersonator
Mall Santa Claus
Marriage Counselor
Mascot
Mattress Salesman
Manure Salesman
Mayor of New Springfield
Mayoral Candidate
Mexican Wrestler
Mini-Golf Assistant for Sir Putt-a-Lot's Merrie Olde Fun Centre
Missionary
Mob Boss
Monorail Conductor
Mountain Climber
Musician
Nuclear Power Plant Manager
NASA Engineer
Navy Reservist
Oil Rig Worker
One Man Band
Opera Singer
Ordained Minister
Outsider Artist
Owner
Paparazzi
Performance Artist
Personal Assistant
Plastic Arts/Conceptual Artist
Police Officer/Police Chief
Prank Monkey for Mr. Burns
Public Speaker

Quiz Master
Roadie
Railroad Engineer
Rollercoaster Rebuilder
Safety Inspector for New England Kandy Company
Safety Salamander
Sailor in the Naval Reserve
Sanitation Commissioner
Security Office of SpringShield
Sideshow Freak
Silhouette Model
Singer
Smuggler
Snowplow Proprietor and Driver
Soccer Referee
Soldier
Softball Player
Stand-Up Comedian
Street Musician
Superhero
Spokesperson/Walking Billboard
Sprawl-Mart Greeter
Talk Show Host
Teacher
Television Producer
Telemarketer
Tomacco Creator/Farmer/Salesman
Tow Truck Driver
Town Crier
Traveling Salesman of Simpson & Son Revitalizing Tonic
Trucker
TV Show Host
Union Leader
Used Car Salesman
Voice Actor
Writer

Town Crier—"Lisa the Iconoclast" (Season 7, Episode 16)

Job Interview: After winning over the election committee for Springfield's centennial celebration, Homer edges out Ned Flanders for the coveted role.

Career Highlights: He abuses his status by ringing his bell willy-nilly all over town, as well as making this declaration about Flanders: "Ye olde town crier proclaimed crappy by all."

Voice Actor—"The Itchy & Scratchy & Poochie Show" (Season 8, Episode 14)

Job Interview: After a decline in ratings, *The Itchy & Scratchy Show* decides to add a new character named Poochie who's a dog with "attitude" and is "totally in your face." After a brief audition process, Homer wins the role of the new cartoon.

Career Highlights: Homer buddies up with fellow voice actor June Bellamy, who voices both Itchy and Scratchy. She tells him, "Very few cartoons are broadcast live. It's a terrible strain on the animator's wrist."

34 Network Notes

Are you ever watching a show on television (or via your computer, phone, or projection onto a bomb shelter wall), and a character will say something like "aw rats" instead of a good old-fashioned "hell," "damn," or "ass?" Have you noticed a show you love being awfully sympathetic toward the GE corporation for seemingly no reason? Well, my friend, these are likely results of network notes. Network notes are often sent down from television executives in order to make a television show as broad and as profitable as possible, often restricting creative decisions and blunting incisive commentary. Mike Reiss even called them "the bane of television comedy" in *The Simpsons: An Uncensored, Unauthorized History* by John Ortved. And *The Simpsons*, for the most part, has not been subject to them.

At the beginning of the show, executive producer James L. Brooks, a highly sought-after talent with plenty of leverage over a newly created FOX Network, was able to negotiate into his contract that *The Simpsons* would be insulated from executive notes entirely, something completely unprecedented at the time. Many writers have attributed the show's unique success and artistic credibility to this very insularity. "Working on *The Simpsons* felt like being in the graduate school of comedy or a great comedy lab, where you could try and do anything, and no one would stop you as long as it was good or funny," said writer and former showrunner Josh Weinstein in Ortved's book.

Former consultant Brad Bird, who also directed the animated movies *Ratatouille* and *The Incredibles*, thought that Brooks' shielding of his staff "allowed good work to flourish."

It's clear that *The Simpsons* voice was protected, especially early on, from network influence, especially in how often they referenced the network they were on, making fun of shows like *Married with Children* and *COPS*.

The Simpsons would go on to parody the idea of the FOX executives mercilessly. In the famous "Itchy & Scratchy & Poochie" episode, network executives create Poochie, a character built out of buzzwords and focus group gibberish. ("You've heard of the phrase 'let's get busy?' This is a dog who gets bizz-ay.") He's voiced by Homer and ends up being kind of racist in a using hip-hop culture-to-sell-things kind of way. Needless to say, Poochie fails miserably and is hated by children.

The writers get even more direct about their feelings in the Season 12 episode "Day of the Jackanapes," an episode based on a show Al Jean ran during his time away from *The Simpsons*. The episode begins with network executives, giving Krusty the Clown notes like, "We're losing male teens. Could you get jiggy with something?" When the executives start actually giving Krusty notes live on air, Krusty announces his retirement from show business on the spot. At the end of the episode, Mr. Teeny casually incinerates the executives with plastic explosives that were designed by Sideshow Bob to kill Krusty.

The paradigm shifted for *The Simpsons* in terms of criticizing the network when FOX News rose to prominence in the early 2000s, as *The Simpsons* has lampooned FOX News much more than the network on which they reside. Never afraid to make a political statement, the show has poked fun at the ultra-conservative news network multiple times, including a reporter saying, "FOX News: Your voice for evil," and having a FOX News helicopter read, "Not racist, but No. 1 with racists."

According to Matt Groening in a 2017 Comic-Con panel interview, this has led to some suggestions from the corporate arm of 20th Century Fox for *The Simpsons* to ease up on their scathing jokes at the cable news affiliate. We suggest watching as much FOX News as possible in order to support the parent company that makes *The Simpsons*. (Just kidding! Please don't do that.)

35 Internet Message Boards

After Poochie's infamous animated debut in The Itchy & Scratchy & Poochie Show, the Comic Book Guy said: "Last night's *Itchy & Scratchy* was, without a doubt, the worst episode ever. Rest assured I was on the Internet within minutes, registering my disgust throughout the world." This is the perfect satire for the world of recap culture where virtually every series has episode reviews that are posted moments after airing. It's hard to comprehend the reality and significance of Internet message boards. Before fans of *The Simpsons* had Frinkiac, dedicated subreddits, and too many podcasts to choose from, these fans, who were living in the pre-net era, would use text-only forums to discuss their favorite (but more often least favorite) moments of the show.

Once reserved for nerds, the Internet has become an integral aspect of life for just about all of us. When everyone is so connected and people's opinions are everywhere, it's hard to imagine there was ever a time that *The Simpsons* writers were in the dark about what people thought of the show. They had the ratings and were obviously aware of the mania surrounding the show, but they had never had access to what real viewers thought. After reading the type of things they were saying, some of the writers may have wished they hadn't.

People use the Internet to say the worst things imaginable. For the authors of this book, the worst thing we can conjure up is a bad review of a classic episode of the show, and that's mostly what you would find on the boards. When Matt Groening admitted to reading the comments, he told *The Philadelphia Inquirer*, "Sometimes I feel like knocking their electronic noggins together."

Ian Maxtone-Graham notoriously called them "beetle-browed" and exclaimed, "That's why they're on the Internet and we're writing the show." Let us tell you, that comment didn't help things. People on the still active No Homers Club still reference that line. While most of the writers were turned off by the commenters, Bill Oakley used to respond to select *Simpsons* fans until it became too much. He explained, "there are people who take it seriously to the point of absurdity."

The groups in question are worth knowing, as they are a fascinating and weird bit of *Simpsons* trivia. The first is alt.tv.simpsons (known as a.t.s.), which was created in 1990, four months after the first episode aired. According to the excellent book, *Planet Simpson*, alt.tv.simpsons was among the most trafficked news groups of the early 1990s. The site nitpicks episodes for inconsistences and was famously critical of the show to such a degree that they inspired the famous Comic Book Guy line, "Worst. Episode. Ever." Comic Book Guy was further used as a semi-mascot/parody of the site when he visits his favorite newsgroup alt.nerd.obsessive. If you're wondering how people could say a single bad word about *The Simpsons* during their golden age, consider one user's belief that "Marge vs the Monorail," which has been regarded as one of the best episodes of comedy was…bad. Thanks, Internet.

"Deep Space Homer" Controversy

Early in *The Simpsons'* development, Matt Groening put his foot down. Despite their animated format, Groening wanted to keep the show grounded. His argument: even though the show could technically detach from reality, was it necessary? Certainly, one could argue that animal charcacters Snowball II and Santa's Little Helper were capable of carrying a scene just as well as Homer or Marge, but they did so with regimented rules—and only a knowing nudge or a simple eye roll. Groening wanted to keep the parameters of their fictional world as simple and strong as possible.

Then Homer went to space.

For years Groening had used this example as a throw-away of what the show "would never do." It's large enough of a stretch to have Homer be employed at all—nonetheless be capable of such a laundry list of incredible accomplishments over the years. At this point in the show's history, Homer had already stumbled into a successful plowing business, been appointed monorail conductor, been hired as Krusty the Clown's stand-in, and yes, singlehandedly and stupidly saved the nuclear power plant. Somehow, zooming Homer to space seemed against all the track the writers had laid out. The show was in a constant contest of bending the boundaries without breaking them, and introducing real stakes such as space travel seemed to shatter everything they had worked so hard to build.

Season 5's "Deep Space Homer" was originally pitched by then-executive producer David Mirkin, who had been chipping away at the idea for a while before presenting it to the room. He reportedly based it on NASA's Teacher in Space Project, which was a program during the Reagan era that launched ordinary civilians into space in order to boost public interest. Thinking civilians don't get more ordinary than Homer, the concept seemed like a natural fit to adapt for Springfield.

Groening wasn't the only one opposed to this concept. In *The Simpsons'* four and a half seasons, there was rarely a controversy that broke the room up more than "Deep Space Homer." Thinking it was too big an idea for the show to wrap their head around, the staff was quickly divided. Given that the show only had 22 minutes to get a story out and the concept of space travel was meaty enough as it is, a solution was soon devised to simplify all other elements of the episode in order to let this premise truly shine.

Early in the development, sillier concepts like making everyone who worked in NASA as dumb as Homer were quickly dashed in favor of a more realistic straight man to stupid Homer dynamic. What resulted was a surprisingly sweet story of Homer's quest to make his family proud and Marge's concern that what Homer's attempting may very well kill him. The stakes were high, but the special sauce of the show seemed to be preserved.

But what would the fans think? The producers weren't sure. They never attempted anything like this before. In the end the episode was a success—and surprisingly so. Its legacy would transcend in ways Mirkin, Groening, and the rest of the writing staff could never have anticipated. For starters, it would birth one of the more prevalent memes circulating around the Internet. When Homer's spacecraft carries ants as an experiment to see how they'll do while weightless, the ant farm accidentally breaks, and insects float throughout the space right into the live cam. When Kent Brockman decides to check in with the crew, the oversized close-up ant is the first image broadcasted, launching the town into a frenzy. When we check back in with Kent, he's prepped and poised to serve whatever dystopian future this image conjures. "I, for one, welcome our new insect overlords," he says. The phrase would later be famously uttered by *Jeopardy!* champion Ken Jennings.

But the most surprising turn of this once-controversial story is NASA's own embrace of this episode. Astronaut Edward Lu requested a copy of it to be sent to the international space system, and the episode continues to be available for astronauts to view. MSNBC deemed it their fourth favorite *Simpsons* episode, and *Empire* magazine declared it a "contender for greatest episode ever."

In what has become an accidental trademark of the show, "Homer in Space" actually predicted the future. In 2014 NASA actually did send ants to the International Space Station, but no word yet on whether or not they tussled among Ruffles in a cataclysmic crash.

Write a Song

As you already know by being a superfan and reading this very book, *The Simpsons* has provided its viewers with a wealth of simultaneously beautiful and hilarious music from the likes of former composer Alf Clausen, theme song writer Danny Elfman, and a long list of famous band members from The Beatles to Wings! Although most fans are completely contented by the copious amount of *Simpsons* songs, other (more selfish) people have yelled, "That's not enough! I need more!" To those people we say, "Boy, do we have a chapter of this book for you."

Here are some our favorite fan songs that already exist.

"The Ballad of Hans Moleman" by MC Lars
Nerd-rapper extraordinaire, MC Lars, whose real name is Andrew "Simpsons Lover" Nielson, penned an inspirational hip-hop ode to Hans Moleman that painted a more heroic portrait of the particularly downtrodden character. Instead of focusing on Hans' more humiliating moments, Lars explains his resilience:

Moleman, Hans Moleman, you can't keep Hans Moleman down

*'Cause he's like Cowabunga dudes, with a skateboard in his
  hand*
Hipster glasses so thick and round
*Moleman, Hans Moleman, you can't keep Hans Moleman
  down*
Even in his iron lung, well, he's still dependable
He's the talk of the whole darn town

The Five-Step Guide to Creating a *Simpsons* Song

Pick a character—Choose which character or characters you'd like to sing about.

Pick a message or theme—Decide what you're trying to say about said character(s). Is this song about redemption, failure, or perhaps a first crush? If you chose a sad character, you can lean into their sadness like I did or put a spin on it like Lars did to Hans.

Pick your favorite character quotes—Make a list of all your favorite character quotes and see if you can find an overarching theme. What story do these quotes tell and how do they help your theme? Make things easy on yourself by combining quotes that rhyme naturally and look for creative ways to make quotes that don't rhyme work together.

Pick a music style—Whether you're an established songwriter or just starting out, finding the style of music you want to use for your *Simpsons* song should be easy and fun. If you don't already have a go-to style, pick a musical artist you love and pretend you're writing in their voice. Use the same chords they use and get cracking! Just remember that the style of song will add to its humor. Part of what makes Okily Dokily so clever is that metal is a stark contrast to what you'd expect Ned Flanders to listen to.

Write away—Now that you have your character, your theme, your quotes, and your music style, the only thing that's left to do is put your song into the world for all to love.

A Ned Flanders-Themed Metal Band

These guys put the metal in metal-diddly-oh neighborinos! Okily Dokily has five members (Red Ned, Thread Ned, Head Ned, Stead Ned, and Bled Ned) who not only dress the part in Ned's green sweater and black slacks combo, but they also have written an impressive 13 songs all in the voice of our favorite church-going Springfieldian. When news of their existence hit the Internet in 2016, fans around the world rejoiced as they could finally bang their heads to the metal treatment of *The Simpsons* they didn't know they needed. Song titles include: "White Wine Spritzer," "Flanderdoodles," "Vegetables," and our favorite—"God Speed Little Doodle."

"Everything's Coming Up Milhouse" by Allie Goertz

Long before our podcast started, I wrote the folk song, "Everything's Coming Up Milhouse," a musical attempt to capture the pure sadness and relatable pathos that is Milhouse Van Houten. Although the phrase "Everything's Coming Up Milhouse" is meant to be met with hope and optimism, this song skewers Milhouse, reminding him that he'll always have unrequited love for Lisa and live in the shadow of his best friend. As the song explains, "Everything's coming up Milhouse, but Lisa still passes him by. Everything's coming up Milhouse, but his flood pants can't keep his eyes dry." Tragic.

All three of these examples demonstrate just how different each *Simpsons* fan song can be from another. Next time you're itching to hear a song about your favorite character, don't just wait around for someone else to write it; use this chapter to learn how to make one yourself. You can bend genres, change narratives, and get as serious or silly as you like while writing your tune. As long as your song is about *The Simpsons*, fans will be sure to sit there groovin' on it.

Watch Other Shows Created by *The Simpsons* Writers

Some of the best television of all time was created by *The Simpsons* writers, and we're not even counting *The Simpsons*. From iconic sitcoms to indie cartoons, here is a list of some of the best television ever, and all were written or created by former or current *Simpsons* folk. And we're leaving out some famous shows that writers worked on *before* joining *The Simpsons*, which includes classic sitcoms like *Cheers* (Sam Simon, Ken Levine), *The Larry Sanders Show* (David Mirkin), and *It's Garry Shandling's Show* (Mike Reiss and David Mirkin).

As a bonus, we're including some of the more unusual shows that never made it big like UPN's unfortunately failed show, *The Mullets*, created by Bill Oakley and Josh Weinstein. The show about two brothers with the same haircut was UPN's lowest rated show but was probably another example of a show that was ahead of its time (a commonality amongst Josh and Bill shows). Just know that it's business in the front, party in the back.

The Critic
Simpsons Folk—Al Jean and Mike Reiss
Al Jean and Mike Reiss left *The Simpsons* after its fourth season in order to create *The Critic*, starring film critic Jay Sherman, who appeared in an episode of *The Simpsons*. Jon Lovitz voices Sherman.

Mission Hill
Simpsons Folk—Bill Oakley and Josh Weinstein
After leaving *The Simpsons*, Bill and Josh created the underrated and cult classic *Mission Hill*. The show followed the misadventures of a group of roommates living in a hip neighborhood and was

way ahead of its time. Despite being jerked around by the network (it was cancelled after two episodes, brought back, then cancelled again after four more episodes), the show eventually found a cult following thanks to Teletoon Unleashed, a Canadian late-night television block, which released all 13 episodes.

Futurama
Simpsons Folk—David X. Cohen and Matt Groening

Come on, you've seen this.

For those who haven't seen it (perhaps you got stuck in a cryonic tube), *Futurama* follows the story of a pizza delivery boy named Fry, who accidentally (you guessed it) cryogenically freezes himself and awakens in the year 2999. Still a pizza boy, Fry explores the planet as the show explores the endless possibilities and absurdity of the future. Assuming you like irreverent comedies with just as much heart as laughter, you will love *Futurama*.

F is For Family
Simpsons Folk—Michael Price

If you're the type of person who fell off of *The Simpsons* earlier in the show's run, you will have missed out on the humor of Michael Price, who started in Season 14 and still works on the show even after co-creating *F is For Family* with Bill Burr. The family comedy set in the 1970s is based on Burr's own life during "a time when you could smack your kid, smoke inside, and bring a gun to the airport." In addition to Burr, the show is impressively cast with Laura Dern, Sam Rockwell, and Justin Long.

The Pitts and Complete Savages
Simpsons Folk—Mike Scully

The Pitts and *Complete Savages* are two live-action sitcoms created by Mike Scully and his wife Julie Thatcher that were cut down before they got a chance to grow. *The Pitts* (cancelled after two months) featured absurd and fantastical plots about a normal family. *Complete Savages*, which was (oddly) produced by Mel Gibson, is about Nick Savage as he struggles to raise his five unruly sons, but the show got cancelled after a season. Don't worry about Mike Scully though, he has *Simpsons* money, *Everybody Loves Raymond* money, and *Parks and Recreation* money. So, he's doing okay.

The Office
Simpsons Folk—Greg Daniels and Brent Forrester
Everybody knows *The Office* (created by Ricky Gervais), but not everyone realizes that the man behind the American adaptation is Greg Daniels, a writer from *The Simpsons*. The show debuted with mixed reviews but eventually became a staple in sitcom history. The show was so popular that Daniels was also tasked with coming up with the spin-off called...

Parks and Recreation
Simpsons Folk—Greg Daniels and Mike Scully
Parks and Recreation evolved into such a unique project that you might have never guessed that it was originally meant to be an spin-off. When the spin-off idea didn't quite stick, the show was retooled to become what we know of it today, which in many ways feels like a live-action version of *The Simpsons*. From the cartoon-ishly food-obsessed protagonist to the Shelbyvillian rivalry between Pawnee and Eagleton, *The Simpsons*-like qualities shine through.

King of the Hill
Simpsons Folk—Greg Daniels and Brent Forrester
After the success of *Beavis and Butt-Head*, Mike Judge wanted to make a show about a family in Texas. The network paired Judge with Greg Daniels, and the two fleshed out the idea and created the show as we know it today. Although still obviously deeply funny,

King of the Hill has a far more grounded quality than *The Simpsons*, making it a nice companion piece to our favorite show.

39 Milestones

You can't talk *Simpsons* shop without talking milestones, and there are some pretty big ones for this series. *The Simpsons* hold various world records in many different categories, cementing their place in the American cultural zeitgeist forever. Let's start with the first major milestone being the moment it surpassed *The Flintstones* as the longest running animated series in the U.S. *The Flintstones* ran for six seasons, airing a total of 166 episodes from 1960 to 1966. *The Simpsons* beat them upon airing episode 167 on February 9, 1997. That episode was "The Itchy & Scratchy & Poochie Show." As we all know, *The Simpsons* went on to have many, many more seasons after that.

In 2001 the word "D'oh" was added to the *Oxford English Dictionary*. This is not a joke. You actually can look it up in the dictionary. Its definition is: "expressing frustration at the realization that things have turned out badly or not as planned, or that one has just said or done something foolish." Yup, that sounds about right.

Within the show itself, a milestone was reached in 2003 when John Swartzwelder wrote his final episode, "The Regina Monologues." Swartzwelder, who has written 59, currently holds the title for most episodes written.

Back in 2009 *The Simpsons* broke the record for longest-running primetime series. This record only goes for most seasons, though, and the show has yet to beat the *Gunsmoke* for the greatest number of episodes. *Gunsmoke* ran for 20 seasons but aired 635 episodes. In 2016 The Simpsons aired their 600th episode during Season 28, and that episode was "Treehouse of Horror XXVIII." In 2016 FOX renewed the show for a record-breaking 29th and 30th season. So, when episode 636 of *The Simpsons* does eventually air, it will hold yet another record. For now, however, the show has to stay just a little bit humble.

Another record for the series includes most guest stars featured in a television series. At around Season 26, it was noted that the series had a total of over 700 guest stars, and that number has only gotten bigger. I mean, come on. Our moms don't even have that many friends on Facebook. Furthermore, from the years 2001 to 2003, *The Simpsons* was the most searched show on the Internet.

The show also currently holds the title for number of Emmys (32) for an animated series. These Emmys include wins for: Voice-Over Performance, Outstanding Animated Program, Outstanding Original Music, and even a few for sound mixing. Hank Azaria and Dan Castellaneta have earned four voice-over performance awards, while Harry Shearer, Yeardley Smith, and Nancy Cartwright each have one. Producer James L. Brooks has earned 20 Emmys, many of which were for *The Simpsons*, and received the Norman Lear Achievement Award in Television in 2017.

Season 2 episode "The Way We Was" marks the first flashback episode for the series. The series' 100th episode aired on April 28, 1994, and it was "Sweet Seymour Skinner's Badaaaasss Song." Episode 200 was "Trash of the Titans" and occurred on April 26, 1998. The 300th episode is actually disputed among fans. According to Season 14's production order, the 300th episode is "Strong Arms of the Ma." However, in broadcast order, the actual 300th episode aired was "Barting Over," which aired on February 16, 2003. We're going to leave the winner of that debate up to you. Then came the 400th episode, which aired on May 20, 2007, and was "You Kent Always Get What You Want." The 500th episode aired during Season 23 on February 19, 2012. That episode was "At Long Last

Leave." The opening credits of this episode featured a very fast reel of every couch gag on the series up to that point.

In 2014 something special happened at San Diego Comic-Con when an attraction called "The Homer Dome" was built. Inside this dome was a paint-by-numbers mural. Any visitor could go in and start drawing, which resulted in a record being made for highest number of people contributing to a single work of art. Is there anything *The Simpsons* can't do?

Accomplishments and Awards

Though having Emmys and Peabody awards under your belt isn't a requirement for a multi-season pick-up, something tells us that having that on your show resume wins favor with FOX. *The Simpsons* has collected a staggering amount of trophies: 32 Emmy awards, 30 Annie awards, seven Environmental Media awards, 11 Writers Guild of America awards, six Genesis awards, eight People's Choice awards, three British Comedy awards, and that's just scratching the surface. In 2000 *The Simpsons* won its own star on the Hollywood Walk of Fame.

The show's acknowledgment from the Environmental Media Association is somewhat unique for a sitcom of its caliber. Since 1991 the EMA committee has assembled to award "the best television episode or film with an environmental message." The EMA is a non-profit, which believes "through television, film, and music, the entertainment community has the power to influence the environmental awareness of millions of people." Some of the more notable episodes that have received acclaim from the committee include "Two Cars in Every Garage and Three Eyes on Every Fish," "Mr. Lisa Goes to Washington," and "Lisa the Vegetarian."

The Simpsons Movie was also nominated for its own laundry list of awards, including a Golden Globe for Best Animated Feature. In 1997 *The Simpsons* became the first ever animated show to win a Peabody. According to the awards committee, their achievement in "providing exceptional animation and stinging social satire, both commodities which are in extremely short supply in television today" won them a seat at the table.

It's hard to detect precisely what may have pushed the Peabodys to finally accept the animated family as one of their own, but something tells us that episodes like, "Homer's Phobia" and "A Millhouse Divided" helped open the conversation. The show has never been one to waver from hard truths and uncomfortable stories, making their achievements well-earned. Since Season 1 the show has grappled with themes of adultery, existential crises, and homophobia. Where another show might project a certain perspective or judgment, *The Simpsons* has famously remained non-partisan.

In fact, "Homer's Phobia," would later be nominated (and win) a GLAAD Media award for Outstanding TV—Individual Episode, the only honor GLAAD has ever given the show in its run. Instead of exploring themes of right and wrong, the show often allows its characters to come face to face with these issues through their own POV. A great example of this occurs in the Season 4 episode "Homer the Heretic," when Homer denounces God and his need for attending church. The episode wraps up not with a message of atheism but rather a statement of religion as personal to one's own spirituality and that messages of right or wrong may be irrelevant.

When *The Longest Daycare* premiered in 2012, it would be the first time the show ever got attention from the Academy Awards. Though the short didn't end up collecting an Oscar, the very fact that *The Simpsons* was nominated speaks volumes to their continued effect on popular culture. The show's awards extend internationally as well. From 2004 to 2009, *The Simpsons* has been nominated for numerous Australian Kids' Choice awards (winning five out of seven nominations). In 1998 it was nominated for a British Academy Television award. In 2007 the show won a UK Kids' Choice Award.

In 2006 writers Al Jean and Mike Reiss received the Animation Writers Caucus Animation award given to writers who "advanced the literature of animation in film and/or television through the years and who has made outstanding contributions to the profession of the animation writer." In 2010 Mike Scully also received this award, in 2012 series creator Matt Groening picked it up, and lastly in 2013, series co-developer Sam Simon received the honor.

Ned Flanders

There is no one within the city limits of Springfield who's as good-natured and well-meaning as Ned Flanders. He bounces with a heightened enthusiasm for life's most banal tasks. He can be almost as easily enraptured by a pair of left-handed scissors as Homer would be from a lifetime supply of Duff beer. Ned's good-spirited approach to life is a natural foil for Homer's life of laziness and self-involvement. In the show's early years, Ned's role was mainly relegated to requesting borrowed leaf blowers and household appliances, which Homer playfully denied him. One could surmise that Ned's happy playing doormat to Homer and to the rest of Springfield because his Christian nature is so immersed within his personality that living to serve is all he needs (that and a white wine spritzer once every six months). "Dear Lord, thank you for Ziggy comics, little baby ducks, and *Sweatin' to the Oldies Volumes One, Two,* and *Four*," Flanders says in Season 4, Episode 11's "Homer's Triple Bypass."

Ned's devotion to his faith is so strong that it even outweighs Reverend Lovejoy, who often regards Ned as a pest. Ned's a Republican, an entrepreneur (owner and operator of the town's market for The Leftorium), and a devoted father of two young boys named Rod and Todd. Ned's interpretation of the bible is taken to a fault, often applying its practices to every life event and leading him to phone Lovejoy at the drop of a hat or at the utterance of a bad word from Bart.

In the Season 8 episode "Hurricane Neddy," we get a closer look at Ned's origin story and how he came to be the blissfully optimistic person he is today. As a child he was actually unruly and reckless, raising hell and running circles around his loose and laid-back beatnik parents. Their parenting style was fairly non-existent, and so young Ned never knew what consequences were until it was possibly too late. Within this episode we witness Ned go through several rounds of child therapy until he eventually tempers his inexplicable childhood anger, learning to stifle it for the sake of becoming an active member of society.

Ned's a widow, having lost his first wife, Maude, rather infamously in a freak accident at Springfield Speedway. In the Season 11 episode "Alone Again, Natura-Diddly," the Flanders family enjoying the racing event due to "the high levels of safety the drivers use." When a squad of cheerleaders fire T-shirts into the crowd, a stray shirt knocks Maude off the bleachers and to her death in the parking lot. This episode was met with mixed reviews—similar to the Armin Tamzarian controversy sparked from "The Principal and the Pauper." Animated shows aren't normally serialized in a way that a character's destruction in any particular episode is echoed throughout the show's run, but the boldness of Maude's death has

In the memorable Season 5 episode, Ned Flanders, along with Ernest Borgnine, lead Bart Simpson's Boy Scout troop. (Fox/Photofest © FOX)

defied that marker. From Season 11 on, Ned's storyline has strayed from his position as a blissed-out believer to a man coping with grief and charging toward a second chapter.

On occasion Ned's positive outer shell has splintered. In the Season 5 episode "Homer Loves Flanders," we see a different, more humane side of Ned as he's eventually exhausted by Homer. In the episode Ned invites Homer to a football game, sparking a sudden friendship between the two men when Homer witnesses the benefits of befriending Ned as opposed to bemoaning his persistent positivity. Homer soon shifts his entire focus on their budding friendship, forcing Ned to grow tiresome of the sudden shift in their dynamic. Since its 1994 premiere, this episode has quickly become a favorite among superfans not just for the expansion in Ned's character, but also because it was the last episode Conan O'Brien pitched for the show before leaving to host *Late Night with Conan O'Brien* on NBC.

Ned's design was constructed by Rich Moore, and his name was inspired by Flanders Street in Portland, Oregon. The first episode that prominently featured the Flanders family was Season 1's "Dead Putting Society." Matt Groening has described Flanders' character as, "just a guy who was truly nice, that Homer had no justifiable reason to loathe, but then did." *The Simpsons* showrunner Mike Scully described Flanders to *TV Guide* as, "everything Homer would love to be, although he'll never admit it."

Flanders is integral to the world of *The Simpsons* as a yin to Homer's fiery yang and a pattern that is echoed throughout the entire town of Springfield. Homer and Ned need each other as adversaries much in the way that Mr. Burns needs Smithers to redeem him from evil or how Marge redeems Homer's oafishness with her love. The decision to make Flanders Christian didn't come until a little later in the first season of the show, but it's difficult to imagine Ned in any other way. His resolve to remain true to his beliefs—hell or high water, hurricane or apocalypse, Homer or no Homer—is a stronghold of the show that grounds the town with a moral compass that gives it life.

Ned is voiced by Harry Shearer, who decided to give him a sweeter-than-usual sound, allowing him to be more endearing than grating to the viewers. Over the years the writers have provided Ned with heaps of surprises to his character, including his inexplicable ripped body ("Stupid Sexy Flanders!"), his high-pitched scream (voiced by Tress MacNeille), and his friendships with random celebrities (part of why Homer decides to become his bestie in "Homer Loves Flanders"). Those qualities have allowed him to add texture and transcend the stereotypical Christian trope.

Make *Simpsons* Food

Food is a prevalent force within Springfield. It divided the dinner table when Lisa became a vegetarian, it sent a fuming Mr. Burns to the press when Marge controversially cooked Blinky, the three-eyed fish and it lures and lassoes Homer into doing pretty much anything. Not only is food often utilized as a story theme, but the inventiveness in which Springfield snacks and sweets are devised are worth their own spin-off show. Who could forget Nuts and Gum (together at last!) or hasn't dreamed of making a concoction as popular as the Flaming Moe? What kind of monsters would we be if we didn't partake in homemade PowerSauce bars?

Lucky for you, fiction is about to become its own scrumptious reality. It's time to dust off your apron, act like your own Lunch Lady Doris, and dig deep into the deliciousness of *The Simpsons*.

Below is a roundup of our favorite appetizing amateur recipes and difficulty ratings, ranging from Maggie to Marge:

Nachos, Flanders-Style (Season 7 episode "Home Sweet Homediddly-Dum-Doodily")
Difficulty: Maggie

Ingredients:
cucumbers
cottage cheese

Instructions:
Chop a cucumber horizontally, forming the cuts into perfectly circular disks. Place them on a serving tray.

Grab a tub of cottage cheese and add a dollop to each cucumber (the sadder the scoop, the better). If you can present these on the saddest station in your home, the better. We're talking on top of a dusty record player, next to a dog-eared copy of the bible, adjacent to a Frog on Skis piece of Grandmother art that haunts you daily because you're terrified to give it up in case your late Grandmother Gladys will be watching.

Other Culinary Ideas

You can most likely McGyver your way around the Internet, finding recipes for the following, but it's important to note that no *Simpsons* feast would be complete without a Gummy Venus De Milo, which can be ordered online. For PowerSauce bars use a normal recipe for spaghetti and then scoop them into bar-shaped ice cube trays or tightly bind them into plastic bags and freeze them overnight. The Homer donut is a must. Purchase a regular pink frosted donut from your local shop and then add accoutrements like sprinkles, gummy bears, M&Ms, and Jolly Ranchers.

Giant Rice Krispies Treat with a Bite Taken Out (Season 5 episode "The Boy Who Knew Too Much")
Difficulty: Homer

Ingredients
6 cups Rice Krispies cereal
3 bags of marshmallows
¼ cup of butter

Instructions:
Grab a giant saucepan and begin to melt some of that butter at a low heat, add the marshmallows, and stir continually until they become properly liquid-like.

Pour in Rice Krispies (bit by bit as you see fit) and swirl together with a spoon until they're a hardened solid.

Pour the mixture into a buttered pan. We prefer a square-like buffet kind of concoction, the kind your Great Aunt Gladys would bring to a church mixer while stalling to sip her hooch.

Let the mixture cool, turn over onto a plate, and voila! Either carve out a bite-like shape to evoke true *Simpsons* goodness or have your favorite friend or relative do the honors. You'll have a treat worthy of the Qumby Compound.

Caramel Cods (Season 9 episode "Treehouse of Horror")
Difficulty: Marge

Ingredients:
1½ cups unsalted butter
¾ cup sugar
1 teaspoon vanilla
3½ cups all-purpose flour
caramel topping
fish-shaped cookie cutter
cookie sheet

Instructions:

Heat oven to 350 degrees. In a large bowl, beat butter until creamy. Add in sugar and vanilla and then beat flour in until blended.

Roll out the dough and cut away with the fish cookie cutter. While rolling it out, make a lot of jokes about the mob or Troy McClure and his romantic abnormalities. Have fun while alienating the other members of your house as you do this task. On a greased cookie sheet, place cookies two inches apart.

Bake 12 to 14 minutes or until brown. Cool off.

Dollop bits of the caramel sauce onto the cookies. Let cool. Place on a tray that allows for the power and grandeur of these bona fide caramel cods to reign, stick a lollipop stick in them, and eat the lamest Halloween treat ever, like a corndog if possible.

Springfield Elementary

With the exception of the Simpsons home and the nuclear power plant, Springfield Elementary has been a prominent ground zero for stories since Day One. Springfield Elementary is where we most often see the other kids of Springfield, including Nelson, Martin Prince, Ralph Wiggum, Jimbo Jones, Sheri and Terri. Principal Skinner reigns over it with a humorless iron fist, Mrs. Krabappel coasts through the day, Groundskeeper Willie greases himself up, and Lunch Lady Doris bides her time between cigarette breaks.

The world of *The Simpsons* is one in which adults are often inept. Chief Wiggum is laughably poor at policin', Patty and Selma celebrate in their DMV schadenfreude, and Mr. Burns can barely be bothered to remember his own employees' names. Yet, the ineptitude contained within Springfield Elementary's walls are of a different breed.

Early in the show's run, the writers crafted Principal Skinner into being a hardened Vietnam vet and were eager to exercise his possible PTSD in whatever opportunity presented itself. In time he's softened to being a humorless boob of a man, praising uniformity and misunderstanding basic human interactions. In introducing a school pageant he decries, "Welcome to an evening of theater and picking up after yourselves!"

Mrs. Krabappel's role in the school is similarly offbase. She represents the heaps of teachers who perhaps once held a passion for emboldening young minds, but by the time we see her, that ship has long since sailed. Her admonishing of Bart's hell-raiser antics is at times both through frustration and bemusement, almost as if she resents her role as an authority figure. Similar to Principal Skinner, Mrs. Krabappel's relationship with Bart is a push-and-pull of codependent caring. Deep down we believe that she wants Bart to succeed but also deep down we know that if she had her druthers, she'd be on a singles cruise faster than you can say, "Salad for one, soup for one, wine…for three."

Contrary to Mrs. Krabappel, Mrs. Hoover is a teacher who seems like she never found a true passion in teaching in the first place. Her role is often playing an exasperated echo to Lisa's know-it-all-ness who is eager to launch herself onto any kind of life raft that gets her as far away from the school as possible. The halls of Springfield Elementary have been plagued by various mishaps and mysteries. We've witnessed the following.

- Lack of funding resulted in a cinder block replacing a tether ball on the playground.
- Lack of funding resulted in Malk being served in the cafeteria instead of milk, and gym mats being ground into

meat. Circus animals, cow testicles and hearts, and shredded newspaper were also used as food.

- Lack of funding resulted in the use of rat milk.
- Lack of funding resulted in gravy that's merely just water dyed brown.
- Lack of funding resulted in overcrowded classrooms, trims in chalk budget, and asbestos pouring from the sky like snow at any given moment.

Basically, the school's strongest quality is its laughable lack of funding. In the Season 6 episode "The PTA Disbands," we see this in full force and as the episode's plot center. After Skinner's obsessive skimping on basic requirements to run a proper school, Krabappel and the teachers hang up their hats and head to the streets, protesting until their rights are rewarded.

Over time in the show's run, the history of Springfield Elementary has been expanded. Before Bart and Lisa attended, the school boasted a swimming pool among its facilities, and Groundskeeper Willie was the swim coach. At one point the school even had winding staircase, leading to a fortification area, which, like many of the flourishes of color and history that the school's been given over time, has never been re-addressed in later episodes.

Part of the fun of Springfield Elementary as a show location is its flexibility. It can host a carnival or a science fair or play sanctuary for Skinner and Krabappel's forbidden love. It's been a meeting place for civilians witnessing a comet and for a brief period in time it did double-duty as a Springfield prison. So let's hope Superintendent Chalmers never quavers from his stronghold of superiority, Hoover never has a positive outlook, and Willie keeps doing what Willie does (whatever that is).

44 Showrunners

We already told you we think *The Simpsons* writers deserve statues, so what do the showrunners deserve? But first what is a showrunner and why do they deserve anything? Okay, we'll slow down and let former co-showrunner Bill Oakley answer that for you. In a live interview with *Late Night Action* host Alex Falcone, Bill explained that a showrunner is akin to a director of a movie who is also the film's writer and producer. "You make every decision about everything," he said. That includes everything from deciding which episodes will be created and who will write them to directing the actors, animators, and sound editors.

Here are all the different people who have run the show over the years and what they brought to the table.

Matt Groening, Sam Simon, and James L. Brooks (Seasons 1–2) It makes sense that the three creators took the reins in the beginning and made all the important decisions that gave the show its initial tone and feel. During these breakout seasons, the show had a more grounded reality than what you'd find as the show evolved. And while *The Simpsons* has always been funny, its comedic sensibility in these seasons were more in keeping with *Life in Hell*'s observational and satirical humor. There's an entire camp of people who believe *The Simpsons* didn't get good until Season 3 or 4, but we say, "Get outta here, stupids!"

Al Jean and Mike Reiss (Seasons 3–4) When these Harvard alums graduated from writers to showrunners, their strong comedic sensibilities—paired with their deep understanding of the characters—allowed them to take the show and its inhabitants to new and more daring places. During their seasons the show started to get the look and feel of what would lead to the golden age of *The Simpsons*.

David Mirkin (Seasons 5–6)

When Mirkin became the showrunner, a huge shift in the writing team took place as many writers left to do other projects. With such big shoes to fill, Season 5 could have very easily been the end of the best show ever. Instead, the new writers—and writers who stayed—churned out some of the most acclaimed episodes including "Rosebud" and the 100th episode, "Sweet Seymour Skinner's Baadasssss Song." The show started to get weirder (in the best way) and take bigger risks with its gags and plot points like Bart getting a pet elephant and Mr. Burns having a childhood teddy bear that had previously belong to Hitler. Still, the show would maintain its core values and come back with the family in episodes like "And Maggie Makes Three."

Bill Oakley and Josh Weinstein (Seasons 7–8)

The iconic pair of writers joined the writing team in the third season after catching attention for their *Seinfeld* spec script. Penning such classic episodes as "Who Shot Mr. Burns?" and "Lisa vs. Malibu Stacy," the writing duo would become showrunners and executive producers who were instrumental in the show's golden years. Where Mirkin had allowed *The Simpsons* to branch out in its level of absurdity, Oakley and Weinstein primarily brought the focus back to the family. That doesn't mean Oakley and Weinstein played it safe. They changed up the entire format with "22 Short Films About Springfield" and addressed network issues in "The Itchy & Scratchy & Poochie Show."

Mike Scully (Seasons 9–12)

After getting his start by writing jokes for Yakov Smirnoff, Scully began writing for *The Simpsons* in Season 6, contributing some of the best Lisa and Marge episodes in the history of the show (i.e. "Lisa on Ice," "Marge Be Not Proud," "Lisa's Date with Density.") When Scully took over as showrunner, he experienced a mass exodus because of the departures of Oakley, Weinstein, Dan McGrath, David X. Cohen, and the tragic death of Phil Hartman. It was a level of change that affected the show irreparably, but Scully still managed to pull off four strong seasons with iconic moments and the level of heart and humor that you could find during *The Simpsons* at its best.

Al Jean and Matt Selman (Season 13–present)

In Oakley's interview with Falcone, he explains the difficulty of the job, rationalizing that this was the reason most people only ran the show for two seasons at a time. Not only did Jean come back for more, but he also hasn't left since. During his long run, he has taken the show through just about every "*Simpsons* did it" situation possible. Over the last decade and a half, he has managed to keep *The Simpsons* in the news with inventive, daring, and head-turning moments and stunts with controversial guest stars, character romances, and hour-long episodes. Jean has often shared showrunning responsibilities with the great Selman, who's been on the show since 1997 and supervised the critically acclaimed Lego episode, "Brick Like Me." The two have accomplished much in their time with the show, but more than anything have kept the family on air. That's got to at least win them a Lego medal.

45 Principal Skinner

All it takes is a rush of color, a defiant deviation from the very rules he so steadfastly scurries toward during every second of his life, and Principal Skinner is surrendered to a puddle. In the Season 7 episode "Team Homer," Seymour Skinner's fight is focused on implementing gray and dull school uniforms, but then they exploded into technicolor the moment rain hits their polyester tri-blend. "Skinner, why aren't these uniforms colorfast?" Superintendent Chalmers bellows. Skinner, desperate to please, thinks hard, and then exclaims, "I don't understand. I buy them at the same place I buy Mother's clothes!" Then he panics: "Oh no! She's in the park!" And then the lecherous comment from Chalmers: "This I gotta see!"

In this brief scene in this one singular episode, everything we know and love about Principal Skinner is displayed: he's eager to please and desperate to bow to any and all authorities in his path. We love his subservience to Superintendent Chalmers, someone who makes him quake in his boots. Throughout the Bill Oakley/ Josh Weinstein years, this was notably explored through their *Odd Couple*-like pairing. It is within their showrunner reign that we get "Principal and the Pauper," but most notable is their vignette in "22 Short Films About Springfield" that typifies their exasperated/ eager back and forth and also invents the concept of steamed hams.

Skinner's a stereotypical mama's boy who lives with the geriatric Agnes Skinner, who keeps her grown-up son on a leash tighter than Homer in hot pants. Principal Skinner's proudly lacking in a sparkling personality, something the show's writers happily highlight some of his favorite things, including Diet Caffeine Free Dr Pepper, Silhouette Night, and the very concept of school.

In the early seasons of the show, the writers wrote Skinner as a hardened Vietnam vet, a man who would sprinkle his sorrows inappropriately into any and all conversations. Since about Season 4, this has been greatly played out. A new Skinner was soon surfacing, leaning more into the comedy of loneliness than that of PTSD. However, Skinner's need for authority figures who boss him around has remained consistent. One might assume that aggressive and snarly Agnes has become a perfect replacement his former officers in the Army.

Most of the time, Skinner has kept a tight wallet around Springfield Elementary, a premise explored through the Season 6 episode, "The PTA Disbands." In this episode the teachers erupt in a protest when Skinner's budget-consciousness reaches extreme heights, going as far as micromanaging chalk usage.

One of the most heartbreaking storylines of *The Simpsons* has to be the saga of the star-crossed lovers Edna Krabappel and Seymour Skinner. First explored in the Season 8 episode "Grade School Confidential," we see their romance run its course over the 22 minutes, but its impact on the show lives on.

Previously prickly, uncharacteristically tender, these two seem to have finally found a reason for the run-around that is their lives. Out of all of the suitors the show's given Krabappel over the seasons (and the lack thereof for Skinner), this by far felt the truest and closest to a soulmate. Yet, part of what makes *The Simpsons* so special is the ambiguity of the episode's ending. After spending the episode fighting for their romance, they win in the end…but still decide to split. When Bart questions their decision, they explain that it "had run its course." We at home accept this because we don't know how to feel. But just when we think the episode's over and everything has been reset, a lingering connection keeps their story alive. Could there be a separate universe where love conquers all?

Principal Skinner was designed to be a simple foil, a stick in the mud for all of Springfield and an adversary to Bart. Though over time what Skinner was shaped up to be was so much more. Soon he had heart, hurt, and a whole lot more to make fun of as a pseudo-avatar for all of the writer's high school teachers.

The Controversy Over Armin Tamzarian

Superfans don't do well with change. They can't handle codas or epilogues or anything dismantling the happily ever after they were once promised. For a group of alleged adults, they sure do spend their lives in a non-stop game of make believe. But when Bill Oakley and Josh Weinstein took the helm of the show, their goal was to push the envelope. Characters that rarely got their place in the sun were soon centerstage. The Season 9 episode "The Principal and the Pauper" is the boldest example of this goal, as they literally rewrote a popular character's history, changing all that we know about him and the world of Springfield itself.

"The Principal and the Pauper" opens with Principal Skinner's 20th anniversary at Springfield Elementary. It's a celebration befitting any treasured member of a community with a packed house, lively decorations, and celebratory treats, of which even Superintendent Chalmers approves, though he notes: "the school normally serves cake only on Thursdays. And I'm also well aware that today is Friday. Nevertheless." Cue Bart and Milhouse wheeling in a special Skinner cake.

The celebrations are short-lived, however, when a man claiming to be the real Seymour Skinner interrupts, and the crowd becomes confused. Most surprising is what comes next: "It's true," Skinner pushes out. "I'm...an imposter."

We soon learn that "Skinner" is actually Armin Tamzarian, a Vietnam vet who fought alongside the real Seymour Skinner and was heartened by his dreams of one day becoming an elementary school principal. Assuming he had perished in combat, Armin took it upon himself to not only carry out Seymour's dream, but also to start a new life to salve his own directionless path. The episode was written by Ken Keeler, directed by Steven Dean Moore, and was actually a holdover from Season 8—perhaps because of its controversial nature. Many people believe the premise of the episode was based on the 1993 film *Sommersby*, and at one point was potentially titled "Skinnersby." However, Keeler clarified that he was more inspired by (and obviously named after) *The Prince and the Pauper* by Mark Twain.

Oakley and Weinstein were excited to dive deep into another Skinner episode, having both written "Sweet Seymour Skinner's Baadasssss Song," and reportedly spent "a month immersed in the mind of Seymour Skinner." Keeler described his process of writing the "real Seymour Skinner" (voiced by Martin Sheen) and not falling into temptation to draw him as a despicable character. The end result is the real Seymour is just...off. The town he left has evolved past his departure, and the vision he once held for his second-life chapter has now decayed and betrayed its romanticized hue.

Sure, the imposter Seymour's not perfect. According to Edna Krabappel, he's "a weenie." But he was *their* weenie. Agnes Skinner adds, "Now there was a weenie you could be proud to call your son." Within the episode we see the disjointedness the real Seymour causes to the town, sparking the community's efforts to get Armin, Seymour, or whomever they've lived with for the past handful of decades, to return.

When the episode aired in 1997, it was received with mixed reviews from both fans and critics. Although the tidy wrap-up of its ending was typical of *The Simpsons'* style, fans felt it was too easy for the complicated premises the episode brought up. According to Chris Turner, the author of *Planet Simpson*, this episode marked "the abrupt plunge of *The Simpsons'* golden age." Many other critics have echoed this sentiment, characterizing this episode as the beginning of the end of the show's flawless run in high quality.

Weinstein, Oakley, and Keeler have long defended this episode as being one of the series' best. In his interpretation this episode doesn't so much dismiss all of the character building the show had done with Skinner up until that point but rather added to his story with a new texture. On the DVD commentary, Keeler describes the Armin Tamzarian debacle as being more about "people who like things just the way they are" and extends it to say that this episode is about "people who hate it."

Much like the angry folks who disapprove of sequels, "The Principal and the Pauper" upsets the order. Though, as Keeler would assert, what good is avoiding creative challenges? Wouldn't it be a worse crime to allow the show to grow risk-averse? *The Simpsons* has never been about bowing to a status quo, and, though Armin Tamzarian was never what the fans expected (or wanted), they can at least rest easy knowing that "everything will be just like it was, before all this happened, and no one will ever mention it again…under penalty of torture."

Milhouse Van Houten

Milhouse is one of the saddest characters in Springfield. Always the perennial punching bag and content in his seclusion from the spotlight, his life in Bart's shadow has been one of the show's standout storylines since Day One. Milhouse is gullible, greedy, insecure, and naive. He's often the puppet of Bart and thrust into the fray of whatever harebrained scheme his spikey haired bestie has concocted. Examples of this are sometimes embarrassingly dangerous.

Milhouse comes from a divorced family, a premise prominently featured in the Season 8 episode "A Milhouse Divided." His dad sleeps in a racing car bed; Homer sleeps in a big bed with his wife. His mother, LuAnn, has since moved onto a splashy post-divorce life that includes sleeping with a dude named Pyro.

There are occasional breaks from Milhouse's subservience to Bart. In the Season 7 episode "Marge Be Not Proud," Milhouse lies to Bart about playing the popular video game *BoneStorm*, so he could have more time with it himself. Within that same season in "Bart Sells His Soul," we see a bolder side of Milhouse taking great joy in leveraging power over Bart's conscience.

Though originally dreamed up as a Springfield side character, Milhouse's impact on the series is manifold. Catchphrases have been coined ("Everything's coming up Milhouse!"), movies have been made (the Season 7 episode "Radioactive Man," and romances have been sparked and sparred.

Over the seasons the writers have had an increasingly soft spot for Milhouse, a fact Al Jean described to *TV Guide* as due to the fact that they're "more like Milhouse than Bart." Perhaps it's this personal perspective that results in Milhouse never winning, and when he does, it's most likely the A-Story of the episode.

Milhouse has a long-running crush on Lisa, which for the bulk of the series was unrequited. In the Season 8 episode "Lisa's Date with Density," Milhouse confesses to Lisa that he likes her after she confesses to liking Nelson. She tells him, "I like you too, Milhouse. But…not in that way. You're more like a big sister." An outraged Milhouse responds: "No I'm not! Why does everyone keep saying that?"

There have been occasional exceptions made to Milhouse's lack of romantic prowess. Milhouse is fluent in Italian, a fact first introduced in the Season 17 episode, "The Last of the Red Hat Mamas." When Milhouse speaks the foreign language, his personality is seemingly transformed into a suave alter-ego of himself, forcing Lisa to have a slight change of heart. When Lisa approaches Milhouse with this news, she soon catches him with another Italian girl named Angelica, and their crush dynamic is suddenly flipped.

But he's often uncoordinated, especially when playing pin the tail on the donkey. He's possibly homosexual, a fact that lies buried within his personnel record at school. He's allergic to honey, wheat, dairy, mistletoe, the red parts of candy, and his own tears.

Over the years, there have been exceptions and nuances given to Milhouse's unrepentant dorkiness. In the Season 3 episode "Bart's Friend Falls in Love," we see Milhouse dating his first girlfriend, Samantha Stankey. One of the more heartbreaking themes of the show is that no matter what kind of pleasure Milhouse receives in life, we know that it's only a matter of time until the other shoe drops. In "Radioactive Man" it's the movie production shutting down; in "Bart on the Road," it's the Knoxville World's Fair being out of commission; and in "Bart's Friend Falls in Love," it's Bart sabotaging Milhouse's budding romance by telling Stacey's strict parents.

What makes Milhouse the saddest character—sadder than Hans Moleman, sadder than Frank Grimes, sadder than Barney emerging from a drunken blackout—is his acceptance of his unfortunate fate. When rejected and left alone, it's easy to see Milhouse assuming this is just how the world is. Any attention he receives, positive or negative, is almost welcomed for the very fact that it's energy from another human.

But there's still a glimmer of hope, even though history has taught Milhouse time and time again that things won't work out, he still seizes the day, hoping that perhaps this time will be the one time that everything will change.

48 Sign Gags

Due to the fact that Springfield is intended to be Any City, USA, the writers were not limited to making regionally specific references, so any landmark, business, or billboard was fair game to add colorful characteristics for the sake of comedy. Having visual jokes stacked on top of already funny scenes is baked into the very fabric of *The Simpsons'* style. It's this blink-and-you'll-miss-it storytelling that speaks to the writers' approach in unknowingly creating a show perfectly suited for DVD re-watches before that concept was ever invented.

Sign gags appear in nearly every episode often as an Easter egg for either an inside joke for *The Simpsons* staff (the Mt. Swartzwelder Historic Cider Mill in the "Burns Baby Burns" episode after *Simpsons* writer John Swartzwelder) or for a simple gag (a sign hanging over the Springfield Elementary Auditorium read "PARENT/TEACHER NIGHT 'LET'S SHARE THE BLAME'"). Even Homer's yearbook quote of "I can't believe I ate the whole thing" is the visual gift that keeps on giving.

Sometimes, sign gags can prompt a character to spiral into despair like Otto Mann's claim of "false advertising" in front of Stoner's Pot Palace. Other times writers use sign gags as an opportunity for a personal jab ("Now Entering Winnipeg, We Were Born Here, What's Your Excuse?") The most famous and frequent sign gag is the marquee in front of the First Church of Springfield. There, you can feast your nondenominational eyes on: "Communion in 30 Minutes or Less or Your Service is Free," "God: The Original Love Connection," or "Next Sunday: The Miracle of Shame," to name a few.

 **Nerds**

On a lesser show, there might be one token nerd, maybe two if you're lucky. The character would have thick rimmed glasses, a virginal demeanor, and a pocket protector that screams "I have social anxiety!" It's easy to imagine that had *The Simpsons* been given network notes, characters like the easily-nauseated Wendell Borton or calculator-gripping Database would be the show's TV-approved nerd representatives. Fortunately, TV-approved is not *Simpsons*-approved. From Artie Ziff to Uter Zorker, *The Simpsons* captures the entire spectrum of nerd nuance. We have our textbook nerds like do-gooder Martin Prince and science-nerd Professor Frink, though according to him, "nerd" stands for "Not Even Remotely Dorky."

Some of the best nerds are Doug, Benjamin, and Gary from "Homer Goes to College." As obsessed with pop culture as they are with science, these three are the quintessential college nerds. Although the episode came out in 1993, their interests (including

Monty Python, *Star Trek*, and *Dungeons and Dragons*) make them indecipherable from present-day nerds, who may have also been mortal enemies of Homer.

Before nerds get the chance to go to college, they have to start out young. In "Bart's Comet" we are introduced to the Superfriends—a highly selective group of people named after their interests. The members include Database, Cosine, E-mail, Report Card, Lisa, and Ham, who was named after his love of ham radios.

You don't have to be book smart to be a nerd. In fact, some nerds could use some help in the brains department. Both the Squeaky Voiced Teen and Milhouse are more nerdy because of their appearance, clumsiness, and unrequited love more than their intellect. There are also toy collectors like Waylon Smithers or Reverend Lovejoy, who plays with model trains in his basement. "If the passengers will look to their right, you will see a sad man. That is all," he says.

The Simpsons household houses nerd-card-carrying Lisa "the Singing Dorkette" as well as Marge Simpson, whose nerdiness transpires in her weird love of Ringo, fear of burlesque, and belief that potatoes are "neat." Marge is an example of someone with a nerdy personality but not necessarily nerdy interests like Comic Book Guy, a perfect parody of the Internet nerd at large because of the arrogance and sarcasm of a 45-year-old virgin who still lives with his parents. He coined the popular phrase, "Worst. Episode. Ever." And once said, "I must return to my comic book store, where I dispense the insults rather than absorb them."

Similarly arrogant is Marge's high school boyfriend Artie Ziff, whose brain is as active as his busy hands. Artie is the egotistical, self-entitled nerd who values intellect above all else. "Fellow classmates instead of voting for some athletic superhero or a pretty boy, you elected me, your intellectual superior, as your king," he informs his schoolmates after being elected prom king. Whereas

Comic Book Guy's arrogance only got him a few dates with Agnes Skinner, Artie returned to Springfield a software billionaire.

In the middle of the nerd spectrum is a rule-loving mama's boy, Seymour Skinner. His nerdiness shines through in his inability to choose a detergent ("Tide...Cheer...Bold...Biz...Fab...All...Gain...Wisk"), his love of science ("You get all the fun of sitting still, being quiet, writing down numbers, paying attention. Science has it all"), and his idea of an ideal night out on the town ("Good evening everyone and welcome to a wonderful evening of theater and picking up after yourselves.") There's Lisa's rival, Allison Taylor, who is a star student and anagram enthusiast who is so advanced that it nearly earned her a hosing of a lifetime from Bart. This brand of nerd can also house the entire Flanders clan (except Maude, a total fox) who are such dorks they don't even swear. Rod and Todd's aversion to violent cartoons and sugar radiates a nerdy sadness.

Frank Grimes—or Grimey, as he liked to be called—was the working man's nerd. He's a deeply relatable character who watched the bullies (in his case, Homer) succeed, rendering his hard work useless. You can tell Grimey is a nerd from his personalized pencils to the pocket protector, in which they were so perfectly stored. Grimes has always been bullied. When Grimes received a degree in nuclear physics, a bird attempts to steal it away. While there are many things that make Frank nerdy, it was ultimately his obsession with meritocracy that ended him. In true nerd fashion, he was upstaged by his accidental bully at his own funeral.

50 Get a Tattoo

There's always a danger when donning a pop culture-themed tattoo. What if the band breaks up or the references run dry? What if you lose interest in the very thing you branded to your body in the first place? That's the beauty of getting a piece of Springfield slapped to your sleeve. All of those concerns need not apply.

The Simpsons has been around so long that it's transcended the pop culture tattoo expiration date. We know that even if the show bows into that last good night, its legacy will continue to outlive us all, so why not have a little fun? The only downside to donning some ink is deciding which deep cut reference best fits your personality. Are you more of a "Stupid Babies Need the Most Attention" kind of guy? Or a drawing of dignity kind of gal? The upside is that there are no wrong answers, and your tattoo will give you instant entry into an inner circle of fellow fans smiling at you from afar, eager to become your new best friend...or at the very least eager to

Co-author Julia Prescott sports a tattoo of the gummy Venus de Milo and its sweet, sweet candy. (Julia Prescott)

engage with you in a passionate conversation in the checkout line for a good 10 minutes.

Thesimpsonstattoo is worth a follow on Instagram. Some of the best tattoos we've seen there include a Knoxville Wig Center roundup with Nelson, Milhouse, and Bart from the "Bart on the

My Venus de Milo Tattoo

This was tattoo numero tres after getting matching tats with my sister at age 19. We got swallows on our feet. (I know, gross), and I got a camp tattoo on my forearm at age 23, which looks like a cult symbol. (I know, gross.) Finally, when I was in my mid-to-late-20s, I found that something needed to be branded on my body to commemorate my undying love for...something. I was searching. I was stoked. For what? I didn't know.

Then as I went through my 227th notes pass on a pilot that would never see the light of day, I found myself chuckling at what was obviously a joke inspired by *The Simpsons*. It hit me: I write comedy because of *The Simpsons*. Every set-up structure, punch-line hit, or even Gore Vidal reference can be attributed to a writers' room bungalow on the Culver City FOX lot by a bunch of nerdy white men.

I wish I could tell you I arrived on the choice of Gummy Venus de Milo because the Sky Daddy above spoke to me through tea leaves, but the fact of the matter is I just always liked that episode, and out of all *The Simpsons'* visual references, that seemed to lend itself best to the old-school tattoo style I was going for. Also, I saw it on someone else's Instagram and figured I gotta have it.

In retrospect, I'm glad I didn't get it on my actual "sweet, sweet can," though that was hotly debated, because I get to display it proudly to the world. Little did I know that the very thought of getting this tattoo would lead me to a friendship, which would lead me to a podcast, which would lead me then to a *popular* podcast, which would then lead me to write this very book with my friend. And it's all because of an episode of television featuring a cartoon feminist and a cartoon man with an insatiable hunger for candy. I tell ya, the world is crazy.

—*Julia Prescott*

Road" episode and Lisa with the quote: "I Am the Lizard Queen."
Another has Troy McClure with "You May Remember Me From
Such Tattoos As This Leg!" There is a Crazy Cat Lady tattoo and a
Malibu Stacy doll with the quote: "Don't Ask Me, I'm Just a Girl,"
making the anti-feminist gobbledygook look cool. A stamp of the
Stonecutters is another winner.

51 Ralph Wiggum

For as highbrow as the show goes, crafting characters with deep
intelligence and an even deeper ability to reference NPR (see: Lisa
Simpson and occasionally Smithers), sometimes all the world wants
is a big, dumb child. For those moments when Homer's dopiness
is not enough to satiate your appetite for stupid, we have Ralph
Wiggum. Ralph is Police Chief Wiggum's only son and is often
characterized as the dumbest student at Springfield Elementary.
He's voiced by Nancy Cartwright and first appeared in the Season
1 episode "Moaning Lisa," though his truest form (and adjusted
design) didn't take shape until the Season 2 episode "Homer vs.
Lisa and the 8ᵗʰ Commandment."

Ralph is most often the punchline of any situation, chiming in
with his special brand of nonsense. Quotes like: "My cat's breath
smells like cat food," "Me fail English? That's unpossible," and "Oh
boy, sleep! That's where I'm a Viking!" can be found prominently
displayed on *Simpsons* merch the world over.

Ralph's popularity is dizzying and defies logic. In 2009 Kid
Robot released their own Ralph Wiggum figurine apart from their
regular run of *The Simpsons* toys. The Bloodhound Gang wrote
a song about him simply titled, "Ralph Wiggum," and the lyrics

Our Favorite Ralph-isms

"If Mommy's purse didn't belong in the microwave, why did it fit?"
"I wet my arm pants."
"My cat's name is Mittens."
"Look Big Daddy, it's Regular Daddy."
"When I grow up, I wanna be a principal or a caterpillar."
"That's where I saw a Leprechaun. He tells me to burn things."
"Hi, Principal Skinner! Hi, Super Nintendo Chalmers!"

are a jumble of their favorite Ralph-isms. Out of any non-family character in the show, *The Simpsons* staff has reported receiving the most amount of questions regarding Ralph.

Why is it that Ralph stands out so? Could it be that Ralph's purpose within the world of *The Simpsons* is to deliver non sequiturs, which make great T-shirt slogans? Could it be is simple design? With a blissed-out gleam in his eye, a frozen smile on his face, and a naiveté that makes Homer look like a Isaac Newton, Ralph's a cool breeze on a hot summer day. His "this tastes like burning" lifestyle can lighten the sourest mood. His presence within the show is a constant reminder to not take things too seriously.

Over the years the writers have attempted to provide shape and structure to his sense of self. In the Season 4 episode "I Love Lisa," we see Ralph front and center with an unrequited (and probably first) crush. His attempts at wooing Lisa are sweet but fruitless. When Lisa finally breaks the news to Ralph (and on national television), we witness Ralph experiencing a sad emotion for possibly the first time. Back in the Simpsons house, Bart slowly narrates Ralph's romantic demise with remote in hand: "Watch this, Lise. You can actually pinpoint the second when his heart rips in half."

Ralph being Ralph, he, of course, recovers. Over time, Ralph's usage in the show can shift. Sometimes he's as dumb as a stapler, other times he can operate that stapler, and on a few occasions, he would like to marry that stapler.

138

Ralph can often represent the cruelty of real life. When Ralph wins, it's almost always seen as a stab at schadenfreude. In the Season 6 episode "Lisa's Rival," Ralph ends up taking home the prize for best book report after Lisa painstakingly hurls herself into the project. When Ralph wins, it's not because he's somehow stumbled upon brilliance but rather misunderstood the assignment, grabbed a bunch of extra *Star Wars* toys, and presented them to the committee who loved the vintage nostalgia and awarded him first prize. This moment soon gives way to one of the most popular Ralph-isms the show has ever scripted: "I bent my Wookie."

52 Bullies

Let's talk about the world's most adorable antagonists. Within Springfield there's a hardened crew of miscreants that split time between spray painting the side of the Kwik-E-Mart and giving swirlies to nerds. Their names are Nelson, Jimbo, Kearney, and Dolph.

Nelson Mandela Muntz is the most notable. Though he's the shortest and youngest of the group, his tenacity and toughness seem to outweigh the others, forcing them to obey his every command. Nelson's been a presence within the show as early as Season 1 and can be most often remembered for his signature, "Ha ha!" It has since become a battle cry for schadenfreude. Martin tears a hole in his pants? "Ha ha!" Old lady knocked upside down into a trash can? "Ha ha!" Bart breaks his leg and he may actually be hurt pretty bad? "I *said* 'ha ha.'" But because this is *The Simpsons*, even the smallest recurring character sets their day in the sun, and there's more to Nelson than meets the eye.

In the Season 8 episode "Lisa's Date with Density," Lisa and Nelson briefly engage in a romantic relationship. Though their love is short-lived and their split amicable, an added texture is given to Nelson's character. From that point forward, Nelson's hardships are honed as reasoning for his antagonistic behavior. We learn that Nelson's parents are divorced, and blame is mostly placed on his mother's cough drop addiction. At one point Nelson yowls, "By the end her breath was so fresh she wasn't really my mother anymore." What better way to put the divorce of Milhouse's parents into perspective?

Another notable bully is Corky James "Jimbo" Jones, Sr. (also known as Jamesbo and Hector Gutierrez). Hot damn, *The Simpsons* writers love to throw a good really long middle name joke in there that only a fan writing a book about *The Simpsons* would ever pick up. Jimbo is known by his trademark skull T-shirt and purple beanie hat, which is placed uncomfortably high on his head. In a later episode, we learn it's to cover up his perfectly sculpted bald spot. When Nelson's not around, Jimbo's often in charge, doling out bad deeds and trying to make it with chicks. Though Jimbo is mostly menacing, he tends to have a tender side not dissimilar to Nelson's. This usually comes out when he assumes no one else is looking or when he's hoping to get some.

In the Season 4 episode "New Kid on the Block," Jimbo becomes the temporary boyfriend of Laura Powers, which baffles and breaks the heart of Bart, who spent the episode pining for her affection. Though Laura jilts Jimbo in the end, his presence as an intimidator in the town is restored as soon as the next episode.

Kearney Zzyzwicz, Sr. is the oldest of the bullies at age 29. Kearney's strong, stupid, and solidly convinced he'll never see the sixth grade. One of the running jokes that follows Kearney is how much older he is than everyone else. He's the father to a 10-year old child that attends Springfield Elementary alongside him and "sleeps in a drawer." Kearney's son looks exactly like the bald Kearney, though a bit more bright-eyed and confident. His upbeat attitude is almost heartbreaking to witness, considering the clustered circumstances in which he was brought into the world.

Dolph Starbeam is perhaps the most mysterious of the group. The son of aging hippies, he's a perfect example of a laid-back, lackadaisical parenting style backfiring into brutality. Dolph doesn't hesitate to shoplift, give swirlies, or swear in front of children. He's the less defined of the bully characters and thus the most traditionally tough without remorse. He's often been described as "the most attractive of the bunch," which is an argument the Internet seems custom-made for. He's named after Dolph Timmerman, one of Matt Groening's classmates growing up. Though the real Dolph wasn't necessarily a bully, he was, according to Groening, "just a cool guy." No word on whether the real Dolph also sported an unrelenting asymmetrical haircut, but we have our hopes.

Visit Knoxville's World's Fair

Sure, it's no Andy Williams in concert, but the road trip destination in "Bart on the Road" deeply deserves your attention. Since its 1996 premiere, the episode has resonated with a wide swath of superfans, sparking both tattoo tributes and road trips to Tennessee. So why not take matters into your own hands? Slip your rental car into cruise control, slide into the backseat with your brethren, and banish all thoughts of whether or not your cover of going to the Grammar Rodeo will play with your parents.

A little bit of history: the 1982 Knoxville World's Fair (formally known as the Knoxville International Energy Exposition) was themed to the premise of "Energy Turns the World." At the time of its debut, it drew in around 11 million visitors, making it one of the most popular world's fairs in history. Some of the fair's greatest features include the Peruvian exhibit, in which an unwrapped mummy was put on display; the Egyptian site, which featured ancient artifacts dating back hundreds of years and valued at $30 million; and a larger-than-life Rubik's Cube from the popular toy's country of origin, Hungary.

When "Bart on the Road" was originally conceived, Knoxville actually wasn't their first choice. Within the writers' room, there was great debate between that location and Fort Lauderdale, Florida. The focus of Bart's spring break trip needed to be a funny, unlikely place that no 10-year-old in their right mind would possibly have interest in. Within the episode, Milhouse is given the reins to sell the site to the group, "Not just a county fair, not just a Europe fair, but a *World's* Fair. The World's Fair in Knoxville, Tennessee!"

Of course, we know that things will not end up being what they seemed. The boys arrive in Knoxville, race to the observation deck, and quickly discover that the last time Knoxville was a necessity for road-side wandering was just shortly after its 1982 celebration.

Similar to the show's depiction, visiting the real Knoxville World's Fair is a decidedly different affair than what you might expect. Knoxville, as a town in and of itself, is a strange corner of Southern hospitality that's one part Austin, Texas, one part Nashville, Tennessee, and no parts Dollywood, which is about an hour away. With a bustling nightlife on its main stretch boasting gastropubs alongside Mom and Pop shops, it's at times both frozen in time, yet soaring toward a pre-packaged future.

But you don't go there for the happy hours on the main stretch; you go there for the World's Fair Sunsphere. Enter through the main floor and you'll be instantly treated to a tantalizing sight of keepsakes from 1982. The giant Rubik's Cube from Hungary rests forever in the lobby, and it's on a rotating mechanism that self plays over time!

Then hurry your happy selves to the elevator and ride it to the top floor, watching the city from 266 feet. During the fair it cost $2 to ride the elevator where fancy folks would wine and dine in its observation deck restaurant. Nowadays, the sphere is a hollow shell of what it once was. Riding the elevator now will treat you to a timeline of how the sphere came to be and the history that's followed. When one of the authors of this here book visited the sphere three years ago, a man with a dog roamed its halls while speaking loudly to his girlfriend on speakerphone.

Though there's no wig store at the top (and thus no way to properly recreate your disillusioned selfie with your wig-wearing besties), knowing that you get to at least touch a piece of *The Simpsons* history is enough to make your friends jealous and your mother confused.

54 Learn "Classical Gas"

If you've ever wondered whether your friend is a keeper, try the Lisa needs braces test. Simply say, "Lisa needs braces," and if your friend replies, "Dental plan," you have a lifelong companion. If they look at you with slack-jawed confusion, it's time to say good-bye and bust out the ol' blues guitar.

In a 1993 episode, Homer becomes head of the power plant's union and leads the workers in a strike to regain their dental plan. While the workers are striking, Lisa plays a protest song on an acoustic guitar. At the end of the song, Lenny approaches her and asks her to play the song "Classical Gas." To play the song by Mason Williams, find the sheet music at: www.classicalgas.com

55 Who Shot Mr. Burns?

"Who Shot Mr. Burns?" was the first (and only) two-part episode of the show, and it originally aired on May 21, 1995. It was based on the popular episodes, "A House Divided" and "Who Done It" of the TV show *Dallas*. In "A House Divided," J.R. Ewing was shot by an unidentified perpetrator. For the eight months that followed that episode, viewers were enraptured with the mystery, and the culprit was eventually revealed on November 21, 1980.

Matt Groening had wanted to reference this episode within the show as a publicity stunt. Rumor has it that, due to the layout of the show's writers' room, Bill Oakley and Josh Weinstein's office was the closest in proximity to Groening's. One day Groening emerged with a glint in his eye and opened the writing duo's door with the simple request of wanting to do an homage to *Dallas*. To this date Weinstein isn't sure if he and Oakley were chosen based on creative prowess or convenience. (We think it's the former.)

From there, the writing staff then decided that the two-parter should be used as the grounds for a worldwide contest with a prize at the end. Oakley and Weinstein had originally envisioned the culprit to be Barney Gumble because they reasoned he could go to jail and not change the dynamic of the show. Showrunner David

Mirkin later changed the shooter to Maggie to not only surprise viewers, but also to keep the story within the core family.

After Part One originally aired, viewers could participate in the contest by calling 1-800-COLLECT and guessing who they thought the shooter was. This contest was hosted by FOX and ran from August 13 to September 10. It was one of the very first contests to tie together television and the Internet, which was still in its infancy. In addition to the call-in number, FOX launched springfield.com, a website on which viewers could read up on clues and study the mystery.

Then this is where it gets a little tricky: the prize for the person who accurately guessed Maggie in the end would be then immortalized (and Simpsons-ized) as an animated character within a future episode. However, due to contest regulations, the winner had to be chosen from a random sampling of entries. In the end the sample FOX chose from didn't actually contain any right answers, and so winner Fayla Gibson of Washington, D.C., won by chance, not by skill. To make matters worse, Fayla revealed that she wasn't even a fan of the show but rather participated in the contest on a whim. In the end she opted out of being animated and decided to take a cash prize instead.

In the years since its debut, most fans regard the "Who Shot Mr. Burns?" contest as a pivotal moment in the show's history. The "Who Shot Mr. Burns?" contest then took the show to the next level by creating a spectacle on a global scale. For anyone tuning in at the time, the mystery was inescapable.

There has never been an event the show has produced quite like, "Who Shot Mr. Burns?" At the time of its production, the staff worked tirelessly to keep the mystery a secret, even going so far as making animation director David Silverman the only one who truly knew—apart from the writing staff. Wes Archer, who was a director on the special episode, only knew so much as he was given to animate and guide his staff. Even the table read for this episode ended before the third act, thus preserving the mystery.

The show had a great deal of fun, laying in several "Easter eggs" and misdirects in Part One, including things like setting every clock to 3:00 or 9:00, having Mr. Burns talk about stealing candy from a baby, and having several Springfield residents stroke guns inexplicably in a town hall meeting, thus heightening suspicion.

To throw off the scent of the trail even more, there were an assortment alternate endings by David Mirkin and recorded by Harry Shearer. Several of these endings aired during the episode "The Simpsons 138th Episode Spectacular" and included characters like Barney, Moe, Apu, and Santa's Little Helper firing away at C. Montgomery Burns.

The reception of "Who Shot Mr. Burns?" was widely positive and remains one of the most popular moments in the show's history. In 2003 *Entertainment Weekly* named the two-part episode as part of their list of "The Top 25 *Simpsons* Episodes of All Time."

The Economic Value of *The Simpsons*

How much is the entire franchise of *The Simpsons* worth? In short, the answer is a lot. A whole lot. Like, a lot a lot. Okay, maybe that answer wasn't so short after all. The real answer is—drumroll please—more than $13 billion. Yes, you read that right. Please pick your jaw back up off the floor.

If that number seems outrageous, think about how long the show has been on air and how many reruns play on so many different channels. All of that equates to revenue for the franchise. If that alone hasn't overwhelmed you, now contemplate the amount of merchandise, books, comic books, games, and even a movie, that exist. All of it generates money. There's a *Simpsons* version of nearly everything, including an entire section of a theme park at Universal Studios (both in Los Angeles and Florida). Back in 2013 it was reported that over $4.6 billion was generated in *Simpsons*-themed consumer products alone, and that number has only grown since.

Outside of merchandise, *The Simpsons* has managed to rake in so much dough that it's broken records for it. When *The Simpsons* movie debuted in 2007, its profits far exceeded expectations of the entire entertainment industry. Homer and the gang broke several records at the time during their opening weekend, earning around $71.9 million. What records, you ask? Well, first off, it broke the record for best opening ever for a non-computer graphically animated film. It also beat *Beavis and Butt-Head Do America* for best opening for an animated movie rated PG-13 or higher. It was also the best opening for a movie derived from a TV series.

In 2013 *The Simpsons* continued to make it rain with their record-breaking syndication deal with FXX. The network paid $750 million to become the cable home of the series, which had 24 seasons and 530 episodes then. That's not far off from $1 billion. Is there a show that will ever surpass such a deal? We think not.

Some other fun *Simpsons*-related deals include three soundtrack albums. The first one, *Songs in the Key of Springfield*, came out in 1997, and that was followed by the release of *Go Simpsonic with The Simpsons* in 1999. In 2007 two more soundtracks were released. The first was *The Simpsons: Testify*, and then the movie soundtrack aptly titled, *The Simpsons Movie: The Music*.

Non-soundtrack *Simpsons* albums also exist because, of course, they do. The music in those albums are all original songs created outside of the series. The first one was the 1990 classic, "The Simpsons Sing the Blues." Two of the four producers on that record were Michael Jackson and DJ Jazzy Jeff, which might help explain how it went double platinum.

Last but not least, another cool moneymaking deal for *The Simpsons* was when 7-Eleven shelled out $10 million to convert 11 of their stores nationwide into temporary Kwik-E-Marts. It was a deal done to help promote the release of the film, and yes, 7-Eleven paid for it. That's how you know you're a hot commodity. That $13 billion makes sense now, huh? As large as that number is, however, bear in mind that Mr. Burns is worth even more—around $16.8 billion.

57 Smithers

It's Smithers, Mr. Burns' condescending right-hand man and Springfield's No. 1 bootlicking sycophant! The yes man's yes man! Listen, if we had our way, this whole chapter would just be a GIF of Smithers shaking his butt during that licorice whip dance from "The Simpsons Family Smile-Time Variety Hour." If a picture is worth a thousand words, that GIF is worth slightly more. But we have a responsibility to unpack all the nuance that goes into one of the longest running secondary characters of the show and perhaps TV's greatest gay nerd.

Maybe you can look at him as a vessel through which the writers use to slip in gay jokes and maybe you're right. But he's a surprisingly more complex character than just a punch line. We've seen him have tender moments with the Simpson kids, drink excessive quantities of Vagrant's Choice Scotch, and, of course, cut loose on Fire Island. There's so much bundled up in his little brown suit and purple bow tie.

*Waylon Smithers is not only Mr. Burns' right-hand man, but he's a longtime...
uh...admirer of his boss as well.* (20th Century Fox/Photofest © 20th Century Fox)

Smithers is voiced by Harry Shearer and debuted on screen in the third episode of the first season in "Homer's Odyssey." There's not much notable about his first appearance. He was in his typical position as the lackey assistant to the most evil man in town, Mr. Burns. Oh wait, we almost forgot, Smithers used to be black! Weird, right? When asked about Smithers' racial history, the writers and producers offer a mixed bag of answers. Groening even told TMZ (sigh, we know) that Smithers being portrayed as African American in his first appearance was "a mistake" but offered no follow-up to clarify if it was a production mistake or a creative one. It, though, is generally believed the show understandably wanted to avoid making a black character subservient to a white billionaire.

Smithers has made hundreds of appearances since turning yellow, and as the show goes on, we get more and more information about his history. We didn't even learn his first name, Waylon, until Season 3. His name was later used as a gag that harkened back to Bart's prank phone calls to Moe's Tavern. Moe promptly hangs up when Bart asks to speak to Waylon Smithers, thinking it's a prank because his name sounds like Wailing Scissors?

As an infant Waylon Joseph Smithers Jr. was presumably orphaned after his father was killed in a nuclear power plant accident. (Homer found his body in one of the more grim backstories.) Mr. Burns took in young Waylon Jr. and acted as a surrogate father figure. This all played out in the Season 13 episode "The Blunder Years." While entertaining, the story is made all the more unsettling when considering Smithers' history of being *extremely* horny for Charles Montgomery Burns.

Smithers' unrequited lust—and love—for his boss has been a long-running theme that's had surprising mileage. It's somehow turned from a cheap joke to one of Springfield's most complicated relationships. Sure, Smithers has nearly nonstop sexual fantasies about a frail and nude Mr. Burns gracefully floating through his window or jumping out of a cake. He's also admitted his love to him on a few occasions. At this point Burns knows the game but still plays coy. I don't know if any other sitcom has had a will they/won't they scenario—where the entire audience really hopes they won't.

In the early 1990s, discussing gay characters on TV was a touchy subject, and needless to say, opinions were a little less enlightened on the topic, but Smithers was always written with his sexuality in mind. There's been significant debate among fans and writers about how exactly to describe Smithers' preferences. Some claim he's strictly attracted to Mr. Burns; others are certain he's gay. There have certainly been hints. In "Homer's Phobia" it's implied he was supposed to go on a date with John Waters. And then finally in Season 27's "The Burns Cage," Smithers comes out (not that it was any of your business).

We finally see Smithers' mom in Season 28's episode "Moho House." While her appearance was brief and she's only known as "Mrs. Smithers," it does continue a beautiful Simpsons tradition of making someone's parent look the exact same as their spouse and child.

Like the best Springfield residents, the more we see Smithers' personal life, the more likable and relatable he becomes. Although he started as a great archetype to skewer the worst brown-noser at your job, he's ended up being a surprisingly three-dimensional character, especially for a two-dimensional one.

58 Mr. Burns, a Post-Electric Play

There are musicals and plays about everything these days. Once reserved exclusively for Shakespeare (a statement we assume but choose not to fact-check), the stage is now filled with things like musical renditions of *Spider-Man* and something called *Moose Murder*, which Mental Floss dubbed "the worst play ever on Broadway." In a world where finding a good play is as safe as a game of Russian Roulette, how do you choose what to see? If you're anything like us, you're going to choose the one that's about Mr. Burns. Both of us have had the privilege of seeing the *Mr. Burns, a Post-Electric Play* and cannot recommend the experience enough. The dark comedy written by Anne Washburn originally premiered in 2012 but has toured sporadically since its debut, which means you should have the opportunity to check it out before you die.

The play centers around a group of survivors retelling the plot points of the epic Sideshow Bob episode, "Cape Fear," following an apocalyptic catastrophe and then goes into how the story has changed seven years later and then 75 years after that. If that sounds crazy, it kind of is. Immediately, the play will suck in *Simpsons* fans by doing what all of us do—quote *The Simpsons* with friends.

As soon as the "Cape Fear" retelling picks up steam and you can imagine yourself actually watching the episode (which many would prefer to watching any play), you are sucked out of the moment by a noise off in the distance—something to remind you that the play isn't actually about *The Simpsons*, but showcasing how we use *The Simpsons* to communicate, distract ourselves, and make sense of the world.

In the second act, which takes place in a different room, we see that the future has evolved (or possibly devolved) in such a way that people are trading accurate quotes from *The Simpsons* for currency, and that groups are putting on episodes complete with commercials as a means of survival. We won't spoil what happens in the third act, but we can assure you that it will be a surprise.

The play received polarizing reviews, and we're not surprised by this. It's bold, bizarre, unusual, and uncomfortable. It challenges you in a way most art doesn't. The *Los Angeles Times* called it "spectacular...weird, creepy, and, as its title character would proclaim it, 'Excellent!'" *Time* called it, "Both scary and sweet, funny but dead serious, unique, and wonderfully theatrical." On the flip side, it has inspired write-ups like, "'Mr. Burns' Might Be The Worst Play...Ever" and "Mr. Burns, 'three hours of hell.'" In the latter review, *The Daily Telegraph* critic writes, "Loosely inspired by *The Simpsons*, this play distresses, discomforts, and dehydrates its audience."

Although it's no ballet (aka a bear driving around in a little car), it's utterly impressive that someone not only wrote a play based on *The Simpsons*, but also made and produced a play to critical acclaim with a continued run that leaves audiences unsure how to feel. This is what art is.

59 The Fox Studios Lot

Like most television shows, *The Simpsons* is primarily produced on a studio lot in Los Angeles, California. As you can probably guess, given that the show has been a major FOX property since its inception, its lot is none other than the 20th Century Fox Studios lot, which is in the Century City neighborhood of L.A. If you ever find yourself there, you'll no doubt come across Stage 20, the side of which is adorned with a massive, colorful mural of *The Simpsons*. Built in 1966 this soundstage was the filming location for classic movies like the original *Planet of the Apes* and less-than-classic television shows like *Two Guys, a Girl, and a Pizza Place*.

Many episode ideas are originally pitched at an annual writers' retreat before the start of each season. Whereas story ideas may have started here, the actual writing of the first draft can take place anywhere. Usually, one writer is responsible for this initial draft and can choose to spend their allotted two weeks of writing time wherever they want: at home, a vacation destination, a restaurant, etc. Original writer John Swartzwelder was known for writing his drafts in a diner while fueled by coffee and cigarettes. When smoking was banned in restaurants in California, legend has it he that he had one of the establishment's booths installed in his home so he could still smoke and write and feel like he was there.

Located at the show's production offices on the aforementioned FOX lot, the writers' room is often referred to more accurately as the "rewrite room" to reflect what's actually going on in there. It is here where the draft goes through drastic changes, as writers restructure the story and, most notably, punch up the jokes. Original writer George Meyer is said to have been so valuable to this rewriting process that he has very few script credits to his name.

Around the ninth season, a second rewrite room was established to accommodate the growing number of writers and to double their efficiency so they could work simultaneously on two different episodes. And while the condition of the writers' room presumably has improved over the years, its status in the early years was notorious for its…ramshackle-ness. Writer Conan O'Brien has likened it to a bad college dorm room—complete with terrible furniture missing springs and a big mashed blob of caramel candy permanently stuck on the ceiling.

After the script is thoroughly worked over in the room and rewritten by the writers and producers, there is a table read (once again on the lot) where the script is actually read out loud for the first time. This is done to gauge response on jokes before one final rewrite. These days it's rare for the entire cast to be available at the same time, so often parts at the table read are read by voice actor Chris Edgerly. In fact, the cast's availability is now so scarce that for the actual recording they are almost never in the same room. In 2015 it was revealed that cast member Harry Shearer was recording his lines via telephone from the United Kingdom. For certain special guests, producers are even willing to travel to them to record their dialogue. Paul and Linda McCartney's lines in "Lisa the Vegetarian," for example, were recorded after showrunner David Mirkin arranged to travel to McCartney's recording studio in London.

Once the dialogue tracks are set, they're then brought to life by the animators at Fox Animation in Burbank, California. For decades this process had previously been done at Film Roman, whose facilities jumped around from Studio City to Burbank to Woodland Hills, all of which are neighborhoods in the greater Los Angeles area. It should be noted the first three seasons of the show (as well as the *The Tracey Ullman Show* shorts) were animated by artists at the Klasky Csupo studios in Hollywood. After the animators start working, there's still some back and forth, as the writers respond to early animation with more rewriting and re-recording. Once all that's done, the animation gets its final touches and coloring done overseas at Akom Studios in South Korea. The ever-meticulous producers of the show can (and do) still make changes after this step, but this is about where the process comes to an end.

A significant part of the episode-making process occurs in Korea of all places, and sometimes dialogue recording happens internationally as well. However, *The Simpsons* is primarily a Southern California production. If you're so inclined, you could take a tour of the 20th Century Fox Studios in Los Angeles and see some of these places yourself.

The Simpsons House

In 1997 the dreams of every fan of *The Simpsons* could soon become reality: one lucky winner would get their own piece of Evergreen Terrace. Contests had been part of the show by this point. Just a couple years earlier in 1995, the "Who Shot Mr. Burns?" contest swept national attention (and boosted Slurpie sales at 7-Elevens). *The Simpsons* House Giveaway contest was announced on July 10, 1997, and was sponsored by Pepsi and constructed by Kaufman and Broad homebuilders. The rules were simple: viewers were encouraged to buy up various Pepsi products branded with a specific number. During the show's 1997 season premiere, one lucky number would be announced, making the winner able to move in as soon as March 1998.

The house would reside at 712 Red Bark Lane in Henderson, Nevada, and would cost $120,000 to construct and design. It took 49 days to build, and designers reportedly spent more than 50

Matt Groening, creator of The Simpsons, *and his son, Will, sit inside the master bedroom of the life-sized replica of* The Simpsons *house in Henderson, Nevada, in 1997.* (AP Images)

hours watching some 100 episodes to study up before their big job. In an effort to amp up audience spirits and satiate curiosity, photos of the design process were promptly leaked to the press. Fans were delighted to find how closely the house resembled a cartoon come to life. Bold colors, bright patterns, and, yes, corn cob curtains were all included to complete the illusion that Marge, Homer, and the kids had just briefly stepped outside while their presence in the house remained warm and cozy.

Then…the winner was announced, and everything changed. Barbara Howard from Richmond, Kentucky, was the lucky recipient, but rather than packing up her moving boxes, she chose to receive a cash prize in the form of $75,000 instead. What a buzzkill.

The walls that designers and construction workers had painstakingly worked on, the furnishings they labored over to make exactly proportional, and the exacting color scheme had been dashed bit by bit as the house's future hung in the balance. The house was located in a subdivision renamed "Springfield South Valley Ranch" and was briefly open to the public during August and September of 1997. During that time, a reported 30,000 fans flocked to visit it, including Matt Groening.

Since the contest results were announced, the house was stripped down and sold off bit by bit. The exterior paint was recolored from a vibrant yellow to a sober beige, and all the furnishings inside were auctioned off to eager fans. However, not all of this story ends in tragedy. At the time of its construction, the land surrounding it was empty and sprawling. Now there's a suburban community that's sprung up around it—not dissimilar to the real Evergreen Terrace.

In a DVD commentary, Groening commented that after the contest came and went, he half-jokingly suggested the house, "be blown up on live television." In reality, the future of the house became just another piece of commercial real estate. Today, fans still find their way to Henderson. Though the lawn is dried out and the neighborhood has shifted, if you squint your eyes and shake your fist hard enough (and shake harder, boy) you may just be able to summon a touch of Springfield.

61 Krusty the Clown

Whether or not there's actually smoke billowing out of his throat, Krusty the Clown speaks with the hardened and gritty cadence of a man who's always mid-cigarette. He approaches life as if he's older than Moses and maneuvered through so many phases of Hollywood mumbo-jumbo that down is up, and up is down.

Krusty's full name is Herschel Shmoikel Pinchas Yerucham Krustofsky. He is one of the few (yet most prominent) Jewish members of Springfield. He was born on the Lower East Side of Springfield, and his father is Rabbi Hyman Krustofski. Krusty is a patchwork of a personality: one part Jerry Lewis, one part classic TV clown, and all parts over it. The fun of following Krusty's various exploits is that he can operate as a pseudo stand-in for Mr. Burns when the episode requires something sinister, he acts paternal when Bart's bellowing for his help in Season 4's "Kamp Krusty," and take us to tender tears when reunited with his father in the Season 3's "Like Father, Like Clown."

Krusty is Bart's favorite entertainer of all time; he worships at his TV altar with the voraciousness of Ned Flanders to God. From shady licensing deals to shifty comedy specials, there's nothing that Krusty can do that would deter Bart from following him. Bart's belief in Krusty's impermeable ability to entertain not only allows Krusty to be a buoyant figure within the show, but it also adds texture to his character when he takes the time to start to believe that himself.

That being said, Krusty may be Springfield's one and only asshole. Similar to how Mr. Burns' lack of empathy rattles true through his emaciated bones, so too does Krusty approach life with a lackadaisical regard, but Krusty's desperate opportunism differentiates the pair. Krusty's asshole-ness seems to be colored within the hue of both exhaustion and exasperation that he's still doing this act all these years later. You get the sense that he wants to be saved into that big Hollywood hot shot halo in the sky—whatever that may be.

One must consider, though, do we want a satisfied, happy Krusty? We get a glimpse of it from time to time. Krusty's reunited with his father and seems to cry real tears, Krusty's remorseful over the consequences of his money-following actions in how they affect his fans, and when Sideshow Bob enacts a murderous plot, Krusty feels partially responsible for his rage.

But the truest form of Krusty comes out when he's not front and center. In the Season 7 episode "Sideshow Bob's Last Gleaming" when all of television is threatened to be extinct by Bob's villainous hand, Krusty scrambles to the studio to live out his dream of being the only TV show on the air. Krusty quickly searches for anything resembling entertainment, going so far as to puppet a scorpion for *The Stingy & Battery Show*. This is where Krusty is most himself. His passion to be on camera is as insatiable as Patty and Selma's love for *MacGyver*.

It's important to note one critical conspiracy theory about Krusty is that he...doesn't exist. Early in the show's run, Matt Groening told NPR's *Fresh Air* that they based Krusty's development on, "the satirical conceit...that *The Simpsons* was about a kid who had no respect for his father but worshipped a clown who looked exactly like his father." An idea for Krusty's "secret identity" as Homer was kicked around in the writers' room, but as the show was further developed over the first couple seasons, it was quickly scrapped. In the end the staff saw the show enduring far beyond that handful of seasons, and a reveal of this nature would have been inappropriate.

The persistence and endurance of Krusty as both famous person, foil, and family man has made him one of the most treasured citizens of Springfield in the show's expansive run. Krusty will always be our favorite perennially mid-comeback star.

62 Sideshow Bob

As the voice of Sideshow Bob, Kelsey Grammer's velvety tones transcend what's required for any normal guest star. They're undeniably distinct, rapturously confident. If *The Simpsons* was a live-action comedy, one might expect him to break the fourth wall by turning to the camera and uttering, "This is my show now…you fools." And you know what? We'd be fine with that.

Bob's been a part of the show since Season 1 and doesn't seem to be stopping anytime soon. He's also one of the few guest characters that's seen a full arc. In the beginning we saw him as a mute sidekick to Krusty the Clown, then an attempted murderer in the Season 3 episode "Black Widower," then a corrupt ex-con hungry for Bart's blood in "Cape Fear," and, finally, a reformed civilian with pure intentions in "Brother from Another Series."

In the Season 14 episode "The Great Louse Detective," we see Bob at his old ways of attempting to murder Bart and later in the Season 17 episode "The Italian Bob" we see Bob again attempting to hit the restart button as he had done before.

Bob's presence is so profound within the show that he's been immortalized with the highest honor for anyone (living, dead, fiction, or real). He was incorporated into a theme park ride. *The Simpsons* Ride at Universal Studios follows the family attending a similarly kitschy theme park, and Bob attempts to thwart their fun and end their lives around every turn. As far as theme park ride stories go, it's pretty advanced. Most often, ride simulators of this sort lean into whatever will get the audience bobbing around and quasi-queasy—without thinking too hard beyond that. When you go on *The Simpsons* Ride, it feels like you're living through a completed episode. If you don't like that, then it's also got episode clips playing on flat screens as far as the eye can see.

Throughout this book we've talked a lot about the inadequacy of adults in Springfield, and Bob's the most capable human presented. He's well-educated, well-spoken, and his falsetto is *anything* but pitchy. Should Bob run for office, he'd stronghold the position with the same ease and finesse of a Season 1 *House of Cards* Frank Underwood.

What could be next for Bob? Where do the fans want him to go? More evil or moving on? According to Al Jean, the answer is all of the above. Bob's development is intentionally cyclical—like Wile E. Coyote relentlessly plotting against a Bart-like roadrunner. Bob's story will never be closed, but we'd still give all we had to see a *Bob and Cecil* spin-off show. Now go off and sing the "HMS Pinafore" and don't tell anyone you only know it because it was featured on an adult cartoon.

Predicting the Future

Many a fan of *The Simpsons* has found themselves in this position: sitting back, relaxing, watching an older season, and then something on the screen pops up that feels a little too timely. For a second you think you might somehow be watching a new episode, even though that's not what you put on. But what's really happened is something far more freaky and far more powerful. *The Simpsons* predicted the future. (Cue the dramatic *dun dun dun*.)

From quick sight gags to full-on episode plots, *The Simpsons* has made some predictions more accurate than any fortune cookie we've ever cracked open. (No offense to fortune cookies, though. Keep doing what you're doing.) In the realm of tech, who can forget that moment in Season 6 when Lisa's future fiancé communicates via a smartwatch? That was back in 1994, 20 years before the first actual smartwatch was introduced to the world. Then, of course, there's our personal favorite, the prediction of autocorrect. It was a one-off gag in the classic episode "Lisa on Ice," but believe it or not, this joke ended up having a hand in the actual design of the iPhone. Seriously. Kearney asks Dolph to make an important note on the now-forgotten Newton, a digital assistant invented by Apple that did not sell very well. The note dictated by a very professional Kearney was supposed to read: "Beat up Martin." Instead, Dolph's device changed it to: "Eat up Martha."

In later interviews former Apple engineer Scott Forstall states that he was in charge of perfecting the iPhone's now legendary touchscreen keyboard. In the hallways of his workplace, the words: "Eat up Martha" would be uttered by him and his employees to encourage them to perfect that keyboard. They did a pretty good job at the end of the day, but hey, nothing is perfect, and we all know that autocorrect can still totally get things hilariously wrong.

Outside of the tech realm, the show gets far more eerily accurate with its prediction of real events. Some of the most memorable ones include the unfortunate eventual reality of a tiger attacking Roy Horn of the famous duo Siegfried and Roy. Of course, on the show this duo was called Gunter and Ernst back in 1993 (Season 5), but we all know who they were really meant to be. Ten years later in 2003, Roy was mauled by one of his tigers. He's okay, though, and the pairing is still going strong. Sadly, the same can't be said for Gunter and Ernst.

Another peculiar prediction is Greece's debt default. Back in 2012 during Season 23, Homer appears as a guest commentator on *Head Butt*. While on it, a ticker runs across the screen that reads, "Europe puts Greece on eBay." In 2015 Greece's debt crisis reached a point where a referendum was held to decide whether or not they'd essentially be forced to leave the European Union. That's basically like putting something up for auction on eBay, isn't it?

It gets weirder from there like in Season 10 when Ron Howard pitches Homer's script to Brian Grazer at the offices of 20th Century Fox. Under the infamous Fox logo, a smaller line under it reads, "A Division of Walt Disney Co." In 2017 that really happened. In a February of 2010 episode, *The Simpsons* had the United States beating Sweden to win the gold medal in curling in the Winter Olympics, and that actually happened in 2018.

But the absolute craziest prediction that no one ever guessed would actually come true in a gazillion years is the one where Donald Trump is legitimately the president of the United States. In the year 2000, "Bart to the Future," another episode, which takes place in the not-so-distant future, aired. In that episode Lisa Simpson becomes president, wherein she gives a now-infamous quote saying, "As you know, we've inherited quite a budget crunch from President Trump." Seeing that nothing in the world really makes sense anymore, here's hoping there's still a chance that Lisa Simpson will be our next president.

64 The Golden Years

Has there been a topic more controversial, more polarizing, more responsible for dividing families, friends, and figurines than this debate? When meeting another superfan, it is often the first question after "You like *The Simpsons*?" It's almost as if the answer can perform double duty as a litmus test on whether or not the conversation can sustain—and for good reason. *Which years represent the golden age of* The Simpsons?

The viewers, who consider the first chunk of seasons to be the show's best, most often banish viewings of the latter seasons because their experience of the show is seemingly frozen in amber. Most often, this debate of the golden years resembles a generational divide akin to politics or pop culture. The old world of fans of *The Simpsons* represent mostly baby boomers or Gen X, whereas the new world consists of bright-eyed and blissed-out millennials. The former's angry that the new kids can't appreciate the nuance of the first two seasons. *It's not slow! They were figuring things out*, whereas the millennial representatives plead with them to give the Carl Carlson episode a chance.

Season 1—1989–90

Showrunners: James L. Brooks, Matt Groening, Sam Simon

Highlights: It includes the introduction of Santa's Little Helper, the infamous jumping the gorge scene, and the entrance of Bleeding Gums Murphy as the best blues musician bestie a little girl could ask for.

What It Says About You: You're weird; there's no way around it. You dig stories about adultery, suicide, and sorry excuses for cheating on IQ tests. You think off-color Smithers is the best kind of Smithers and relished in the show being entertaining *and* educational. You are lonely, but that only means that the people who share your beliefs will similarly savor their time spent soaking up their sorrows at Moe's in the Universal theme parks where they will no doubt gripe about millennial fans who "don't know their history."

Seasons 2–9—1990–98

Showrunners: James L. Brooks, Matt Groening, Sam Simon (2–3), Al Jean and Mike Reiss (4–5), David Mirkin (6–7), Bill Oakley and Josh Weinstein (8–9)

Highlights: On the early end, we get Dancing Homer, the arrival of Flanders' Leftorium, and the infamous "Streetcar Named Marge" episode that infuriated New Orleans and sparked a controversy. On the later end, we get the "I Didn't Do It" episode where Bart becomes an overnight celebrity and the beautifully poetic, yet unfortunately titled, *Pukahontus* during The *Critic* crossover with Jon Lovitz's Jay Sherman.

What It Says About You: You're a '90s kid, that's for sure. Each week, you ran—not walked—to the TV set and basked in its comforting glow like Homer during "Treehouse of Horror V." As a kid you only knew two kinds of people: Barts and Lisas. And you identified as one and refused to accept the possibility of any overlap. As a high schooler, you secretly crushed on Jimbo Jones. As a college student, you tried (and failed) to dub your apartment, "Kamp Krusty." To you Barney will always be a fall-down drunk, and Moe will always be lonely. You desperately wish you could play, "Classical Gas." Your politics are firmly, "Down with Homework" and "Up with Miniskirts." You refuse to concede.

Seasons 10–20—1998–08

Showrunners: Mike Scully (9–12), Al Jean (13–20)

Highlights: It includes "Tappa Tappa Tappa" during Season 10's "Lard of the Dance," the creative clip episode "Behind the Laughter," the earth-shattering explanation for Homer's slowness due to a crayon lodged in his brain from Season 12's "HOMR," and the star-studded "How I Spent My Strummer Vacation."

What It Says About You: You like loopier fare. You're all about diving deep into the backstories of some of the best background characters. You've been around long enough to see Selma smooch Grampa and learn that Homer's friendship with Lenny, Carl, and Moe stretches back much further than that first round of beer. Your eyes glaze over whenever any older *Simpsons* fan references the time period Homer and Marge met. You've learned over years of side glances to keep your mouth shut over your secret appreciation of the band Sadgasm.

Seasons 21—2009-infinity

Showrunners: Al Jean

Highlights: It includes Season 24's, "The Saga of Carl," in which we learn Carl Carlson's heartwarming cultural backstory, Season 25's ambitious Lego-centric "Brick Like Me," the even *more* ambitious "Homer Live" that included a unique East Coast and West Coast feed, and the show's first ever non-"Treehouse of Horror" Halloween episode.

What It Says About You: You're a contrarian at heart. Who's to say if your defiant devotion to the show comes from a puckishness you enjoy lording over the Season 2-9ers, or if you genuinely believe the show has gotten better with age? (We believe that for most of you: it's a little column A, a little column B.) You're the kind of person who roots for new rollercoasters at theme parks and sees no issue with reboots. "The more the merrier," you might decry, as the superfans around you groan while typing into their message boards.

Start a Lisa Simpson Book Club

You'd be hard-pressed to find a fictional character more well-read than Lisa Simpson. Her passion for the written word is unparalleled—almost as if she emerged from the womb with a determined glint in her eye and a dog-eared copy of *Breakfast of Champions*. Her role throughout *The Simpsons'* storied tenure has been as a staunch protector of knowledge, educating all those within her vicinity.

Lisa to a book is analogous to Homer to a cold beer, Bart to a slingshot, Maggie to a pacifier, and so on. Though the expansiveness of her personal library is seemingly endless, that shouldn't discourage you. For the *Simpsons* superfans who want to expand their mind while still remaining true to their toon roots, this is the kind of book club for you. Who knows? Maybe by the end, you'll be reading at the 78th grade level, too. Below are a couple of Lisa-approved highlights to get you going.

The Telltale Heart by Edgar Allan Poe
From Season 6, "Lisa's Rival"
Synopsis: A short story published in 1843 chronicles an unnamed narrator desperate to convince the reader of his sanity as he can't escape the thumping of a phantom heart.
Simpsons **Connection:** *The Simpsons* has an obsessive fascination with Edgar Allan Poe that goes from book projects to

bone-chilling segments in "Treehouse of Horror." Lisa's diorama project was thwarted at the last minute with a real cow heart.

A Separate Piece by John Knowles

From Season 7, "Mother Simpson"

Synopsis: A coming-of-age novel that focuses on morality, patriotism, and loss of innocence.

***Simpsons* Connection:** One of the best moments of this fan-favorite episode is when Mona Simpson and Lisa bond over their mutual distaste for John Knowles. In this scene Lisa's relieved to see the strength and intelligence in her estranged Grandma Mona, who "didn't dumb it down" when chatting with her and agrees that Knowles' novel is "preschool" stuff.

Charlotte's Web by E.B. White

From Season 2, "Lisa's Substitute"

Synopsis: Children's novel from 1952 that you've *definitely* already read, but for those in need of a trip down memory lane, it's about a spider named Charlotte and the pig named Wilbur who protects her.

***Simpsons* Connection:** Lisa looks on in awe (and love) when Mr. Bergstrom nearly tears up while reciting a passage in this stand-out Season 2 episode. It's this appreciation for literature and emotional availability that cements him as the perfect first crush.

Ethan Frome by Edith Wharton

From Season 3, "Brother, Can You Spare Two Dimes?"

Synopsis: A novel set in a prolonged flashback focusing on the life of Ethan Frome. That's it. You'll really test the resolve of your book club with this one, but at least you'll feel one inch closer to the Harvard-heavy *Simpsons* writer's room when you're done.

***Simpsons* Connection:** This is the first volume of, *The Great Books of Western Civilization* that Herb gifts Lisa when the family discovers he's Homer's long lost half-brother. According to Herb, Lisa's to receive a new book every month, "from *Beowulf* to *Less Than Zero*." Lisa gleefully clutches the book in her arms, acting at the intersection between child preciousness and adult-like preco-ciousness and exclaims, "Finally! A copy of *Ethan Frome* to call my own," which kind of feels like a line from *Ethan Frome*.

The Simpsons: A Complete Guide to Our Favorite Family
created by Matt Groening, edited by Ray Richmond
     From Season 15, "Today, I Am a Clown"
     Synopsis: Please, this is slightly self-explanatory.
     Simpsons **Connection:** In what would become a more promi-nent running joke after Season 10, *The Simpsons* busts out a meta moment by way of Lisa, who refers to the *Simpsons Guide* when dealing with a familiar premise. This is the book you bust out when you're all out of options, but it's the one that will elicit the biggest applause.

Troy McClure

Few side characters can resonate as strongly as Troy McClure. Troy's impact on the show is manifold: he's the voice of a has-been Hollywood actor, the face of educational films, and the spokesper-son for silliness from TV to the big screen to the Broadway stage. In contrast to other celebrities like Krusty the Clown and Rainier Wolfcastle, there's a polished charm and enthusiasm that Troy exudes. Whether it's forced or fully genuine, Troy's almost always the most professional performer in all of Springfield.

Troy is a mishmash of washed-up Hollywood B-movie actors, a spiritual love child of Troy Donahue and Doug McClure. According to the writers, Troy would often be used as a panic button of sorts when an episode was reaching a standstill. His character is most fleshed out through the Season 7 episode "A Fish Called Selma," in which he and Selma Bouvier are wed in an effort to save his career and get those "fish rumors" put at bay.

Troy's famously voiced by comic legend Phil Hartman, who Matt Groening described to NPR's *Fresh Air* as being perfect for the role since he was able to pull "the maximum amount of humor" out of any line he was given. Hartman's association with his cartoon counterpart was so strong that his posthumous biography was even titled *You Might Remember Me: The Life and Times of Phil Hartman*. Hartman died in 1998. His wife, Brynn Hartman, shot him before killing herself.

After Hartman's passing, the show retired both McClure and Lionel Hutz, the corrupt ambulance-chasing lawyer Hartman also voiced. McClure's last appearance was in the Season 10 episode "Bart the Mother" in an education film titled, *Birds: Our Fine Feathered Colleagues*. The episode was dedicated to his memory.

During the show's run, a rumor of a live-action Troy McClure film swirled around the writers' room, a project that Hartman was reportedly very excited about. In the movie Hartman would have played McClure, and the rumored plot would focus on his triumph through washed-up has-been Hollywood to a place that's…slightly less washed-up and slightly less has-been. Even decades later, Troy McClure and Phil Hartman's contribution on *The Simpsons* remains unwavering, and he'll forever be one of the show's most beloved supporting characters.

Complete List of Troy McClure's Oeuvre

"Hi, I'm Troy McClure. You might remember me from…"

Films

The Boatjacking of Supership '79
Calling All Quakers (with Dolores Montenegro)
The Contrabulous Fabtraption of Professor Horatio Hufnagel
Cry Yuma
David Versus Super Goliath
Dial M for Murderousness
The Electric Gigolo
The Erotic Adventures of Hercules
Give My Remains to Broadway
Gladys the Groovy Mule
Good-Time Slim, Uncle Doobie, and the Great "Frisco Freak-Out"
The Greatest Story Ever Hulaed
Here Comes the Coast Guard
Alice Doesn't Live Anymore
Hydro, the Man With the Hydraulic Arms
Jagged Attraction
Leper in the Backfield
Look Who's Still Oinking
Make-Out King of Montana
Meet Joe Blow
The Muppets Go Medieval
"P" is for Psycho
Preacher With a Shovel (with Dolores Montenegro)
The President's Neck Is Missing
Radioactive Man
Radioactive Man II: Bring On The Sequel
Radioactive Man III: Oh God, Not Again
The Revenge of Abe Lincoln
The Seven-Year-Old Bitch
Sorry, Wrong Closet
Suddenly Last Supper
They Came to Burgle Carnegie Hall
Today We Kill, Tomorrow We Die
The Verdict Was Mail Fraud
The Wackiest Covered Wagon in the West

Educational Films

60 Minutes of Car Crash Victims
Adjusting Your Self-O-Stat (with Brad Goodman)
Alice's Adventure through the Windshield Glass
Alice Doesn't Live Anymore
Birds: Our Fine Feathered Colleagues
The Decapitation of Larry Leadfoot
Designated Drivers: The Lifesaving Nerds
Dig Your Own Grave and Save
Earwigs, Ew!
Firecrackers: The Silent Killer
Fuzzy Bunny's Guide to You-Know-What
Get Confident, Stupid!
The Half-Assed Approach to Foundation Repair
Here Comes the Metric System
Lead Paint: Delicious But Deadly
Locker Room Towel Fights: The Blinding of Larry Driscoll
Man Versus Nature: The Road to Victory
Meat and You—Partners in Freedom
Mommy, What's Wrong with That Man's Face?
Mothballing Your Battleship
Phony Tornado Alerts Reduce Readiness
Shoplifters: BEWARE
Smoke Yourself Thin
Someone's in the Kitchen with DNA!
Two Minus Three Equals Negative Fun
Young Jebediah Springfield (A Watch-and-Learn Production)
Whoa! Don't Touch Me There

TV Specials

Alien Nose Job
Carnival of the Stars
Five Fabulous Weeks of The Chevy Chase Show
Let's Save Tony Orlando's House
Out With Gout '88
The Miss American Girl Pageant
The Simpsons 138ᵗʰ Episode Spectacular
The Simpsons Spin-Off Showcase

TV Series
AfterMannix
America's Funniest Tornadoes
Buck Henderson, Union Buster
Handel with Kare
I Can't Believe They Invented It!
The Candy Bar That Cleans Teeth
Eyeball Whitener
Spiffy, the 21st Century Stain Remover
The Juice Loosener
Shortland Street
Son of Sanford and Son
Troy and Company's Summertime Smile Factory

Cartoons
Christmas Ape
Christmas Ape Goes to Summer Camp

Celebrity Funerals
Herschel Shmoikel Krustofsky
André the Giant, We Hardly Knew Ye
Shemp Howard: Today We Mourn A Stooge

Travel Guides
Hats Off to Fargo
Pinch Me, I'm in Boise
Duluth, It'll Grow on You
Suddenly, Tulsa
Smother Me in Shreveport
Living and Loving in Lubbock
Bredonia: Gateway to Wichita
Fairbanks Needs Women
Eeeny Meeny Miny Murfreesboro
Yuma, It's Senoirific
Rancho Relaxo
Springfield Knowledgeum Welcome Video
Welcome to Springfield Airport
Where's Nordstrom?

67 Springfield's Entertainers

Since its debut, part of *The Simpsons'* signature style was its meta-commentary on consumerism and pop culture. Due in part to the show's basic premise depicting an All-American family, the show's creators posit that naturally this All-American family is as obsessed with TV as the show's viewers would be, and thus Springfield-specific entertainers were born. Early in the show's run, the writers dreamed up their own fictional pop culture such as *The Itchy & Scratchy Show* and *Radioactive Man*. The world of *The Simpsons* felt more intimate and insular. In later episodes this contrasted starkly when celebrity cameos became more prevalent throughout the voice cast; soon Lady Gaga and The Who would touch down on Evergreen Terrace.

There were of course exceptions to this original pop culture rule. Michael Jackson is the uncredited guest star in the Season 3 episode "Stark Raving Dad," and this episode alludes to a reality where Bart bopped his head to "Beat It." Marge's sisters Patty and Selma are fan-obsessives of the TV show *MacGyver* and are almost always prepped to drop everything to bask in its Richard Dean Anderson glory. Though overall, *The Simpsons* creatives' trigger finger seemed to be more dominantly placed on creating their own action star to make fun of than quipping to an animated version of Jean Claude Van Damme. Here are some of their best original stars.

Rainier Wolfcastle

Rainier is loosely based on celebrities starring in various action movies in the early 1990s. He's one large dose of Arnold Schwarzenegger, another part Chuck Norris. He stars in the fictional *McBain* movie franchise, which often sees him negotiating with fugitives and firing off a hefty machine gun in every location from bank heists to comedy clubs. In *McBain: Let's Get Silly, The Simpsons* writers make a sly nod to Schwarzenegger films like *Kindergarten Cop*, in which a strong action star struggles with the softness of civilian life. Wolfcastle began his career as a child spokesperson for bratwurst and has a daughter named Greta, who, of course, like all kin in *The Simpsons* world, looks just like him.

Kent Brockman

Kent is more or less Springfield's Edward R. Murrow (when he hasn't had his danish). His dry, matter-of-fact reading of the news is intermittently interrupted by his diva-like behavior, and his spineless qualities render him useless whenever anything above a traffic jam is reported from his news desk. His ridiculous wealth allows for him to be a callous character within Springfield, often pushing his fellow man before him in order to benefit directly. Though due to the fact that he's seemingly the only reporter (unless you count Arnie Pye of "Arnie Pye with Arnie in the Sky," reporting from a helicopter), he is omnipresent in any calamity that hits the Springfield community.

Disco Stu

Disco Stu is one of the first examples of a character that was originally created for a one-off joke, but due to fan reception, he has since been becoming more of a regular. In the episode "Two Bad Neighbors," Marge lifts up an old jacket of Homer's that spells "DISCO STU" in studs on the back. "Who's Disco Stu?" She asks. Homer replies, "I was trying to spell 'Disco Stud,' but I ran out of space." The frame then widens to reveal a *real* Disco Stu shopping nearby, and boom: a new character was born. Disco Stu runs Stu's Disco. Disco Stu does not advertise. Disco Stu likes to speak in the third person.

Belle

Belle is described as an "entrepreneuse" and "proprietor" of La Maison Derrière, the only burlesque house in Springfield. She was first introduced in the Season 8 episode "Bart After Dark," in which Bart gets an after-school job assisting Belle in the day-to-day operations of her sultry storefront. Belle's character is loosely based on Dolly Parton in *The Best Little Whorehouse in Texas*. Her styling is vaguely reminiscent of Victorian-era women, particularly Lady Tremaine in Disney's *Cinderella*. She's strong in her self-assuredness and firm in her belief that she runs an honest business despite town outcry over its moral ambiguity. In the song "We Put the Spring in Springfield," she successfully convinces Springfield of her positive effect on the community.

68 The Legend of John Swartzwelder

Which of his fellow writers on *The Simpsons* did Jeff Martin describe as looking like Clark Gable, so much so that he assumed an attraction between the writer and guest star Elizabeth Taylor? Al Jean? Conan O'Brien? Bill "You Mean Bob" Odenkirk? The actual Clark Gable?

It was John Swartzwelder, *The Simpsons* writer known for being as eccentric as he was prolific, and, boy, was he both of those things. Swartzwelder was the author of 59 episodes, the most of any writer of *The Simpsons*, including fan favorites like "Homer at the Bat," "Whacking Day," "Itchy & Scratchy Land," and "Rosebud." Swartzwelder wrote for the first 15 seasons of the show and went on to co-author the script for *The Simpsons Movie*. Swartzwelder is even credited by Al Jean and collaborator Mike Reiss with adding an appreciation to *The Simpsons* for things "old-timey American," like gangsters, hobos, and antiquated phrases.

A native of Seattle, Washington, Swartzwelder first got into comedy writing by mailing jokes to the writers of *Late Night with David Letterman* but didn't include a return address where he could be reached. This forced Letterman writer Jim Downey to call Swartzwelder's mother in order to track him down and offer him a job interview. In Mike Sack's book, *Poking a Dead Frog*, Downey recalled Swartzwelder's interview as "one of the most spectacularly awful in history," where Swartzwelder entered Letterman's office without permission, smoked, drank, and described the current state of television as "shit." While Swartzwelder was not hired at *Late Night*, Downey later hired him for two seasons at *Saturday Night Live* in the mid-1980s.

After SNL Swartzwelder went to write for George Meyer's *Army Man* magazine, where he was among the first of many writers of *The Simpsons* pulled away from the magazine by producer Sam Simon. Meyer, a legendary part of *The Simpsons* staff in his own right, said Swartzwelder seemed to embody the now legendary underground comedy tomb. "The quintessential *Army Man* joke was one of John Swartzwelder's: 'They can kill the Kennedys. Why can't they make a cup of coffee that tastes good?' It's a horrifying idea juxtaposed with something really banal," Simon said. "It's illuminating because it's kind of how Americans see things: life's a big jumble, but somehow it leads to something I can consume."

This kind of joke that Swartzwelder wrote, which was profound, clear, and dumb all at once, would show itself in some of his most famous lines from *The Simpsons* like "Why won't those stupid idiots let me in their crappy club for jerks?" Another classic is: "To alcohol! The cause of…and solution to…all of life's problems." As if his writing alone wasn't cause for his cult hero status,

Swartzwelder's J.D. Salinger-esque reclusiveness has made him a mysterious figure on par with Thomas Pynchon. (We're sorry for getting so highbrow, so we'll dumb it down: Thomas Pynchon is sort of the J.D. Salinger of writers. Does that help, dumb dumb?)

Swartzwelder has never done an interview, and there are very few available pictures of him online. He has refused to participate in any of *The Simpsons* DVD commentaries and has made very few media appearances. HIs shyness from the spotlight has even led to some fan theories that Swartzwelder isn't a real a person but instead a fictional character the other writers use as a pseudonym.

Swartzwelder was even reclusive from his own writers' room. Starting in Season 6 of *The Simpsons*, Swartzwelder was allowed to skip rewrites and send in his drafts and notes from home. This was in no small part due to his constant chain-smoking in the writers' room, coming into direct conflict with an indoor smoking ban. Later, when the state of California banned smoking in restaurants, Swartzwelder bought the booth out of his favorite diner and had it installed in his home so he could continue to smoke and write in his trustiest seat.

Since leaving *The Simpsons*, Swartzwelder has penned several self-published novels starring bumbling detective Frank Burly. Swartzwelder chose to self-publish in order to preserve the integrity and sense of humor of his books, which couldn't seem more apt. We recommend reading all of them, as it's all the Swartzwelder you're gonna get.

 **Moe**

"They used to call me 'Kid Gorgeous.' Later it was 'Kid Presentable,' then 'Kid Gruesome,' and finally 'Kid Moe.'" Moe Syzlak's description of the nicknames he cycled through as an amateur boxer perfectly epitomize what makes his character so funny and so tragic. The description of Moe is worse than gruesome. In other words Moe has his rock bottom so many times that he actually is the rock bottom.

Moe is the owner of Moe's Tavern, Springfield's primary watering hole. He also may be the only bartender in Springfield. He is also the allegedly ugliest, saddest, and quietly the most depraved character on *The Simpsons*. He has been involved with an insanely long list of seedy behavior, which includes, but is not limited to, panda smuggling, bootlegging, running a game of *Deerhunter*-style Russian Roulette, watering down the alcohol in his bar, some kind of whale hiding, gambling on youth sports, kidnapping Hans Moleman, committing insurance fraud, attempting to murder fellow child actor Alfalfa, causing arson, and registering as a possible sex offender.

And that doesn't even include Moe's low points in terms of loneliness, self-loathing, and desperation. While strapped to a lie detector test, Moe reveals that his plans for the night were to go on a date with a woman except that he was actually ogling the women in the Victoria's Secret catalogue—only it was the Sears catalogue. Moe once got offended that a group of hillbillies had no interest in "*Deliverance*-ing" him. Moe once robbed Homer, his best customer, of the very pants he had on. Giving up on finding his soulmate, Moe once proposed to a WNBA human mascot, knowing full well that inside was town schlub Gil Gunderson.

179

Lovable loser Moe Szyslak (far left) is the bartender for a gaggle of regulars, who are the town drunks. (Fox/Photofest © & Fox)

If it isn't clear that *The Simpsons* writers use Moe as a harbinger of some of their darkest jokes and feelings, Moe's suicide attempts on *The Simpsons* have become so numerous that the joke is now in their consistency. In a Season 24 episode "Whiskey Business," Moe looks in on a noose hanging in the liquor closet and remarks "Not today, old friend." One of Moe's suicide attempts is foiled when he catches a falling Maggie Simpson, who had been thrown from the Simpson family car in a fender bender. That episode, "Moe's Baby Blues," is centered around Moe developing an attachment to Maggie and reveals a softer, more redemptive side. What makes Moe such a rich character is that he's also capable of this kind of sweetness, like when he saved the owner of King Toot's music store and his wife from a flaming car, or when Moe streaks across a baseball field to help Bart attempt one more catch. Moe also reads at the children's hospital and volunteers at a soup kitchen.

Like most ancillary characters of the show, Moe started out with much less depth and backstory and more as a mechanism for joke delivery. In Season 1 Moe is introduced as the bartender who's on the receiving end of Bart's prank calls. Much like Duff Man, Comic Book Guy, and even Waylon Smithers, the elevation of Moe Szyslak from side character to center stage has been one of the show's kindest trademarks. Moe can serve many functions: victim to Bart's antics, shoulder to cry on for Homer, or as the saddest sap in Springfield.

70 Mix *Simpsons* Drinks

Whether you go wild with a white wine spritzer Flanders-style or swill some Duff, any time's a good time to brush up on your bartending skills for a bona fide celebration of *The Simpsons*. You don't have to have the skills of Moe Syzslak to spruce up some liquor-heavy libations. To fix the following classic beverages, all you need are some basic bar necessities and a room filled with thirsty superfans.

The Flaming Moe

In the Season 3 episode of the same title, we witness its creation. Late one night Homer was skipping out on entertaining Patty and Selma and so he built an everything-but-the-kitchen-sink alcoholic salve with all that he had available, including its "secret ingredient" (Krusty-brand cough syrup). From there the drink becomes a sensation, transforming Moe's into the go-to drunk tank to get sloshed in Springfield. You'll find that with a few fine-tuned palatable hacks, even you can get drunk on the divine within the confines of your own home.

Ingredients:
1 ounce brandy
1 ounce peppermint schnapps
1 ounce sloe gin
1 ounce blackberry liqueur
1 ounce strawberry juice
Cough syrup

Instructions:
In the cocktail glass of your choosing (and one you may not miss should it inexplicably melt), pour all of the ingredients except for the cough syrup. Stir for a bit, add the cough syrup, and then grab a lighter…and ignite! Then blow. Then be merry.

Skittlebräu

Don't let Apu discourage you because Homer's idea for a drink can and will exist even if the Kwik-E-Mart doesn't carry it. And it will get you buzzed to blitzed, and that's only accounting for the sugar high.

Ingredients:
1 can of beer
1 pack of Skittles

Instructions:
This one's pretty straightforward but still worthy of your skills. Grab your tallest pint class, scatter some Skittles on the bottom, and then pour over your beer just right to ensure that the foamy head on top shimmers with the colors of the rainbow.

Illegal Bathtub Hooch

Get revved up to rip into this prohibition-era bathtub hooch as if Rex Banner himself was after you. From bathtub gin to prison wine, there are several options you can serve, but we're opting for the latter so we can achieve maximum dirtbag effect (and because the ingredients were phenomenally easier).

Ingredients
1 bottle of 100 percent fruit juice (preferably grape)
¼ teaspoon (1 oz) of champagne yeast
Optional: added sugar as you see fit

Instructions:
So maybe don't mix this in your bathtub after all but do pour out about two ounces of juice from your juice bottle (to prevent over-flowing), mix the yeast in, and swirl it around. Top it off with a balloon to allow for fermentation and place it in a warm spot over the next three to five days. Replace the balloon with the original bottle cap, place in your fridge, and voila—one glass of scuzzy wine coming up!

A Single Plum Floating in Perfume Served in a Man's Hat

This is for the effervescent host who longs to be prepared for anything—unexpected visitors, picky eaters, and Yoko Ono herself, who asked for this very drink at Moe's Tavern. Of all of these recipes, this is the one you should have really started off with first.

It's simple, it's silly, and it doesn't require looking in longing at your prison wine over the course of a single work week.

Ingredients:
1 bottle of perfume
1 plum

Instructions:
Grab the finest (or firmest for the sanctity of sipping without spillage) man's derby hat you can find. Pour the perfume inside until at a reasonable level, then drop the plum, and watch it sink to the bottom because you realize in that moment—and only in this moment—that *The Simpsons* is an animated show that takes creative license while detaching from reality, and plums don't float. (They just don't. Why would you possibly think they would?)

71 Barney

"Don't cry for me. I'm already dead." Who can forget the classic line uttered by Springfield's lovable town drunk, Barney Gumble? This one line sums up why we adore this former alcoholic. Inspired by Barney Rubble, Fred Flintstone's best pal with whom he regularly had a dabba doo time (a gay old time), Barney is one of the original characters from *The Simpsons*, appearing in the first full-length episode "Simpsons Roasting on an Open Fire," where he is a sadly sodden Santa. Voiced by Dan Castellaneta (who once recorded the perfect belch before realizing he could never equal it again, so he had the editors simply splice it in whenever needed), Barney at first seems like just a drunk loser holding up the bar at

Moe's. But over the course of the series, we began to see the hidden depths in Barney, and perhaps he best represents the hidden depths behind *The Simpsons'* regular silliness.

We learn, for example, that Barney was a straight-A student in high school...until the fateful day when he has his first beer. Like the Wolfman exposed to the light of the full moon, Barney is instantly transformed from Springfield square to an inveterate Duffer. Homer and Barney were best buds in high school, and Homer himself struggles with his booze intake. The two characters are in many ways mirrors of one another.

But while Homer is a well-meaning dope who has made it through life on a mixture of luck and the love of others, Barney is actually an enormously competent, emotionally deep human being who has one terrible failing: his love of Duff. For example, when Homer and Barney ended up in the NASA astronaut training program, we saw that when divorced from the drink, Barney made an excellent candidate to be a spaceman. Drunk or not, Homer remained ever Homer. Barney's competence even shines through when he's not sober. Even as a drunk, he was able to beat Homer's Mr. Plow at his own game (but the two lifelong buds came back together at the end much to God's chagrin).

Barney is also responsible for one of our favorite exchanges:

Woman: "Excuse me, did something crawl down your throat and die?"
Barney: "It didn't die."

Barney also has the ability to sing like an angel. He joined the "Be Sharps," helping propel the barbershop quartet to unlikely fame. The joke is always that Barney is unexpectedly good at something, but the show goes further, letting us see how tragic it is that Barney's addiction keeps him from truly following any of these paths.

Perhaps no episode revealed more about the Barney behind the booze more than "A Star Is Burns." This is a controversial episode. Matt Groening even took his name off the credits due to FOX forcing a guest starring appearance from Jay Sherman, star of the Al Jean-created cartoon *The Critic*, but it nevertheless gave Barney a chance to reveal his inner self. When Springfield hosts a film festival showcasing local works, Barney submits an arty, haunting black-and-white film described as "savagely tender," which probes his own battle with the bottle, featuring the heartbreaking quote at the top of this chapter. This work of extraordinary beauty is called *Pukeahontas*. The success of *Pukeahontas* convinces Barney to give up drinking and focus on his art...until in an ultimate O. Henry-like twist, he learns that his movie has earned him a lifetime supply of Duff.

This is where the magic of *The Simpsons* really shines. When Barney was created, portraying alcoholism as a joke was a significant taboo (actually, it still is). That inspired Groening and his team of mischievous malcontents to really go for it with the town drunk, but these folks are unable to just stay on the easy joke and so over time they expanded Barney's character to a place where his essentially tragic nature became clear. And yet they never gave up on the jokes! Even when Barney got sober in a plot turn created by Castellaneta, who wrote the episode where Barney quit drinking—a development that shockingly lasted for many seasons—he remained a steady source of laughs. His Duff drinking was replaced with a jittery addiction to caffeine.

Whether we're sober or sauced, we love Barney for his actions that are both ridiculous and sublime. At his lowest we recognize our truth. After all, who among us has not looked another human being in the eye and asked that eternal question: "Excuse me, can I throw up in your bathroom?"

72 Make Art from *The Simpsons*

From a painted sculpture of Poochie to a can of nuts and gum (together at last), making *Simpsons*-inspired art can be anything you want it to be. If you need inspiration, look no further than *The Simpsons*-themed art show, "Eye on Springfield" hosted at Meltdown Comics in Los Angeles in 2015. The show was curated by Nico Colaleo and Julia Prescott (one of the authors of this here book) and featured an array of artists, including some animators from *The Simpsons*.

There was a stupid sexy Flanders watercolor, an inanimate carbon rod oil painting by Kati Prescott, a watercolor map of Springfield, A Simpsons family portrait of them as zombies, a rec-reation of a classic *Itchy & Scratchy* cell, a recreation of the nude portrait Marge painted of Mr. Burns, a hyper-realistic photo of a man posing as a grizzled Krusty the Clown, and the Simpsons family's likeness interpreted through succulents. And that's just scratching the surface.

What's great about *The Simpsons* art is that because the show's been on for as long as it has, the wide swath of superfans range in age and approach. But if you're intimidated and still feeling crummy about never quite getting crafts as a youngster, not a problem. Below is a list of *Simpsons* art you can easily make:

A Portrait of Moe aka "Mr. Stinky"

This is from the Season 7 episode "Bart Sells His Soul," in which Moe converts his crusty and dank tavern into a Springfield version of TGI Fridays. While an exhausted and exasperated Moe makes the customer rounds, a sweet little girl hands this sketch to Moe, and it's the straw that breaks his incredibly hairy back. What's great about this work of art is that it's supposed to be cruddy on *purpose*!

Homer's Nuclear Power Plant Project

Collect your construction paper, nab some cardboard, and grab that glue stick because you're about to have an old-fashioned good time acting like a kid again and making the shittiest interpretation of the Springfield nuclear power plant there ever could be. This was featured in the Season 8 episode "Homer's Enemy," and once you finish this bad boy, you can rely on that reward of a blue ribbon from Mr. Burns himself.

Nuke the Whales Poster

This one could get a bit tricky, but stick with us here. Whether it's a portrait of Homer with slightly-too-small pupils or a picture of Lisa with the wrong number of hair spikes, whenever you're doing a direct recreation of a prop in the show, you open the door to the option of fudging it up. But the takeaway of all artistic pursuits is no risk, no reward. Attempting the Nuke the Whales poster that lives on the walls of Nelson's room (as seen in the Season 8 episode "Lisa's Date with Density") is a great choice for two reasons: it's a deep-cut reference and it's just fun. Bonus points if you creatively interpret this poster with anything but mechanical pencil and some colored markers.

73 The Town of Springfield

The Simpsons live in a small town called Springfield. Though its exact geographical position has never been properly confirmed, many believe that it exists within the state of Oregon, where Matt Groening grew up. The purpose of Springfield is to exist as an every town, where old-timey ice cream shops co-exist with grimy dive bars. You can attend a Spinal Tap concert one night and visit the cracker factory the next. For the most part, it exists to us as a suburb. The next big town over is glitzy Reno-esque Capital City, and even farther than that is run-down thrift store-heavy Ogdenville.

Springfield is named after pioneer-era founder Jebediah Springfield, whose likeness stands tall and proud as a sculpture in front of City Hall. Many young Springfieldians are forced to memorize his story and his uplifting quote: "A noble spirit embiggens the smallest man." The story of Springfield begins when Jebediah and Shelbyville Manhattan squabbled over the principles of the new town they planned to create. Shelbyville's goal was to found a community where they could "marry their attractive cousins." The two men split, forming Springfield and neighboring Shelbyville.

Shelbyville exists as a kind of parallel universe to Springfield. Every element of it is a shoddier version of its counterpart. The town of Shelbyville would soon become a geographical foil to the kind community of Springfieldians, something most explored through the Season 6 episode "Lemon of Troy," where Bart dives over city lines to reclaim a beloved lemon tree. Within Shelbyville we're often greeted by characters that are similar to the Springfieldians we know and love—but slightly off. Bart goes

189

toe-to-toe with Shelbyville's resident hell-raiser, Nelson faces off with the Shelbyville version of himself, and when Milhouse meets another Milhouse, he exclaims, "So this is what it's like when doves cry."

In the Season 7 episode "Lisa the Iconoclast," Jebediah's legacy comes under scrutiny by the middle Simpsons child when she discovers that Jebediah is no hero but rather a lecherous pirate who adopted a new persona before founding the town. In the end Lisa decides to keep her discovery secret so as to not ruin the joy the story of Jebediah brings her fellow Springfieldians.

Springfield's local government is headed by Mayor Quimby, whose mannerisms and extramarital affairs mirror stereotypes of corrupt politicians, especially the Kennedys, and his voice acting is mishmash of Ted and John F. Kennedy. Quimby is slick and opportunistic. He has little regard for the safety and sanctity of the town as long as it doesn't cost him the next election. His main duties are often devoted to awarding characters keys to the town, sleeping with women who aren't his wife, and announcing Springfield-specific holidays.

Though the good citizens of Springfield seem to celebrate every major holiday from Christmas to St. Patrick's Day to Halloween, Springfield-specific holidays are a different category altogether. Most notable is Whacking Day, which allegedly began with Jebediah Springfield and his camp during the town's founding. Every year on May 10, citizens gather and drive the town's snakes to the main square, where they then whack them to a pulp until they're dead. Despite its gruesomeness it's meant to be a family affair.

Similar to "Lisa the Iconoclast," the truth behind Whacking Day's origin may be murky. The holiday historically conflicts with a Revolutionary War battle Jebediah took part in, making its creation not specific to Springfield. In the episode Bart rallies Lisa to gather the snakes to safety with the help of velvet-tongued Barry

White. (No snake can resist the deep bass tones of his sweet, sweet sound.) As Barry sings through speakers placed on the ground, the town is outraged to find their festivities temporarily halted. Unlike "Lisa the Iconoclast," the truth about Whacking Day soon comes out, leaving Springfieldians dismayed to learn that its origin actually began in 1924 as an excuse to beat up the Irish.

Despite all of the hiccups of its history, Springfield remains to be one hell of a tight community. When strife or struggles slam into the town, we often see its citizens rallying together either as an angry mob to defend its honor, or as a kind group working together to help through misfortune.

74 Celebrity Cameos

When Dustin Hoffman signed on to do the voice of Mr. Bergstrom in Season 2, he used the pseudonym (Sam Etic) in case being associated with a cartoon might be bad for his career. Decades later *The Simpsons'* roster of celebrity cameos is comparable to that of *The Tonight Show* and *Saturday Night Live*. With celebrity guests like Meryl Streep, Leonard Nimoy, Glenn Close, Rodney Dangerfield, Mickey Rooney, Michelle Pfeiffer, Jack Lemmon, Buzz Aldrin, John Waters, Jeff Goldblum, Steve Allen, Bob Hope, Mark Hamil, Cloris Leachman, Penny Marshall, Stephen Colbert, Mel Brooks, Joe Namath, Willem Dafoe, Kirk Douglas, Danny DeVito, Martin Sheen, Alec Baldwin, Kim Basinger, Ron Howard, and more, you have to wonder if Hoffman regrets his moniker. (We think he might regret a lot of things.) The more than 500 guest stars range from Oscar-winning actors, sports superstars (Burns' entire softball team from "Homer at the Bat" is littered with future Hall of Famers), directors, writers (Stephen King and J.K. Rowling), singers (Sting and Bono), public figures (Neil deGrasse Tyson and Dan Rather), and everything in between.

The use of celebrity talent has changed over the span of *The Simpsons*. The first two big names, Marcia Wallace and Kelsey Grammer, are examples of celebrity guests who were more about the characters than the actors themselves. There were no gimmicks to the appearances, and when a big celebrity did appear, there was a grounded rationalization to the choice. For example, Marge's crush on Ringo added to her character and justified his being there. A huge shift in the show was created when Michael Jackson did a voice for the show. Even though he went under a pseudonym, getting Jackson was huge deal and opened the door for the caliber of guests they could get.

Season 5 began a trend of celebrities playing themselves in a way that would become commonplace for the show. Cameos would allow actors to make self-deprecating jokes in a way that simply hadn't been done before. Before *Family Guy* had Adam West playing himself, *The Simpsons* had Adam West playing himself on the show, saying such great lines as, "Why doesn't Batman *dance* anymore?" In this era the writers would find clever ways to weave the stars into the plot. In "Homer and Apu," James Woods worked at the Kwik-E-Mart as research for an upcoming role as an uptight clerk, and in "$pringfield" lounge singer Robert Goulet would put his stamp on "Jingle Bells, Batman Smells" as the hired performer at Bart's treehouse casino.

Season 6 marked a predominant shift with the controversial move to have a crossover with *The Critic* in "A Star is Burns." Matt Groening pushed against the decision so heavily that he removed his name from the credits and publicly went on record as not liking the idea, though many view that episode as a classic.

Starting around Season 10, guest stars would seem to drop in, tell a joke, and then leave, almost as if they were out-of-town comedians dropping in to do a set. When Blink-182, Britney Spears, Tony Hawk, *NSYNC, and the like showed up in Springfield, there are undeniably people who loved it, but there are also those who miss the cameo days of yesteryear when the guest stars really had to earn it.

Recently, guest stars like *Flight of the Conchords*, Patton Oswalt, and Ben Schwartz have given the show more indie cred. Where guest stars like Lady Gaga were seen as stunt-casting, former guests took the show to a new place creatively. There's no telling how the show will continue to evolve. We're personally looking forward to the episode where Dame Judy Dench plays opposite Bart.

Watch *The Problem with Apu*

When looking at the many types of nerds in *The Simpsons*, we touched upon the importance of representation in television, explaining that having one token nerd character would have been beneath the show and demonstrated a limited world perspective. Although *The Simpsons* was great at showcasing the nuances of nerdiness, it failed to show the same level of care in providing multiple characters of the same non-white race. In the 2017 documentary starring Hari Kondabolu called *The Problem with Apu*, *The Simpsons* gets called out for its portrayal of Apu and explores the ways it perpetuates negative stereotypes about South Asians.

When Hari made his first public critique on *Totally Biased*, he explained, "Hank Azaria is a white guy doing an impression of a white guy making fun of my father." From Apu being voiced by a white guy to the many stereotypical character choices, including having him work at a convenience store and being in an arranged marriage, there are many problems with Apu and how it affects the view of South Asians to the masses. For many viewers during the show's heyday, Apu was their only insight into South Asian culture. That's insane to think about. When you contextualize the character in this way, you realize how much better it may have been had Apu worked at the power plant (he's clearly smarter than the current safety inspector) or at least *owned* the Kwik-E-Mart.

In the documentary Hari interviews fellow South Asian actors, performers, and writers about their own problems with Apu and discovers a shared negative experience among them. Kal Penn revealed that he hates Apu and therefore hates *The Simpsons*, and that resonated with us as gigantic fans of the show. *The Simpsons* brings joy to so many but has simultaneously hurt marginalized groups thanks to a handful of insensitive creative choices that could have just as easily not existed. According to Hari, the original script with Apu didn't specify that the convenience store clerk was Indian. Azaria's Indian impression was an improvised moment that got a big laugh in the room and inspired the character as we know him today.

As is sadly and often the case, it takes a minority explaining their plight for privileged people in power to realize there's a problem. In sharing his struggle with the character in the documentary, Hari shed a light on an issue that might have continued to be swept under the rug had he not spoken up. Even though Apu is smart, funny, and beloved, there are issues with the character that the show shouldn't have needed a documentary to realize.

Azaria publicy opened up with an earnest response, offering to step down from the voice and providing hope that *The Simpsons* hire Southeast Asian writers not only for the voice of Apu, but also for the show overall.

Months after the film's release, the show indirectly responded to the documentary with a controversial and polarizing moment in the episode called "No Good Read Goes Unpunished" in which

Lisa and her mom discuss an outdated children's book that has become problematic over time. With a framed photo of Apu on the nightstand behind her, Lisa then breaks the fourth wall, looks into the camera, and says, "Something that started decades ago and was applauded and inoffensive is now politically incorrect. What can you do?"

For fans of *The Simpsons*, who resent having to challenge this aspect of the show or just prefer not to think about it, we still urge you to check out the film. Hari loves *The Simpsons* and simply asks that the show takes accountability for the problem of Apu. As Hari says, "You're allowed to be critical of something you love. Whether that thing is *The Simpsons* or America—that's part of what love is."

The Doctors of Springfield

Hi, doctors in *The Simpsons*! Whether you're in need of a routine check-up, working through a fear of plane-related trauma, or need assistance removing gag items from your face, there's a doctor in Springfield who can help. If you're as troubled as the Simpsons family, you will find yourself needing a wide range of therapists, doctors, and counselors, but there's no shame in getting help. Just be careful who you go with or you might end up like Mr. McGreg, who has a leg for an arm and an arm for a leg!

Dr. Marvin Monroe, the psychotherapist from Season 1, was first introduced in "There's No Disgrace Like Home." Even if you don't remember all the specifics of his debut, you will likely recall the electroshock therapy session Monroe puts the Simpsons through. Monroe is a character who faded away, as the show continued to take shape and come into itself, and there are many references to his death in the seventh season. During the "138th Episode Spectacular," the question is posed: "What important *Simpsons* characters have died in the past year?" The answer: "If you said Bleeding Gums Murphy and doctor Marvin Monroe you are wrong. They were never popular."

If you want popular, we'll give you popular. Let's take a doctor's visit to the affable Dr. Hibbert, whose chuckle is so infectious he should seriously get it checked out. Julius Hibbert made his first appearance in "Bart the Daredevil" and has been a staple on the show since. When writing partners Jay Kogen and Wallace Wolodarsky sent in the script for the episode, Dr. Hibbert was written as a woman named Julia Hibbert. When *The Simpsons* got the primetime slot that put it in direct competition with *The Cosby Show*, the writers decided to change the character into a parody of Dr. Cliff Huxtable. From his sweaters to his idyllic family life, it's a near one-to-one comparison. Although Dr. Hibbert is a just as good-natured as Huxtable, he's never shied away from his high prices, which were sometimes *so* high that the Simpsons family would be forced to turn to Dr. Nick.

Dr. Nick is as incompetent as he is affordable, so when you're in a pinch, the Hollywood Upstairs Medical College grad may be your best option. After all, as his slogan goes, "You've tried the best, now try the rest!" If you're interested in seeing Dr. Nick, you can find out more from his many infomercials or calling 555-Nick or 1-600-DOCTORB. ("The B is for Bargain.") Dr. Nick has little regard for ethics or his patients' health, but he continues to get steady work, including when he assisted Dr. Hibbert during Bart's appendectomy (in which he accidentally anesthetized himself). Whereas Dr. Hibbert was modeled after a famous character, Dr. Nick's appearance was inspired by the co-founder of Klasky Csupo, Gábor Csupó. Although the animators believed Hank Azaria was doing an impression of Csupó, he was actually doing a bad Ricky Ricardo impression. Babalu!

Last but not least on the list is Marge's therapist Dr. Zweig. Voiced by the incredible Anne Bancroft, Dr. Zweig had an unparalleled coolness about her that set her apart from the other medical professionals in Springfield. Her demure demeanor and collected calmness made her a perfect partner to Marge as they worked through her fear of flying. In addition to helping Marge recover repressed memories from her past, she taught us that "The Monkees weren't about music…They were about rebellion, about political and social upheaval!" (Sing it, Dr. Zweig.) Although she only appeared in one episode, her effect is long lasting.

While these medical professionals made the biggest splash in the series, there are two others who deserve honorable mentions. First, the unnamed veterinarian who spent his life saving animals that can't even thank him. "Well, the parrots can," he noted. We'll never forget his attempt to save a hamster's life with CPR. He, though, does save Santa's Little Helper when the dog is afflicted with a twisted stomach. Lastly, let's raise a toast to the man who sat by Homer's side as he divulged his insecurities about Marge not being his soulmate. "This really goes beyond my training as a furniture salesman," he tells Homer.

Play *Simpsons* Games

Since the franchise is reaching its third decade, there have been a lot of video games based on *The Simpsons*. Should a die-hard fan like yourself check out all of them? No! Most of them are incredibly bad. I'm looking at you *The Simpsons: Skateboarding*, *The Simpsons: Wrestling*, *The Simpsons: Bowling*. (Basically anything that involves *The Simpsons* doing an activity or hobby likely means the game will not be good.) But luckily there are several really fantastic video games that are worth your time and money.

The quintessential video game that probably most of you have played is *The Simpsons Arcade*, a side-scrolling beat 'em up developed by Konami and released in 1991. The game follows the same template of countless arcade games inspired by *Double Dragon*. You jump and punch your way through countless levels until you rescue Maggie from evil Mr. Smithers. (Okay, maybe *The Simpsons Arcade* is the only one of its kind to follow that plot.) Players are able to take control of Homer, Marge, Bart, or Lisa as they fight goons across a number of series locales, including Krustyland and Moe's Tavern.

What's impressive about *The Simpsons Arcade* is that the game came out after only a single season of the show had aired and still managed to capture so much of its charm. Konami definitely took a lot of liberties with the source material. (Marge doesn't usually fend off zombies with a vacuum cleaner.) But it works as a perfect blend of insanity and delight. It's no wonder The Verge called it "the best video game ever based on a TV show." So the next time you're at a garishly carpeted arcade, be sure to play this game.

Another one worth checking out is *The Simpsons: Hit & Run*, a send-up of the popular *Grand Theft Auto* series that came out in 2003 for the Playstation 2, Xbox, and GameCube. *Hit & Run* is one of the most authentic games of the show made to date. You get to play as multiple characters in an open-world Springfield that you can explore on foot or by driving a huge variety of cars that fans will recognize from different episodes throughout the series (even The Car Built For Homer). The cast supplied voices for the characters, and the series' writers even wrote the story and dialogue for the game. The game came out during a time where there was a particular spell of bad video games of *The Simpsons*, and developer Radical Entertainment really nailed this one. And while it's not nearly as polished as *Grand Theft Auto* or other open-world action-adventure

In addition to arcade games, The Simpsons *has spawned a wealth of video games.* (Joe Kwaczala)

games that use *GTA* as inspiration, none of those games let you drive a Laramie Cigarettes stock car off a jump.

A personal favorite of ours is *The Simpsons: Virtual Springfield*, a 1997 Windows/Macintosh computer game that lets you explore a pretty spot-on replication of Springfield with the goal of collecting hidden character cards throughout town. It doesn't really qualify as a point-and-click adventure game since there is no real story, objective, or puzzles to solve, but it is an incredibly authentic sightseeing tour created during the series' heyday and features dialogue from cast members. And it takes no time to finish at all. This is worth checking out, especially if you don't consider yourself a gamer in the traditional sense (and good for you because most of them are insufferable).

A more recent video game is the 2012 free-to-play city builder mobile game *The Simpsons: Tapped Out.* In the style of games like *SimCity* and *Farmville* (remember *Farmville?*), the player is tasked to rebuild Springfield's roads, homes, and landmarks by accruing revenue and purchasing them. As you progress you unlock more characters, costumes, buildings, and decorations. It's fun, addictive, and easy to play. Like many recent games, it features voice-over work from the cast, and *Tapped Out* is even headed by longtime *Simpsons* writer/producer J. Stewart Burns, who employs 10 staff writers from the show to create gags and jokes for the game when it's regularly updated. The one drawback of *Tapped Out* is—like many free-to-play video games—that it counts on players spending their real money to incur fake money (in this case donuts) and purchase the games' many collectables. And while there is nothing wrong with spending your money however you'd like, freemium games' revenue structure is a predatory business tactic that giant video game publishers like Electronic Arts use to rake in millions of dollars off of many young video game players who don't understand they're spending real money. So, if you're a parent with a child who is fanatical about

The Simpsons, maybe don't link your credit card information to *Tapped Out*. Otherwise, it's a really fun and authentic mobile game.

And if you happen to be a 100-year-old weirdo who still plays "board games" (whatever those are), there are plenty of games that cash in on *The Simpsons'* likeness, including *Monopoly*, *Clue*, *Life*, and *Operation*. Plus, there are lots of trivia games, including *Scene It?* So if you're a fan of *The Simpsons* and a gamer, then you've really got it made in the shade.

78 Bad Guys

The first, and arguably most famous, of the show's villains is Sideshow Bob (voiced in Shakespearean glory by Kelsey Grammer in a staggering 21 episodes). Sideshow Bob has an impressive collection of crimes under his belt, including framing Krusty the Clown, rigging an election, attempting to kill Selma in an inheritance scam, and trying many times to have "Die, Bart, Die" happen.

Our next rogue in the gallery is none other than everyone's favorite gangster from this series, William "Fat Tony" Williams. Voiced by veteran actor Joe Mantegna in 29 episodes, Tony is a staple to the show. Tony made his debut in the Season 3 episode "Bart the Murderer" as the upstanding bar owner who hires Bart as a general errand boy for the Springfield mafia. Although he's responsible for many a bad deed, there's a sweetness to Tony and his love of Bart. Over the course of a stellar villainous career, Fat Tony takes out opposing food trucks to benefit Marge (which is pretty sweet if you overlook the personal gain), puts a hit out on the mayor, tries to kill Homer, and sadly dies himself only to be replaced by his fit cousin, Fit Tony. That man eventually eats his way, nay, earns his way into getting the name Fat Tony for himself. Fat Tony is dead, but long live Fat Tony!

We would be remiss to not mention Russ Cargill, the villain of the 2007 theatrical *Simpsons* movie. Head of the EPA, at least in this universe, it is Mr. Cargill's motive and action to put the ever-intimidating dome on the admittedly cesspool pond that Springfield has become. Voiced by Albert Brooks, Russ eventually runs afoul of the Simpson family and learns what all other series villains learn. Even with 10,000 tough guys, you can't win against the Simpson family.

You can make a case for a lot of other villains through the series, like Artie Ziff, who tries to steal Marge back from Homer (like he ever had a chance against Mr. Plow); Snake, who is a petty thief but somehow good enough to be out of jail pretty much constantly; or Rex Banner, who obviously lives in a film noir but has time to try and stop the beer baron himself. He is launched out of town on a catapult, which shockingly isn't a metaphor. Finally, the most frightening creature to ever come out of Matt Groening's mind was Robotic Richard Simmons. Truly terrifying.

Frank Grimes' Death

Few characters within the world of *The Simpsons* are as polarizing and controversial as Frank Grimes, but that's precisely what the show intended. On the DVD commentary, former showrunner Josh Weinstein said he and Bill Oakley emphasized a goal every season to "push the envelope conceptually." Through their tenure we see this in "Who Shot Mr. Burns?" a take on "Who Shot JR?"; "The Simpsons 138th Episode Spectacular," a riff on clip shows; and

"22 Short Films About Springfield," which twisted and turned the very format of an episode of *The Simpsons* on its head.

Then, there was "Homer's Enemy." For years Homers implacability as a bumbling imbecile provided him an ever-present safety net from social consequence. Often described as "a human puppy," his idiocy was often rewarded by the world, inadvertently becoming the mascot for failing up. Homer lights himself on fire, yelps out "D'oh!," is fine by next scene. Repeat. This soon became a trademark of the show's charm.

Oakley originally conceived of Frank Grimes as a real-world co-worker, who would see Homer for who he truly was. Everything that was sloppily beloved by Springfield would soon become a grating irritation to Grimes. Grimes was an orphan; Homer had a loving family. Grimes worked his way through school; Homer barely had a high school education. Their opposite traits could rattle on for days.

Fans would later recall this episode as being the first moment "Homer as villain" was sincerely explored through the show. By the time the second act hits, Grimes' gripes with Homer soon become our own, and the moral ambiguity of where to lay our loyalties is as large as Homer's bald spot. Then, just as soon as the show introduces the new adversary, they twist the episode into tragedy. While outlining the very reasons why Homer's insufferable in a grand, passionate speech in front of an audience of co-workers, Grimes accidentally electrocutes himself.

According to Weinstein, when the episode first aired, fans believed it was too dark, lacking humor, and portraying Homer as "overly bad-mannered." Weinstein credits this to the episode's humor perhaps being too sharp. The writers weren't trying to cause an upset in Springfield for the purpose of an upset but rather explore new terrain for storytelling that would inevitably diversify the kind of stories they were able to tell within the world of Springfield while also adding dimensions to their main characters.

To say that "Homer's Enemy" is a break in the chain of the show is accurate but not unfortunate. It forces us to consider at what lengths and limits the show's meta-commentary exists. Does Grimes point the camera back at the viewer, judging them for carelessly laughing at the lovable buffoon? Does it puckishly break the format to jostle the auto-pilot nature of sitcom writing as a whole? Or, more simply, was it a funny premise that John Swartzwelder felt worthy to explore through his infamous script?

Hindsight through the show's storied history will provide "Homer's Enemy" and the story of Grimes with more of a legacy than Weinstein could ever have predicted and for good reason. Their intention to bend and break the conventions of the show, to push the limits of its own predictability is the kind of trademark creativity that's helped the show endure for as long as it has. Mention Grimes (or "Grimey," as he liked to be called) to any fan of *The Simpsons* and you'll be treated to an instant shorthand of inner-circle understanding. Whatever you felt about the episode at the time, its timeless relevance to the show and its fans is proof enough that the writer's risk most certainly paid off.

80 Love Affairs

If the characters on *The Simpsons* aged in real time, in 2018 Homer would be 68 years old, Marge would be 65, and they'd be celebrating 38 years of marriage. We know that's not how time in the show really works, but it's still nice to think about, considering the major storms their marriage has weathered. (Terrifying side note: in 2018 Ned Flanders would be 89 years old.)

In Season 1 Homer buys a bowling ball with his name on it and gives it to Marge for her birthday. For many wives this would gift would be returned, but not Marge! She takes that ball straight to Barney's Bowlarama and keep rollin'. Marge is wooed by her bowling instructor, Jacques, who was voiced by the incredible Albert Brooks and whose lines were almost entirely improvised. Homer and Marge begin to drift apart, Bart tells his father to keep his mouth shut to prevent the situation from getting any worse, and Homer can't bring himself to eat a sandwich because it's all he has left of his wife. Marge reaches a fork in the road, chooses her husband, and the episode ends with a sex joke that was lost on all of us below the age of 13. "Life on the Fast Lane" would go on to win the 1990 Emmy award for Outstanding Animated Program, edging out both "Garfield's Feline Fantasies" *and* "Garfield's Thanksgiving."

Just two years later, the only episode fully credited to Matt Groening would scare the crap out of fans of *The Simpsons* across the globe. In "Colonel Homer," an argument between Marge and Homer leads to Homer driving off alone into the night, stopping at a strange bar, and introducing himself to an attractive waitress. That's the first act. I omitted some important details, but still, what the fuck?

Homer goes on to manage the singing career of Lurleen Lumpkin, who's voiced by Beverly D'Angelo and whose song "Your Wife Don't Understand You" mirrored his mental state note-for-note the first night he heard her perform. Homer is blissfully unaware of Lurleen's developing crush—even as Marge grows more and more suspicious—and Lurleen writes a song literally called "Bagged Me a Homer." Have you ever thought that Homer is kinda dumb?

Anyway, he eventually figures it out, sells Lurleen's contract for $50, and returns home to his wife, which seems less an act of faithfulness than blatant financial irresponsibility. Again, Homer is kinda dumb. The episode ends before Marge finds out.

Only a year later, Homer is tested again in "The Last Temptation of Homer," when a beautiful woman voiced by Michelle Pfeiffer is hired to work alongside him at the power plant. Unlike Lurleen, Homer is immediately attracted to Mindy and does his best to quash the whole thing by avoiding her at all costs. Showrunner David Mirkin didn't want Mindy to come off as flirty or seductive, preferring to tell a story about two good people who are thrown into a situation and "can't help that their libidos are going crazy upon seeing each other."

Homer would again question his marriage in the season eight episode "El Viaje Misterioso de Nuestro Jomer" (aka "The Mysterious Voyage of Homer"), where a chili pepper-induced space coyote implores him to find his soulmate. (What a fun sentence that was to write!) Homer's search ends happily, of course, as Marge is able to track him down in a lighthouse due to their... soulmate powers?

Oh, and then there was the "Three Gays of the Condo" episode, where Homer is kissed by his gay roommate, prompting him to jump out a window. Homer is then treated for alcohol poisoning and reconciles with Marge. This one felt less subtle than the others.

81 Go to Simpson Land at Universal Studios

For decades, fans the world over have thought that stepping foot into a real, actual Springfield would be the stuff of dreams. What would it be like to cozy up at Moe's Tavern? How high can they score on the Love-o-Matic? And most importantly, is a Flaming Moe as disgusting as it sounds? (Spoiler alert: it kind of is.)

Then, back in 2007, it finally happened. Universal Parks and Resorts made a special announcement: the world would see a theme park version of their favorite fictional town, and you bet your Bumblebee Man bee-hind it would have rides.

Plans were quickly drawn, rides were re-dressed (R.I.P. *Back to the Future*), and space was saved for Disco Stu's Disco to make its three-dimensional debut.

In addition to *Simpsons*-themed stores, restaurants, and carnival games, the park had big plans to roll out special edition merchandise, treats, and more. Fear not, this is the one place on Earth that would *not* sell out of Bort license plates. In both the California and Florida parks, giant, human-head-sized pink glazed sprinkled donuts ("The Homer" has become the park's top seller in snacks) can be bought and shared (or not) everywhere from gift shops to restaurants. Sip beers from the Duff Brewery Beer Garden while staring at the sober folk as you and your cohorts laugh the day away. Munch on burgers (both meat and non-meat) at Krusty Burger, where a "Clogger Burger" (as depicted in *The Simpsons Movie*) complete with heaping helpings of bacon is a featured meal. Channel your inner yokel at Cletus' Chicken Shack, where fries and thighs unite in deep fried decadence. Still hungry for dessert? Satisfy your sweet tooth at Phinneas Q. Butterfat's, though no word on whether they honor your birthday with a teeny tiny sundae.

Often when theme parks feature attractions linking to actual pop culture, the attempt to imitate the source material often feels forced and hollow, as if your well-meaning stepdad designed a whole land based on the two references he's picked up from your carpool conversations. Perhaps Universal knew this, which is why they quickly tapped *Simpsons* executive producer Matt Selman and longtime writer Matt Warburton to put their genius minds to the test and make sure everything from sign gags to snacks were given the show's official stamp of approval.

This is what makes this land distinct not only for Universal, but also for theme parks as a whole. There's something fun and loose about this crass and creative corner of the world. It's a wild commentary on Disneyland's dreamy designs that are both critical and kind. Much like in the "Itchy & Scratchy Land" episode, which riffed on everything from Disney dollars to Disney jail, Springfield's sharp commentary is apparent, but it's clear that—much like *The Simpsons'* more satire-skewering episodes—everything's approached with love and appreciation at its core. Its main walkway feels like an off-design Main Street USA. Instead of glossy storefronts with old-timey sayings, guests are treated to

Lard Lad Donuts and Duff Brewery are two popular attractions at Universal Studios in Florida. (AP Images)

spray paint from El Barto and the front door of Patty and Selma's DMV.

And it shows. Step into *The Simpsons* Ride and you're instantly treated to a trail of nostalgia. Like most theme parks, every corner of the line has ways to distract you from the dullness of 40-plus minutes of standing. What makes this ride stand out is that flat screens flank every angle, playing clips from the show itself. There should be a word for the elation you feel laughing as a group of sunburnt strangers stare at the same Lionel Hutz quote.

From the bright colors to the constant soundtrack of *The Simpsons* albums playing on a loop as you stroll with your own Patty and/or Selma, it's an immersive experience one will want to have again and again.

Visit All the Springfields

Part of what makes *The Simpsons* such a rich and vibrant TV world is that for years its home base of Springfield was undefined in its geography. Springfield could be anywhere from the desert plains of Texas to the lushness of Yosemite. Depending on what the episode required, the Simpsons family could be transported across every single ecosystem (sometimes in a single episode).

Though fans have collected clues over time on where the *true* Evergreen Terrace may be (the most popular theory credits the Pacific Northwest), you might as well hedge your bets, hop in your car, and hope for the best that the *Simpsons*-brand Butterfingers you bought off the Internet aren't woefully expired. Currently, there are 41 different American towns that go by the name of Springfield, but here's a roundup of the best places to spend your dollaridoos:

Springfield, Illinois
Check out the Abraham Lincoln Presidential Library, which is located here. Let's hope that no squirrels resembling the former president have been assassinated.

Springfield, Idaho
It's time to nibble on some spuds and honor Marge who "just thinks they're neat." This unincorporated community may not have the flashiness of North Havenbrook or Ogdenville, but we believe that one day, by golly, we'll put them on the map.

Springfield, Florida
Regrettably there's no "Royal Frat Inn," in which you can hang your hat. Also know that Springfield is in the panhandle, meaning it's more than a five-hour drive to Orlando, where you could enjoy various *Simpsons* rides. Bummer that it's not a bit closer.

Springfield, Louisiana
Giddy up those gators, we're going into swamp country. Springfield is just an hour from New Orleans, so belly up to beignets and blast through waters on awesome airboats. If you keep your eyes peeled long enough, you may dig into a dalliance with "Big Daddy" while you're strolling with your "Regular Daddy."

Springfield, Wisconsin
There are *five* Springfields in the state of Wisconsin. So cruise around and enjoy the perfect excursion if "you're ready to get Duffed," as Wisconsin is known for its breweries, including the Miller Brewery Tour in Milwaukee. Although there is no Duff

Brewery, we still encourage you to engage in Duffman-like pelvic thrusts from time to time.

Springfield, New York
If you're hoping to have your trip mirror "The City of New York vs. Homer Simpson," note that Springfield is in upstate and more than a three-hour drive from New York City. So, hopefully you won't run into trouble with parking tickets as Homer and Barney did.

Springfield, Colorado
Prep yourself for a hero's welcome when you roll into this district, or, more specifically, a hero's slow clap. Some superfans may choose to get medicated in that Colorado way. And you won't need a traumatic crow-induced eye injury to do so.

Losers

One of the most defining characteristics of Springfield is how densely populated it is with sad, downtrodden characters. Adults are inept (Chief Wiggum), hopelessly drunk (Barney Gumble), and sometimes downright deadly (Dr. Nick when within 500 feet of medical equipment). This is part of what makes Lisa Simpson such a curiosity. Her strong morals and smarts contrast starkly against the landscape of luddites she's forced to live with.

But there's something about the more pathetic characters that strikes a particular funny bone within both *The Simpsons'* writers' room and fandom alike. Viewers have witnessed that the saddest people in Springfield seem to be the ones with the longest day in the sun. Characters, who once may have been thought of as one-offs, have since given way to multi-part story arcs. Fans have endeared themselves to how these poor souls endure despite being repeatedly dumped on by this crazy thing called life.

True to *The Simpsons'* style of laughing *with* rather than laughing *at* things, these characters are always presented with kindness and sympathy, making their relentless underdogdom that much more noteworthy. Here are a few of the most lovable losers.

Lionel Hutz

Famously voiced by the late Phil Hartman and first appearing in the Season 2 episode "Bart Gets Hit by a Car," Lionel Hutz soon became the go-to for the Simpsons' legal counsel. He's been called a "shyster" by Lisa, had his competence questioned by Marge, and even been asked to babysit on occasion.

One of the striking characteristics to Hutz's humor is his relentless spirit and detachment from reality. He'll march into any courtroom with confidence—even if he has absolutely no idea which side he's fighting on. Most of the humor that comes from Hutz has its roots firmly in 1990s cable access pop culture—perhaps as an allusion to the common space they occupy if Hutz ever got his act together and shot a late-night infomercial. We see this expressed through the title of Hutz's business ("I Can't Believe It's Not a Law Firm!"), his business card ("when wet, it turns into a sponge"), and even in his side gigs ("cases won in 30 minutes or your pizza is free!") The fact that Hutz's law firm resides in a shopping mall is no coincidence.

In addition to being vastly underqualified for his profession, Hutz is pathetic because his many vices sprinkle their way through the seasons. Hutz is a recovering alcoholic whose homelessness is referenced, and he has a hard time locating his pants. He's ignorant, greedy, and can grind any conversation to a halt. We feel bad for him but have a hard time believing he ever feels bad for himself.

Similar to Homer's wide-eyed puppy-like spirit, Hutz's bouncy obliviousness bonds him to us rather than repelling him away for being the scumbag he so obviously is. When you pair that that with Hartman's upbeat voice, it seals the deal in making him more lovable than lecherous.

Hans Moleman

Is there a sadder phrase in the English language than "No one's gay for Moleman?" We imagine so, but we're not stoked to search. First appearing in the Season 2 episode "Principal Charming," Moleman's fate was fixed to be short-lived and originally intended to be named "Ralph Melish" (a reference to *The Monty Python Matching Tie and Handkerchief*). According to the DVD commentary on the episode, Matt Groening said Hans looked so shriveled and unrealistic that he was unmistakably "like a mole man" and so a *Simpsons* fan favorite was born.

From there on *The Simpsons* writers took a liking to this lumpy loser, establishing a series-long runner of him being the receiver of catastrophic wrongdoings. Whatever ailment you can imagine, Moleman reps it in spades, including cataracts, almost-near-total blindness, and living in a house under a dam (as seen in "Brother from Another Series"). His character is a magnet of misfortune.

One of the most memorable details the writers gave Hans is how old he *actually* is. In the episode "Duffless," Homer finds himself slogging through an Alcoholics Anonymous meeting, of which Moleman's present. When the hypothetical conch is carried to Hans, he claims that, "Drinking has ruined my life. I'm only 31 years old!"

One of the wildest parts of Moleman's character is how many times he's witnessed (and cheated) death. His car has exploded. He's been lit on fire; given the electric chair; hit on the head with a bowling ball; buried alive, left, and forgotten in a morgue; drilled in the brain by Mr. Burns; and that's only as many as we can recall off the top of our heads. Above all, Moleman's a fan favorite because he's repeatedly unfazed by his fate.

Gil Gunderson

Sometimes called "Ol Gil" but most often "Gil," he is the weakest of the weak that forms our pathetic peak. Gil was first introduced in the Season 9 episode "Realty Bites" as Marge's co-worker in Lionel Hutz's Red Blazer Realty. From the start we detect his sorry situation, and he delivers many memorable lines like: ("Let's not forget old Gil! The wolf's at Old Gil's door" and "C'mon, what's Old Gil gotta do to sell you this car? Aw geez, it's on fire again!")

Gil's character is based on Jack Lemmon's character Shelley Levine in the film *Glengarry Glen Ross*. Similar to our other lovable losers, Gil too was meant to be a throw-away bit. Former showrunner Mike Scully said that despite the writers' original intentions with Gil, Dan Castellaneta was so strong at *The Simpsons* table read that they soon invented excuses to revisit his sorry storyline.

Gil's a clear standout not only within the pool of pathetic people but of Springfield residents as a whole. Similar to Lisa, he maintains a self-awareness that separates himself from otherwise-blissed out Springfield residents. Though where Lisa has a healthy relationship to how the world is as a whole, Gil's is a grueling grind where he's persistently one degree off from his next big break. You get a sense that the moxie he musters to get up every morning is its own staggering feat.

Similar to our other lovable losers, it's Gil's perseverance that pairs him to our other pathetic people. Since the retirement of Phil Hartman-voiced characters like Troy McClure and Hutz, Gil's risen as being the Simpsons family go-to for everything under the sun (and, yes, that includes lousy legal services).

Gil's track record for terrible jobs is expansive and it includes the consistency of him being fired. Where Hutz was blindly confident, Gil is bumbling and crippled by his insecurities, as he depicts when memorably asking Lisa in "Lisa Gets an A" in Season 10, "How many can I put you down for? A lot? Please say a lot. I need this."

 # Rivals

The concept of rivalries is one that's frequently visited on *The Simpsons*. In the early days of the show, it wasn't uncommon for the "vs." to pop up in an episode title like "Bart vs. Thanksgiving," "Marge vs. the Monorail," or "Lisa vs. Malibu Stacy." In these examples, the characters face off against more conceptual opponents, but the characters also have individual rivals. As Lisa Simpson said, "Everybody needs a nemesis. Sherlock Holmes had his Dr. Moriarty. Mountain Dew has its Mello Yello. Even Maggie has that baby with the one eyebrow."

Given Homer's main personality traits (loud, dumb, drunk), it's safe to assume that he's the one with the most enemies in Springfield. Is his next-door neighbor Ned Flanders ever introduced without Homer expressing some sort of disgust? Ever the forgiving and God-fearing Christian, Flanders seems to have an at times unconditional love for Homer, making this a rather one-sided rivalry. Not so for he and Marge's sisters Patty and Selma. Homer hates them with the same intensity that they hate him back. From the time they met him, Patty and Selma were firmly in the corner of another rival of Homer's, Artie Ziff, whom he vied with in high school for the affection of Marge. Of course, there's a whole episode titled "Homer's Enemy," in which new power plant employee Frank Grimes is driven to insanity by his hatred for

Homer. Speaking of the power plant, Homer has also been at odds with his boss Mr. Burns plenty of times. But who hasn't?

That leads us nicely into the next rivalry—Mr. Burns and pretty much everyone. Remember when we said Homer probably has the most enemies? Nix that. Mr. Burns is literally an evil villain. The whole reason "Who Shot Mr. Burns?" is such an effective mystery and cliffhanger is that everyone in town had a motive for killing him—even lovable guest star Tito Puente! Mr. Burns is at odds with plenty of other characters in many other episodes, too. In "Lady Bouvier's Lover," it's between him and Grampa Simpson as potential suitors for Marge's mother, Jacqueline. In "A Star Is Burns," he competes against several other aspiring filmmakers in Springfield's film festival.

Each of the Simpsons children have had their share of rivals, too. Bart's main rival may be the most perilous. About every other season, he finds his life on the line as he has to outsmart the conniving, vengeful Sideshow Bob, who wants nothing more than to murder him. Lisa has been a bit luckier. Nobody's tried to murder her, but she did face the formidable foe of Allison Taylor in the aptly titled "Lisa's Rival." Allison was able to tap into Lisa's raging jealousy by besting her in the category most important to her: smarts. Dialogue-less Maggie barely gets any storylines, but one recurring thread for her is that she has an enemy: a one-eyebrowed baby named Gerald, who has appeared in the show numerous times, and his and Maggie's rivalry drives the narrative of the Academy Award-nominated short film *The Longest Daycare*. Even Santa's Little Helper had a rival. In "The Canine Mutiny," he was all but forgotten when the perfect, seemingly infallible dog, Laddie, entered the Simpsons' lives, immediately taking the spot of favorite pet.

One of the things that makes *The Simpsons* great is that it has the ability to reflect humanity—warts and all. Who hasn't had someone in their life they consider an enemy on some level?

Clearly, the citizens of Springfield are no different. The town as a whole even has a rival, the neighboring city Shelbyville. Screw those guys.

Nameless Characters

There are so many characters in *The Simpsons* that if you were to try to remember all their names, your nose would bleed to the point of passing out while swerving into oncoming traffic. (By the by, you really shouldn't be compiling a list of characters whilst driving. What's wrong with you?) Well, thank Jebus that there are some characters in this helluva town whom the writers never bothered to name. Was this because of laziness or an attempt to lighten the load that superfans have to memorize? Whatever the reason, here are the ones to know:

Blue-Haired Lawyer

The blue-haired lawyer is the Itchy to Lionel Hutz's Scratchy, the Barney's movie to his football in the groin, the Crab Juice to his Mountain Dew. This long-necked litigator's clientele ranges from defending an all-you-can-eat seafood buffet against Homer, a remorseless eatin' machine, to putting the kibosh on anyone mimicking the antics of Charlie Chaplin. His shrewd, professional demeanor and the fact that his law firm is not located in a mall make him the esquire you should hire. Despite his appearing in more than 60 episodes, the writers haven't given the blue-haired lawyer, who also wears glasses, a proper name. Though if they did, I imagine he would object to it on grounds of hearsay.

Old Jewish Man

Here are a few facts we know about the old Jewish man: he's a former Warner Brothers studio exec who was responsible for watering down the ending of *Casablanca*, he became an overnight sensation with his pants-less rendition of "Old Gray Mare," and most importantly, he wants some taquitos. This deteriorated denizen of the Retirement Castle is always eager to roll with Grampa and Jasper—even if he feels like a bit of a third wheelchair. While the rest of these characters surely have names that we just haven't heard, his nom de birth is such a mystery that he has been verbally addressed only as "Old Jewish Man." Unless, of course, his name is actually Old Jewish Man, in which case, disregard this paragraph entirely. Instead, you could take this time to ponder why old gray mares ain't what they used to be, ain't what they used to be, ain't what they used to be.

Mayor Quimby's Bodyguards

When you're more corrupt than a magnetized hard drive, everyday carries the risk of assassination attempts. To avoid such just comeuppance for his sleazy criminal ways, the Springfield mayor, "Diamond" Joe Quimby, needs to be bookended by a quarter ton of rock hard, affordable muscle. Quimby's bodyguards are a top-notch brunette duo who are skilled in both protection and anonymity. Nothing will squash their unwavering dedication to keeping Quimby safe...except that one time they didn't and then Homer became Quimby's bodyguard.

The "EEE-Yeeeeeeeeeessssss?" Guy

The "EEE-Yeeeeeeeeeessssss?" guy is proof that you can have a one-dimensional character whose whole thing is just saying one word in a weird, semi-annoying way...and still put him in the show nonetheless. Looking like a cross between legendary comedic actor Frank Nelson...and, well, legendary comedic actor Frank Nelson, the "EEE-Yeeeeeeeeessss?" guy is best known for his catchphrase, "EEE-Yeeeeeeeeessss?" as well as utilizing a similar inflection to that of legendary comedic actor Frank Nelson. After first meeting Homer in Season 10 and explaining the reason for his uncanny vocal resemblance to legendary actor Frank Nelson was the result of poor blood flow to the brain causing brain cell degeneration, the "EEE-Yeeeeeeeeessss?" guy went on to become a semi-recurring character, much in the way legendary comedic actor Frank Nelson did in many television…Look, this guy's basically Frank Nelson. That was the whole point of this.

Have we beat this dead horse long enough?

Wait for it.

Wait for it.

Yes.

86 Lenny and Carl

Laurel and Hardy.
Martin and Lewis.
Lenny and Carl.

The 20th century gave us the cream of the crop when it came to iconic duos, but few are as simple and satisfying as Homer Simpson's workmates. Lenny Leonard and Carl Carlson first began as simple straight men to Homer's wild and unruly antics. After all, in order to wriggle around in Homer's goofy chaos, we need some realistic parameters to ground us first. Sometimes they pull in the reins of Homer's absurd ideas, but more often than not, they conspire as contented co-enablers for what is essentially "The Homer Show."

When Homer gets a hanger stuck in his shirt, they're front row center and when Homer gets his hand stuck in a vending machine, they abandon him with very little conscience. Their fair-weather friendship to Homer is often played for laughs, but one gets the sense that a true love and appreciation lurks beyond the conventions of forced work companionship. Why else would they tolerate him? Especially considering their access to so many inanimate carbon rods.

In later seasons Lenny and Carl's characters both blossomed. We discovered their true full names, and Carl's lineage even got a full episode treatment in "The Saga of Carl" (Season 24, Episode 21). But despite their added backstory over the years, their "side character trope" was often the root of their character development. Lenny and Carl represent the office friends you feel most intimate with yet know virtually nothing about. In Season 12's "A Tale of Two Springfields," Homer even wrote "Lenny = white; Carl = black" on his hand as a way to remember which one is which.

Lenny is a Chicago-born Buddhist, a war hero, a three-time juror, a descendant of slaves in a Soviet labor camp, and a member of the Springfield Stonecutters (with rank over Mr. Burns), who has been promoted, demoted, and noted for his viability of taking presidential office more than once on the show.

Carl is a black Icelandic Buddhist who holds a master's degree in nuclear physics and whose membership as a Springfield Stonecutter allows for even more "Lenny time." Though it's never been explicitly stated in the show, a running narrative for Lenny and Carl is their romantic lingerings. In "Fraudcast News" (Season 15, Episode 22), Lenny creates his own newspaper called *The Lenny-Saver* with just one headlining story, "THE TRUTH ABOUT CARL: He's Great!" When Lenny sees heaven in "Treehouse of Horror XVI," it appears to him as an angel's chorus of Carl singing, "Hurry up, Lenny. We'll be late for work at the plant."

In Season 18's "Ice Cream of Margie (with the Light Blue Hair),'" Carl says, "See, statements like that are why people think we're gay." And then there's the most famous Lenny and Carl moment of them all, the one that made 2013 Internet aflutter. In the episode "Whiskey Business" (Season 24, Episode 19), we find Marge, Homer, Moe, Lenny, and Carl all en route to cheer up Moe with a trip to Capital City. As Lenny and Carl stand and look out through the limo's moonroof, there's a blink-and-you-miss-it moment showing the two men sweetly holding hands for barely a second—nothing more than a sweet reassurance that they're there for each other. Is this proof of the nature of their relationship? A more important question may be: does it matter?

87 Animation Evolution

When was the last time you watched one of the original shorts of *The Simpsons* that ran on *The Tracey Ullman Show*? If it's been a while or if you've never seen them, they're all on YouTube. Go ahead and watch some of them, specifically the ones from the first batch in 1987. They're pretty scary, right? Sure, there's a simple charm to them, but they look like monsters, unrecognizable monsters.

Even creator Matt Groening wasn't expecting them to look so crude; he expected the animators would clean up and improve upon his initial rough drafts of the character models. Yet there they were for those first several shorts, just as Groening had drawn them. So you can't say the animators screwed up, as they were only being faithful to what they thought was Groening's vision. By the end of the *Tracey Ullman* run, the designs did indeed improve, and the characters more closely resembled their established look, though there would still be plenty of changes made over the next several years.

The animation for these shorts, as well as for the first three seasons, was produced by Klasky Csupo Studios. This studio's aesthetic is a little wackier than what would eventually be needed to fit the show's sensibility, but this collaboration did result in one iconic look for *The Simpsons*: the characters' yellow skin. Groening recalls first seeing an animator's choice to color the characters yellow and immediately loving this choice for its potential in catching a casual channel flipper's eye. Colorist Gyorgi Peluce is frequently credited as the animator to make this choice, along with the one to make Marge's hair blue. Apparently, other off-the-wall suggestions were made and nixed—like trees being purple—but the yellow and blue obviously have stuck.

There are conflicting accounts on why exactly this happened, but *The Simpsons* switched over to Film Roman Studios, starting in the fourth season, and stayed there until 2016. It's during this era that the show's sometimes crude animation style was smoothed out and eventually perfected into a consistent style. This process wasn't entirely completed until Season 6 or 7. You'd think the switching of animation studios would result in some sort of visual shift that viewers could pinpoint, but that's not the case. This is probably because the show was able to hold onto their excellent stable of directors like Wes Archer, Rich Moore, Mark Kirkland, and David Silverman. The latter is perhaps the show's most important animator, as he directed the original shorts, directed many episodes during the classic era, and continues to direct episodes and animate scenes to this day, including the 2007 feature film.

The other major change to *The Simpsons'* animation was when the show switched to a high-definition format for the start of the

20th season in 2008. Not only did this switch obviously result in a crisper look (in 720p), but this also meant the show was now broadcast in a wider 16:9 aspect ratio for the first time. This change was also accompanied with a special treat; for the first time since 1990, there was a new opening sequence, which was long overdue. The old sequence had grown outdated—both in animation style and how it reflected what the show was. Watch it and you'll spot one-episode character Jacques, as well as Bleeding Gums Murphy, a character who died in the show yet stayed in the opening sequence for 13 years after his death! Also, Apu's dog is in there. Did you know Apu has a little dog? We're pretty sure he doesn't, but we looked back at the opening titles while writing this chapter, and there it was.

The look of *The Simpsons* is not likely to go through any more changes, as it's remained extremely consistent for the past few decades or so. However, if you're looking to see your favorite characters in a different style, the show has been outsourcing its couch gags segment to outside directors in recent years. You can find many of these online. We recommend checking out the ones done by Bill Plympton, Michael Socha, Sylvain Chomet, and Don Hertzfeldt.

88 One-Time Characters

From the shorts on *The Tracey Ullman Show* to the present-day version, the world of *The Simpsons* has grown exponentially. Outside of the core family, *The Simpsons* universe is made up of hundreds of characters, and some of our favorite characters have left a lasting impression after only visiting the screen once.

Hank Scorpio isn't just the best one-time character of *The Simpsons*, he's one of the best one-time characters of all time. Voiced by Albert Brooks, Hank is a charming, sugar-pocketing, Bond-esque villain. He's so great he even has a theme song: "Scorpio! He'll sting you with his dreams of power and wealth. Beware of Scorpio! His twisted twin obsessions are his plot to rule

Voiced by Phil Hartman, Lyle Lanley (far left), who appears in the classic "Marge vs. the Monorail" episode, is one of the authors' favorite one-timers. (Fox Network/Photofest © Fox Network)

the world and his employees' health. He'll welcome you into his lair, like the nobleman welcomes his guest. With free dental care and a stock plan that helps you invest! But beware of his generous pensions, plus three weeks paid vacation each year. And on Fridays the lunchroom serves hot dogs and burgers and beer! He loves German beer!"

Speaking of beer, Rex Banner appeared in "Homer vs. the Eighteenth Amendment." Rex's old-timey slang and disdain for banana kabooms make him an absolute delight that we wish we could have seen more of. He delivers hilarious lines like: "Listen, Rummy, I'm gonna say it plain and simple: where'd you pinch the hooch? Is some blind tiger jerking suds on the side?" Another one-timer who has a problem with alcohol is the surprisingly bleak Shary Bobbins, who turns to booze when realizing she can't fix the Simpsons. She may not have been able to stop Marge's hair from falling out, but she inadvertently taught the family to be okay with their shortcomings—all through the power of song and dance.

A lesson-teaching one-timer is from the emotionally charged episode "Lisa's Substitute." The bittersweet episode stars Dustin Hoffman as the sensitive, Jewish cowboy, Mr. Bergstrom, who teaches Lisa the importance of being herself with the famous note: "You Are Lisa Simpson." Mr. Bergstrom wasn't the only character to help Lisa realize her strength and potential. Stacy "Now I'm too drunk" Lovell, voiced by Kathleen Turner, sobered up just long enough in "Lisa vs. Malibu Stacy" to help Lisa follow her dreams of creating a feminist Malibu Stacy doll.

Where most of the characters on this list have entire episodes dedicated to them, Guy Incognito only appears for a moment. Guy is Homer's exact double who had the misfortune of visiting Moe's Tavern immediately after Homer was banned from the bar. Guy may have gotten the beatdown of a lifetime and been overshadowed by a dog's puffy tail, but he remains a fan favorite. Another example of a great one-episode character with little screen time is the totally in-your-face Roy from "The Itchy & Scratchy & Poochie Show." This entire episode was a screw you to the executives, who suggested the show add a cool new character, and Roy was the perfect example of the exec-approved addition. With his backward hat, indoor sunglasses, and attitude, it's clear that Roy is what *The Simpsons* has been missing for all these years.

Our second favorite one-timer is Lyle Lanley from the Conan O'Brien episode "Marge vs. the Monorail." Inspired by Harold Hill from *The Music Man*, the conman is voiced by Phil Hartman. Lanley is not only brilliantly funny, but also full of quotable lines like, "You know, a town with money's a little like the mule with a spinning wheel. No one knows how he got it, and danged if he knows how to use it!" Lanley is just one of the incredible one-time characters, but there's simply not enough space to list them all.

89 The Many Loves of Selma Bouvier

Few storylines within the world of *The Simpsons* are as consistent as Selma Bouvier eagerly awaiting a love to make her life whole. Contrary to her cynical sister Patty, Selma maintains an optimism for love that defies all odds. Think about it. If literally every person you've ever tried to shack up with either tried to kill you, tried to use you, or was the Comic Book Guy, you may lose interest in a having relationship. But not Selma.

The Simpsons writers' kindness toward Selma and her struggles are part of what make the show special. In the Season 3 episode "Black Widower," we're first fully introduced to her quest for a soulmate. "Aunt Selma has this crazy obsession about not dying alone, so in desperation she joined this prison pen pal program,"

Patty Bouvier explains. As a result, Sideshow Bob sashays into the Simpsons' lives right out of prison, and, though Bob claims he's reformed and well-intentioned, Bart suspects something else is afoot—and, of course, he's right. The wedding appears too quick, Bob's temper hangs by a thread, and when the family watches a (weirdly shared) video of Selma and Bob's honeymoon, a dispute with a hotel bellboy over the gas line sparks an idea in Bart to suss out the situation.

In the Season 7 episode "A Fish Called Selma," Selma upgrades from ex-con to ex-Hollywood star by marrying Troy McClure. While getting his license renewed at the DMV, a simple flirtation strikes an opportunistic romance, and soon Selma finds herself thrust into the limelight as McClure angles to save his career. Though a life with McClure would guarantee her some modicum of success, she eventually realizes that a loveless marriage can't be enough for her to simply check a box in life. When Selma realizes her romance with Troy is a sham, she knows she can't continue with it, even though it technically gives her "everything she wants."

This episode comes to us during the Oakley/Weinstein Years, the seasons Josh Weinstein and Bill Oakley co-ran the writers' room from Seasons 7–8. In several interviews Weinstein has declared his sympathy for Selma, identifying with her cosmic quest for belonging and allowing her story to not be one of unrequited repetition but rather of letting it have its own ups and downs similar to any other realistic love story in the world.

But because this show is still a comedy, there was still great fun to be had. Selma's romantic history ranges from Sideshow Bob and Troy McClure to Lionel Hutz and Disco Stu, Abraham Simpson, and, yes, even Fit Tony. In addition to that, she's dated Hans Moleman, Moe Szyslak, and, begrudgingly, Barney Gumble.

When Selma finally gets the opportunity to adopt a child from China (in the Season 16 episode "Goo Goo Gai Pan"), we get a sense of closure to her quest. After experiencing the onset of menopause, Selma decides that it's now or never to "not die alone" and so she sets her sights on adoption. When Marge suggests an international adoption, Selma sets off for China and finds Ling Bouvier, a prodigy in the making, is the perfect accompaniment to Selma's ongoing story.

90 *Simpsons* Pets

When you think of the Simpsons family, who pops in your head? Homer, Marge, Bart, Lisa, the baby Maggie. That's all of them, right? Wrong! You're forgetting about the damn pets. The Simpsons' pets are an intergral part of the family dynamic and have had many episodes and plotlines focused on them.

Santa's Little Helper, the family's former racing greyhound, is without a doubt the most notable pet of the series and had been the backbone of some of the sweetest Bart episodes. He made his debut in the series premiere "Simpsons Roasting on an Open Fire," when Homer and Bart adopt him as a Christmas present for the entire family. Santa's Little Helper's defining features are chewing newspapers, destroying furniture in the Simpsons household, and accuring credit card interest. He is also one of Bart's closest friends besides Milhouse, whom he treats much worse than Santa's Little Helper.

Santa's Little Helper is the focal point of many great episodes of the series, including "Bart's Dog Gets An F" (Season 2 in 1991), "Dog Of Death" (Season 3 in 1992), "Two Dozen And One Greyhounds" (Season 6 in 1995), and "The Canine Mutiny" (Season 8 in 1997).

Lisa's beloved black cat is Snowball II. Named after the Simpsons' first cat, Snowball I (who is referenced as having passed away in the series premiere but is never seen), Snowball has never taken the spotlight in an episode like Santa's Little Helper. She mostly appears in the background or for a quick gag. The heaviest role Snowball II plays into a plotline is in the episode "I, (Annoyed-Grunt)-Bot" (Season 15, 2004) when she (sadly) dies and is replaced by a series of other cats. Eventually, Lisa gets a fifth Snowball but decides to rename it Snowball II and never references the events of the episode again.

But the Simpsons family has owned many other animals besides the cat and the dog that have come and gone over the years. One of the most popular ones is Bart's beloved pet African elephant Stampy from the episode…wait for it…"Bart Gets An Elephant" (Season 5 in 1994). While on paper it sounds like a tired, we're-already-out-of-ideas premise, it's actually a hilarious script written by John Swartzwelder. Matt Groening considers it a quintessential episode.

Another one is Homer's pet pig Plopper (perhaps you know him better as "Spider-Pig"), who first appeared in *The Simpsons Movie*. Like Santa's Little Helper, Plopper also had a lasting impact on the family, as Homer's ownership of the pig causes the events that take place in the film. It is probably the first and only time in cinematic history that a silo full of pig waste can be called the MacGuffin of a movie.

Homer's bad luck with animal ownership was arguably foreshadowed in the episode "Girly Edition" (Season 9 in 1998), in which Homer adopts a helper monkey named Mojo, who quickly becomes susceptible to Homer's unhealthy lifestyle. He even delivers the best joke to come from an animal who ever appeared on the series: "PRAY…FOR…MOJO."

Santa's Little Helper had a litter of 25 puppies in the *101 Dalmatians* send-up "Two Dozen and One Greyhounds." In the episode Bart and Lisa have to foil Mr. Burns from turning the puppies into a fur coat. It features one of the best musical numbers of the entire series, "See My Vest." If the Simpsons didn't have any pets, we wouldn't have that song. So, thanks for that, guys.

The family got another dog in "The Canine Mutiny," where Bart gets a credit card in Santa's Little Helper's name (as "Santos L. Halper") and purchases a border collie wonder dog named Laddie, who can perform amazing tricks, do household chores, and use the toilet. The family eventually forgets about their old dog, and when repo men come to take back everything Bart purchased on the fraudulent credit card, he gives them Santa's Little Helper instead. Ridden with guilt, Bart goes out to get his dog back. It's a very sweet episode that perfectly showcases the bond that the Simpsons family has to their pets. Even when they aren't the best behaved, remember animals are a lot like people. Some of them act badly because they've had a hard life or have been mistreated. But, like people, some of them are just jerks.

Directors and What They Do

It's impossible to comment on the look and feel of any episode of *The Simpsons* without mentioning their directing staff. Since the show's first day of production, an incredible array of talented directors have come through and contributed to its style—often led by *Simpsons* supervising director David Silverman.

Most people don't consider directing animation to be akin to directing live-action, but the process is nearly identical—save for a few crucial details. In animation the "actors" are, of course, the characters themselves, but, more specifically, the "actors" are often code for storyboard artists. They sketch out what the characters are doing, what expressions to utilize, how to angle "the camera" to best tell the story. The director is the person who guides them down that path. In the early days of animation, when the form was looked at as more of an experiment than an expression of storytelling, there were no "camera angles." Instead, all attention was paid to getting the basics, resulting in a flat, two-dimensional loop of a figure evolving before the audience's very eyes. In today's modern animated world, every possible element is used to tell the best story and get the most laughs. Just as an actor can amp up a joke with a single head nod or pull on the audience's heartstrings with a solemn glance, so too can the animation of the show hinge on the animation direction.

Even though one could surmise that a finished script disallows further meddling, there's still plenty of visual wiggle room to work with once the animation directors get handed the torch. Everything from sign gags to bonus background characters are an open field for the animators to contribute their two cents. Most notably, key scenes that rely heavily on visuals conveying the joke are the moments where the directors most shine.

The storyboard stage is where the episode's planning takes place. Storyboard artists sketch out a rough assemblage of what the episode's going to look like, often referring to it as "the blueprint of the episode." In addition to the storyboard artists, a crew of other animators work together to design the props, backgrounds, and characters that are unique to the episode. In the beginning these drawings were done on paper, but they were later changed to "animatics" (sketches paired to voices for editing purposes) and, most recently, switched entirely to digital.

In the Season 4 episode "Homer's Triple Bypass," supervising director David Silverman personally constructed its pivotal scene. Due to the fact that the episode's subject was particularly grim (hovering over the premise of death and all), the staff appointed

Silverman to inject much needed humor. Silverman went all out, drawing humorous expressions for Homer to run through as he experiences a heart attack in Mr. Burns' office. Silverman soon became known for his eye for detail as well. For example, when Homer has an out-of-body experience in this same scene, his foot is still touching his body, signifying that he's not quite dead yet. Silverman holds the record for directing the most episodes of the show. He belongs to a tight crew of other supervising directors, including Gábor Csupó (one half of animation studio Klasky Csupó) and Mark Kirkland.

Supervising directors oversee the overall direction of the show and often guide episodic directors to get the nitty gritty details right on their particular script. Key episodic directors in the show's history include Jim Reardon ("Itchy & Scratchy & Marge," "Homer at the Bat," "Homer's Enemy," as well as the Pixar film *WALL-E*), Wes Archer ("Moaning Lisa," "Bart the Daredevil," "Who Shot Mr. Burns? Part Two," as well as *King of the Hill*), Mike B. Anderson ("Lisa the Iconoclast," "You Only Move Twice," "Homer's Phobia"), Susie Dietter ("Bart Gets Famous," "Bart's Girlfriend," "Radioactive Man," as well as *Futurama*).

The Simpsons Movie

The most surprising thing about *The Simpsons Movie* is that it took so long to exist. Any successful TV show gets looked at, especially one owned by a network that also has a major movie studio. Matt Groening said in interviews as early as 1991 that he assumed they'd make a movie when the TV show got canceled, but such a notion, of course, was killed by good ratings.

Several film ideas came and went. Then 20th Century Fox officially greenlit the project in 1997, but it was several years before writing began. The plot that the writing team settled on was a pitch from Groening, which centered on Springfield's water supply getting ruined by pig feces.

The script went through more than 150 rewrites and was briefly even a musical. Major changes occurred until very late in the process. Notably, the prophecy from Grampa originally came from Marge, but the writers thought it was too dark to have the family to ignore their mom falling over in church and speaking in tongues—whereas ignoring Grampa seemed light and fun.

Changes also led to cutting enough cameos to fill an A-list party, including not using Minnie Driver, Edward Norton, Isla Fisher, Erin Brockovich, Kelsey Grammer, and a song by Dave Stewart of the Eurythmics.

Notable celebs not cut from the film were characters played by Albert Brooks and Joe Mantegna plus as-themselves appearances by Tom Hanks and Green Day. The team just happened to be looking for a band to make an appearance and talk about the environment when a letter arrived from Green Day's management, saying they wanted to be involved in the show. As a thank you, the writing staff depicted the band drowning in sewage.

As the release neared, the staff remained incredibly secretive about the plot. After each table reading, the producers personally shredded the scripts. Writers leaked fake plot details to the press, including a major accident at the nuclear plant and Bart losing his virginity. (Although the latter wasn't at all related to the film, Bart's penis does have a surprising amount of screen time.)

The marketing avoided revealing much plot. Instead they focused on showing the same jokes so many times that you'd be forgiven for thinking the movie was going to be 90 percent Homer making up songs about Spider-Pig. For the premier a contest was held pitting the different Springfields around the U.S. in an online vote, and the winning city would get the first screening. After originally being left off the list, tiny Springfield, Vermont, lobbied to be included and then—driven by state pride and a lot of local TV coverage—won the contest with more than 15,000 votes. It was an impressive feat for a town of just 9,000 people.

A successful cartoon doesn't guarantee a good movie, just ask the people who made *The Flintstones* or *The Last Airbender* or *Garfield* or *Smurfs* or *Alvin and the Chipmunks* or *Transformers*... Fortunately, it is. It's really good. Reviews were generally positive. Noted film critic Roger Ebert said that, though the plot was a little thin, it was a fun and funny movie. It was also a big hit with fans, pulling in more than $500 million at the box office.

It was also a big hit inside our hearts. Marge and Homer's relationship is portrayed with incredible depth. (If you have the ability to feel human feelings, Marge's video should bring you to tears.) And it's packed with funny gags and fan service, using the large format to great effect for both the sequence with Bart's penis and the torch-bearing crowd scene. Not all of it holds up incredibly well—the scenes with Homer and the big-boobed Eskimo, for example. And president Arnold Schwarzenegger was a funny idea in 2007 that now seems too close to the reality of having a former *Apprentice* star as a national leader.

During the ending credits, Maggie says "sequel." That line and FOX's bottom line both indicate a sequel is inevitable. That idea is a little terrifying, as many fans worry about the team blowing it, but James L. Brooks has publicly stated that they're not actively working on it because they're pretty busy, so hopefully that thing that kept everybody from rushing into a first film will keep them from rushing into another.

93 Musical Guests

The Simpsons has long been known for its original musical numbers (like the monorail song and *Planet of the Apes, The Musical*), but every once in a while, a musician/band will appear as Springfield versions of themselves. The first musical guests didn't appear until Season 2, but they were good ones: Tony Bennett sang an ode to Capital City in "Dancin' Homer," and Ringo Starr played himself responding to Marge's fan mail in "Brush with Greatness." Ringo would be the first of three Beatles to make appearances on the show. George Harrison leaned out of a car window in "Homer's Barbershop Quartet," and Paul McCartney provided Lisa with sage advice in "Lisa the Vegetarian." John Lennon, unfortunately, was murdered in 1980, nine years before *The Simpsons* premiered.

Perhaps the most notable cameo by a musician came in the Season 3 episode "Stark Raving Dad," wherein Homer is sent to a mental institution and shares a room with a large, white man who believes he is Michael Jackson. "The King of Pop," himself, was a fan of *The Simpsons* and had personally called Matt Groening to ask for a guest spot. Due to contractual reasons, Jackson was credited as "John Jay Smith," and his involvement in the episode wasn't confirmed until years later. To further the confusion, he also stipulated that he would not sing (he wanted to play a joke on his family), so soundalike Kipp Lennon was brought in to perform all the musical numbers. You may also remember Lennon from his other performances on the show, including the Betty Ford musical number "I'm Checking In" from "The City of New York vs. Homer Simpson" episode and the *Cheers* theme song parody in "Flaming Moe's."

Speaking of "Flaming Moe's," Aerosmith was the first band to make an appearance on the show, and Hank Azaria flew to Boston to record all his lines as Moe and help the band with theirs. To play over the credits, Aerosmith also recorded a shortened version of "Young Lust." One of the best cameos from a musician actually contained no music at all. In the ninth episode of Season 8 called "El Viaje Misterioso de Nuestro Jomer" (aka "The Mysterious Voyage of Homer"), Johnny Cash lent his voice as Homer's spirit guide, a talking coyote. Bob Dylan had also been asked to voice the coyote but ultimately turned the role down. Dylan was previously asked to play himself in the Season 7 episode "Homerpalooza" but turned that down as well.

In "Homerpalooza" the producers aimed to bring in artists to represent several genres: hip-hop (Cypress Hill), alternative rock (Smashing Pumpkins and Sonic Youth), and classic rock (Peter Frampton). Artists who turned down the chance to appear included Neil Young, Pearl Jam, Courtney Love, and, of course, Dylan. In a just world, Dylan's Nobel Prize would be rescinded.

Another notable music episode "How I Spent My Strummer Vacation" features Homer attending a Rock and Roll Fantasy Camp led by Mick Jagger, Keith Richards, Elvis Costello, Lenny Kravitz, Brian Setzer, and the late, great Tom Petty. We could write an entire separate book about the incredible musical guests who have appeared on *The Simpsons*. The big names include Ramones, James Brown, Sting, Spinal Tap, Tom Jones, Barry White, David Crosby, Bette Midler, Robert Goulet, James Taylor, Tito Puente, Paul Anka, Dolly Parton, Elton John, R.E.M., Willie Nelson, The Who, and The Red Hot Chili Peppers.

Crossover Episodes

The Simpsons has often been a show about making shows, including the maddening process of appeasing humorless execs, the futile efforts to cater to superfans, and the skewering of television's self-congratulatory nature. This last concept couldn't be more blatantly expressed than in the crossover episode.

Crossovers are episodes in which two pre-existing fictional properties collide. Though they have existed for more than a century (1829's *Don Juan und Faust* and 1943's *Frankenstein Meets the Wolf Man*, for example), they didn't really pick up steam until 1970s television. Audiences began to see an onslaught of specials such as *The ABC Saturday Superstar Movie* where Looney Tunes characters would freely fraternize with Filmation creations in *Daffy Duck and Porky Pig Meet the Groovie Ghoulies.*

When *The Simpsons* did their own crossovers, they treated them with equal prodding and praising for the TV tradition. Sure, it may feel like a forced obligation to appease superfans of the two shows, but there could still be a real story in there. Here is a list of the biggest fan favorite crossovers the show has ever done:

"A Star Is Burns"

In perhaps the most natural crossover of all, *The Simpsons*' own Al Jean and Mike Reiss' cult hit creation, *The Critic*, slams into Springfield for its first annual film festival. At the time of this episode's 1995 airing, *The Critic*'s future was murky. This episode was devised as a way to leverage the show out of a ratings slump (and live out writers' fantasies of Jay Sherman going toe-to-toe with Homer in a belching slob battle). Though it didn't necessarily work

(*The Critic* was cancelled shortly after), this episode stands firmly as the pinnacle of cross-promotional episodes done right.

"The Springfield Files"

When an alien encounter rattles Springfield, the natural solution is to bring in the paranormal big guns: Agent Mulder and Agent Scully (voiced respectively by David Duchovny and Gillian Anderson). The episode debuted at the peak popularity of *The X-Files* and was a ratings boom for parent network FOX. In the episode Homer thinks he sees alien life, which swoops the town into a supernatural spectacle. It's later discovered that the alien was just Mr. Burns wandering the night, glowing from his nightly skin treatments. "The Springfield Files" gets an added boost of crossover power by also featuring a stoic hot dog-eating Leonard Nimoy, warning us to "keep watching the skies."

"Simpsorama"

To fans, it was inevitable. For creator Matt Groening, it was only natural. Groening's other pet project, *Futurama*, smashes into Springfield and adds a splash of sci-fi. When radioactive ooze collides with a time capsule in the Springfield town square, the answer could only be real actual time travel from the flunkiest member of the flunkiest crew of future miscreants. Of course, this could only be Bender, and, of course, he instantly becomes Homer's newest drinking buddy. From there, the episode goes predictably and playfully off the rails, landing the Simpsons family at *Futurama*'s own Planet Express and living it up between the two similar-yet-different worlds of Groening's creation.

"The Simpsons Guy"

Perhaps the most infamous of all: Homer finally meets Peter Griffin. Though technically an episode of *Family Guy*, this television event was so notable and meaty that it was expanded into a whopping 45 minutes. In the episode the Griffins shack up with the Simpsons after their car is stolen near Springfield city limits, and soon worlds collide. Bart shows Stewie how to sling-shot, Lisa tries to tap into Meg's inner talents, but when Homer discovers Peter Griffin's beloved Pawtucket Ale is nothing more than a watered-down Duff rip-off, friendly spirits between the two shows are soon shattered.

Meme'd Hams

The Simpsons has always had an interesting relationship with Internet culture. Becoming popular in the early days of widespread access to the web, it was one of the first shows to be quickly picked apart online by an adoring legion of nerds. This first generation of fandom was known for obsessive list making, ranking, transcribing, and cataloguing every granular detail of the show, which led to the creators poking (mostly) good natured fun at its fans.

The rise of social media, however, has led to a boom of an entirely different set of fans: meme creators. Creatively obsessive, these artists have created thousands upon thousands of videos, songs, art, fan edits, and other endeavors that both celebrate and deconstruct their favorite show.

This new wave of memes is possible largely due to the creation of Frinkiac, which has literally every single frame and line of *The Simpsons* uploaded and cataloged for easy searchability! That is a certifiably *insane* thing to do, and the Internet is a better place for it, thanks to creators Paul Kehrer, Sean Schulte, and Allie Young. Due to the fact that up until recently *The Simpsons* wasn't easily streamable or available for purchase online, you'd have to do a ton of work just to upload that screen grab of Jasper lovingly clutching a moon pie to your Tumblr, which is downright criminal. The creators of Frinkiac did all the work and passed the sabings on to us (the b stands for bargain, Dr. Nick). If *The Simpsons* is the Internet's collective pop culture memory, then Frinkiac is the *Black Mirror* episode that allows us to scan through literally 30 years of jokes with zero negative consequences.

Twitter accounts such as @simpscreens, which posts a random screengrab from *The Simpsons* every 30 minutes, take a look at the macro via the micro. The screengrabs they post aren't big, flashy moments that we all remember. They're generally shots from the middle of animation cycles or of strange off-model poses. Because of how the eye processes information, these bits of animation that would normally be impossible to see (without going frame by frame like a total nerdlinger) are put front and center. They're interesting both because they can often be funny and also force the Twitter user to think about how much work goes into any given episode of *The Simpsons*, as any single shot is the result of hundreds of hours of work for hundreds of different people. The fact that this is an automated process adds another layer, as it removes any possibility of the human hand guiding it toward a more classically interesting shot.

The most recent *Simpsons* meme to have exploded is the revival and deconstruction of the "Skinner & The Superintendent" part of "22 Short Films About Springfield," aka Steamed Hams. This remix meme follows in the footsteps of the Internet's bizarre obsession with chopping and screwing Jerry Seinfeld's seminal 2007 *Bee Movie* or remixing/re-tuning "All-Star" by Smash Mouth. The format is simple, but the results range from delightfully silly to incomprehensibly weird. The meme states: "It's steamed hams, but" And the "but" could be followed by literally anything. It could be a joke like "but every time Skinner lies, he descends 7 percent more into the Netherworld," or an impressive stylistic re-cutting that turns Steamed Hams into a scene from the PS1 classic *Metal Gear Solid*.

The Steamed Hams meme is also home to some of the most impressive, if questionably used, displays of talent by creative fans of *The Simpsons*. A personal favorite is "Steamed Hams But It's A Piano Dub" by YouTube musician Finn M-K, who scored the entire scene, creating a melody for every spoken word, action, and sound effect, and it still manages to be shockingly catchy.

Steamed Hams finally went full circle when an actual creator joined in. Former executive producer of *The Simpsons*, Bill Oakley, tweeted: "Steamed Hams, but it's the original first draft in a thread," followed by screen grabs of a shockingly unchanged script, and the Internet collectively lost its mind.

96 Controversial Moments

You don't become the world's longest running animated show without making some enemies. From upsetting the president to offending entire countries, it seems *The Simpsons* has perfected the art of getting people angry. Of the things the show has done to upset people, some of the most notable are: having Bart be a bad role model, perpetuating a harmful stereotype (Apu and Brazil), perpetuating a not-so-bad stereotype (Australia), killing off a classic character (Maude), killing off a new character (Frank Grimes), changing characters' timelines (Homer and Marge), and changing a character's background altogether (Principal Skinner). Although we can look back on some of the instances in which *The Simpsons* ruffled feathers and realize they were strokes of genius or acts of boundary pushing, there are other moments that remind us that even the best show with an incredible, well-meaning staff can make and learn from their own mistakes.

On the heavier side of the controversies lie the political and sociological missteps, which affected entire groups of people. It's not fun nor particularly enjoyable to talk about these matters when we could just skip straight to how mad people got about Grimesy despite it being a perfect episode of television. But it's important to not deny the problematic moments and approach them with honesty and, when applicable, humor. Remember the time in which the show started and that *The Simpsons* has often held up a mirror to society, reflecting and often providing commentary on the good and the bad.

In many ways, *The Simpsons* was ahead of its time, especially in its fight for equality, or at least, the fight against inequality. Compared to other shows of the era, *The Simpsons* cast was particularly diverse in its characters' religion, ethnicity, and sexuality. In the award-winning and critically acclaimed episode "Homer's Phobia," Homer confronts his systemic homophobia when he realizes his new friend John (John Waters) is gay. When the episode aired in 1996, Homer was representative of many straight Americans who had not had many knowing encounters with openly gay people. John's affable and sincere personality helped Homer, who again represented those not-always-progressive-middle-Americans, take his homophobia to task and expand his perspective for the better. It's crazy to think that a show that could introduce audiences to such a polarizing topic (at the time) with such nuance and affection would years later make jokes where transpeople were the punch line. Although the show was on the same page as society back then (meaning, the show wasn't more transphobic than other sitcoms or late-night shows), we argue that it was un-*Simpsons* like to miss the mark so disappointingly.

On the lighter side of the controversies...how about the then-president of the United States wanting our country to be less like

MATT GROENING

Some fans ignore this character's controversial backstory, preferring not to think that Seymour Skinner ever was Armin Tamzarian. (Fox/Photofest © & Fox)

The Simpsons and more like the boring ass Waltons? Do you see a book called *100 Things Waltons Fans Must Know and Do Before They Die?* To George H.W. Bush's credit, however, the Waltons never killed off a character with a shirt cannon like *The Simpsons* did to Maude Flanders in "Alone Again, Natura-Diddily." Fans love to debate the show's jump-the-shark moment, and whether you think that was it, Maude's death, which followed a payment dispute involving the incredible voice actress Maggie Roswell, was downright cruel to fans and the character. Many never even saw this episode because they stopped watching after the Armin Tamzarian controversy of "The Principal and the Pauper."

Whether the controversial moments turned you off or made you laugh, we encourage viewers to revisit the episodes and see how they stand the test of time. Will jokes that made us laugh 10 years ago make us cringe today? Conversely, could anyone see Bart as anything other than a sweet and normal kid by today's standards? Let these be a mini-history lesson in the way comedy adapts over time.

97 Product Tie-Ins

Whether you're bereft without your Butterfinger BB's or you crave Krusty O's nightly, there's a *Simpsons* promotional tie-in product for everyone. Within the spirit of *The Simpsons* merch world domination that sparked with the Bart hell-raiser era (and later gave way to the Bootleg Bart trend), product tie-ins featuring characters from *The Simpsons* were a natural evolution. Over the years *The Simpsons* have slapped their silly selves onto heaps of products from hair gel to Halloween masks, but few products held enough weight in *The Simpsons* world to have their own commercials. Cue the ad campaigns that chronicled our youth and the commercials that'll never quite go away. Here is a list of the greatest tie-ins that either tortured us or tantalized our taste buds:

Butterfinger BB's

The Simpsons has been featured in a whopping 150 commercials for the candy bar since 1988. Most spots followed a similar story: Homer's mouth is watering over the premise of pigging out on the candy, but Bart is just too quick for him. In 1999 Bart's catch-phrase was changed to from "Nobody better lay a finger on my Butterfinger" to "Bite my Butterfinger" and then "Nothing like a Butterfinger!" The campaign's seen the rise and fall of several Butterfinger products, most notably butterfinger BB's, which were a pellet-sized version of the regular snack.

Burger King

In 1990 Burger Kings around this great nation offered a set of toys simply titled, "Meet the Simpsons." This would spark a decades-long relationship between the show and the fast food giant, leading to promotional toy tie-ins for their episode, "Call of the Simpsons," in which each family member was decked in camping gear. Later in 1992 Simpsons wheelie toys were offered, and each character had a personality-specific prop. Lisa rode high on her sax, Bart raced off on his skateboard, Marge flew…on her laundry basket? (Author's note: yes, seriously, a laundry basket.) Most of the time, these product tie-ins defied logic or the sensibility of the show but catered more to fast food product culture. Most notable is how many commercials declare, "The Simpsons are *now* at Burger King!" An overlooked but amusing detail is that Lisa was featured eating Burger King meat, even though she's been a vegetarian since Season 7.

Intel

"Inside Homer's Smarter Brain" was a spot created in 2008 in conjunction with Intel Inside. One of the commercials features doctors operating on Homer as part of "their greatest challenge." If they can get the world's dumbest man to increase his knowledge through Intel, then, surely, Intel could save the world from intellectual incompetence. The commercial decried: "Now anyone can have all the brain power they want!" It wrapped up with a hyperintelligent Homer delivering a college lecture.

CC's Chips

Because *The Simpsons* is a global brand, their likeness has been lent to international chains as well. Most notable is Australia's own CC's Chips, which has featured the family in promos since 1998. The premise of each spot would more or less follow a similar structure to the Butterfinger ads: Homer would pine for the CC's Chips, Bart would steal them from him, and madness would ensue. Most often Bart would goad Homer into performing some kind of dare, ranging from running through the power plant naked to escaping a water tank while constrained by a straitjacket.

Church's Chicken and Kentucky Fried Chicken

Somewhat bafflingly, *The Simpsons* leant their likeness to competing fast food chicken chains throughout the 1990s and early 2000s. Kentucky Fried Chicken first began to feature the family in commercials in 1993. The commercial was titled "The Big Steal." Though the spots only played in Canada and Australia, they notoriously awarded customers a free 7-UP whenever they purchased a 15-piece bucket of chicken. Around that same time, the Church's Chicken commercials began to play in America. The first spot features the family enjoying a picnic with Church's Chicken as the main entree, but when Homer's fingers are too sticky from the BBQ sauce to hand back Kearney's lost football, he's chased across the park until it's wrested free. It should be noted that vegetarian Lisa is chowing down on chicken just as much as her family—similar to the Burger King ads.

C.C. Lemon

Another international ad for the animated family features Japanese soda C.C. Lemon and perhaps is the most mystifying of all. The commercial begins as if it's a new episode of the show. The title card emerges from the clouds, but it has the added text of "C.C. Lemon." We're then zipped to the Springfield football stadium, where Homer attempts to get the attention of a C.C. Lemon vendor. As the soda's passed from vendor to Lisa to Bart to Marge, they all take a long swig of the soda, leaving Homer with a single drop and an empty bottle. As he slurps it back, he soon realizes he's on the stadium's Jumbotron, collapsing into an embarrassed grin. What's interesting about this ad—in comparison to its American counterparts—is the lack of a fleshed-out story. Where the Butterfinger and Burger King ads play out as almost their own sub-genre of short film, the C.C. Lemon's to-the-point expediency almost suggests that the very fact that the Simpsons were telling you to buy this product was good enough. We, though, think it would be more effective if they had included a Mr. Sparkle reference.

98 Explore the DVDs

For a sweet little period of time, DVDs with bonus features were everything to pop-culture obsessives. Commentaries, deleted scenes, and other extra features made the wait for a movie or show to come on DVD a much-anticipated event. Now, before we get into the gold on each disc, we should point out that *all* of the episodes are now on FXX, and many of them include commentary. So…why would you want to explore the DVDs instead of just pop open an app and watch to your heart's content? Well, there's something authentic and original about the DVD experience that will provide its own joys.

The commentary (originally recorded for the DVDs) ranges from insightful to hysterical and usually is a bit of both. Each episode usually has the writer, director, a voice actor, and possibly Matt Groening, and you feel like you are in the room with them. It's evident that the commentaries were as enjoyable to record as they are to listen to. And by doing the latter, you will have learned some great nuggets like "Kamp Krusty" was originally going to be a movie, but the writers had a hard time stretching it out into an episode, let alone a feature. In "Another Simpsons Clip Show," Matt Groening, David Mirkin, and David Silverman walk you through the process of making an episode of the show. In "New Kid on the Block," Conan O'Brien regales us with tangential stories, including how Don Rickles was supposed to be a guest star.

In addition to the commentary, the DVDs had an impressive collection of bonus features. There were outtakes, animatics, clips from documentaries, *Tracey Ullman Show* shorts, production sketches, original scripts, music videos, award show moments (Nancy dressed as Bart at the American Music Awards, and

The Simpsons were animated on stage at the Emmy Awards), Butterfinger commercials, and more. The DVDs are jam-packed with trivia, insight, and fun features that could make you the most knowledgeable of fans.

Now that you know what's inside, let's talk about the outside. The cases for the first five seasons are simplistic, beautiful, and share a cohesive theme. Each has a unique colored background and the iconic rabbit ear TV with the Simpsons clan doing their thing on the couch. They're different yet similar enough for it to feel like a proper collection. Seasons 4 and 5 went out on a limb and updated the TV so it wouldn't have rabbit ears any more.

It's important to remember that many people had elected to have the DVDs sent to them as soon as they were released, and you wouldn't know what the DVD would look like until it came to your house or you picked it up at the store. Therefore, when the Season 6 DVD came out, many fans were taken aback to see a drastic change had been made. Not only was the theme thrown out the window in its entirety, the shape of the box was completely disregarded. You can't even call it a box because there was not a square corner in sight. For Seasons 6–10, the DVDs were released in the form of a Simpsons head. Except for the Marge DVD, each Simpsons head had "The Simpsons" written in red on their forehead, making it appear as though someone had carved into their yellow flesh a la "Die, Bart, Die."

The reason the shift in design was upsetting to many fans wasn't because they feared change, but because it was not practical for collectors who wanted to display their DVDs on a shelf. The awkward, clunky head shape made it cumbersome to do so. The creators or someone on the team clearly knew their audience. Inside the head-shaped box was a note that said, "For all those that fear change…For all those anal-retentive nerds who like their DVD boxes to line up perfectly on the shelf…For all those who dislike storing their digital media inside a hallowed-out human head, have we got a deal for you! Just call [redacted] for a very derivative, old-style, just-like-before box with almost nothing new or creative to annoy or terrify you. Enjoy!"

Music

There's a song on *The Simpsons* album *Go Simpsonic* called "Blessed be the Guy That Bonds (*McBain* end credits)." Like most tracks on these show albums, its running time is minuscule compared to a normal full-fledged pop song. On the record's staggering 53 tracks, it's a blink-and-you-miss-it moment waiting to happen. What's incredible about "Blessed be the Guy That Bonds" is that despite the fact that its fate was to be featured only during the end credits is it's fully produced and profoundly funny. To composer Alf Clausen, the same effort and energy would be applied to the opening credits as to the end. It didn't matter if the song played for two seconds or 20; it needed to be a masterpiece. Sure, several TV shows have incorporated musical comedy, but there's something profoundly distinct about *The Simpsons'* approach. The music within the show balances perfectly between cinematic flourishes and full fake musical numbers.

One of the most recognizable theme songs in TV history was originally composed by Danny Elfman and took a reported three days, two hours, 48 minutes, and 19 seconds to create.

Throughout the show's run, the theme song has been occasionally altered to fit the tone of the show to play over the end credits. For the Season 7 episode "Who Shot Mr. Burns?", an African/Cuban version of the song plays over the end credits. During the course of its run, an "Australian version," a *Hill Street Blues* version, and even a *It's a Mad Mad Mad Mad World* version has been written and performed.

But it's the extra songs that forge a personalized path, the ones that no one would expect, the kind that stick with you long after they originally aired. When Apu gets fired from the Kwik-E-Mart and shows up on the Simpsons' doorstep, his sorrow soon turns to song with "Who Needs the Kwik-E-Mart?" It's a melody steeped in the style of a classic Broadway song.

Even their song parodies are decidedly original. When Mr. Burns sings "See My Vest" (to the tune of *Beauty and the Beast's* "Be My Guest"), it makes the dark topic of slaughtering for style snappy and silly. Lyrics include: "Like my loafers? Former gophers. It was that, or skin my chauffeurs."

Then there's the *Simpsons'* original musicals themselves. "Kickin' It: A Musical Journey Through the Betty Ford Center" is a fully-fledged play over the course of a minute and forty-three seconds. "The Garbage Man Can" is a blissfully buoyant ode to *Willy Wonka*. The crown jewel is, of course, the Mary Poppins-skewering episode "Simpsoncalifragilisticexpiala(D'oh)cious," where songs like, "Cut Every Corner," "A Boozehound Named Barney," and "Happy Just the Way We Are" poke fun at the Disney classic over the course of 22 minutes.

In the Season 4 episode "Krusty Gets Kancelled," Krusty does a heart-wrenching rendition of Stephen Sondheim's "Send in the Clowns" from the musical, *A Little Night Music*. Sure, the fact that he's a clown may make a pretty direct case for why they chose this song, but let's not forget this is an animated comedy show. They're not repping old-school Sondheim on *South Park*.

100 Follow the Writers on Twitter

On August 21, 2014, a remarkable thing happened that changed the course of history. At 7:00 AM that morning until 8:30 PM on September 1, FXX aired every single episode of *The Simpsons* in order, and *Simpsons* fans all over the world united. Thanks to reruns, illegal downloads, and DVDs (some of which were infuriatingly head-shaped), re-watching episodes after they aired has never been a difficult feat. Yet the ability to watch every episode ever at the same time as other fans was magical, especially for fans who have mostly just streamed the show. During the marathon fans used the hashtag #EverySimpsonsEver to live tweet episodes and create a community to connect over their love of the best show of all time.

The community experience wasn't just for the fans. The most exciting part of the marathon for many was seeing the show's writers and voice actors join in on the conversation, sharing behind-the-scenes moments from their years on *The Simpsons*. Some writers, like Jon Vitti, created an account solely to partake in the FXX discussions. Others are highly active on Twitter and should be followed immediately. Whether they're sharing insight of their time on the show or giving theories on how to save McDonald's, the following accounts are really funny. (Duh, they wrote on *The Simpsons*.)

Front and center is Josh Weinstein (@JoshStrangehill), who has provided fans with insight and never-before-seen scenes that were from scripts. The DVD commentary hadn't even mentioned them. Josh posted deleted moments, including a one-page Moleman story from "22 Short Films about Springfield," a scene in which Bart and Skinner go to a carnival in "Sweet Seymour Skinner's Baadasss

Song," and what happened to Kirk Van Houten after he was fired from the Cracker Factory as written in Steve Tompkin's first draft. (Turns out seagulls were supposed to take his crackers, and Kirk was going to scream: "My severance package.")

Fans who follow Josh will also benefit from his well-curated retweets, which share further information like this pearl from TV writer Jim Dauterive: "Nerd fact. The Simpsons invented this clean, easy to read script formatting with single-spaced action, double-spaced dialogue and boldfaced slug lines. Greg Daniels brought it over to King of the Hill. It naturally made its way to Bob's Burgers. Yet another legacy of the Simpsons." We are also big fans of his non-*Simpsons* tweets, including his frequent pictures of odd signage like the "Stairwell to Walgreens" sign, which he refers to as his favorite Led Zeppelin song.

Josh's then-writing partner and fellow showrunner Bill Oakley (@ThatOakley) shared copious commentary during the FXX Marathon, using references from the show to get political. During the 2016 election, he tweeted: "Please don't compare Sideshow Bob's term as Mayor to Donald Trump's term as President. Sideshow Bob is less evil and much MUCH smarter," and the deeply wise, "We are all Superintendent Chalmers now, the last lone sane ones surrounded by a sea of fools, shysters, and Wiggums." Bill also turned heads for his business tip for McDonald's. His three-point plan of "INNOVATION, QUALITY, and NOSTALGIA" was detailed in a series of tweets that we can't believe were given away for free.

Simpsons executive producer Matt Selman (@MattSelman) co-hosted the FXX Simpsons Marathon Livefeed with Ben Schwartz, and special guests (including many of the best writers of *The Simpsons*) provided never-before-heard stories and feedback on episodes to help kick off the marathon. He's used his account to share advice from the late, great unsung hero of *The Simpsons*, writing "Essential advice to writers from the late Sam Simon: 'Love your characters'" and has posted pictures of celebrities at table reads from upcoming cameos. After the news that Disney would be purchasing FOX, he turned to Twitter to reveal another *Simpsons* predicted the future moment with a screenshot of the 20th Century Fox sign and the words, "A division of Walt Disney Co" underneath.

For pure laughs and insight on humanity, follow Tim Long (@MrTimLong). He tweeted: "When comedians die, why does everyone tell them to 'make God laugh'? You wouldn't order a dead carpenter to 'make God some bookshelves.'" Mike Scully (@ScullyMIke) tweeted: "Would love to do a Trump family sitcom, but would have to make up a character to be 'the smart one.'" For the deeply irreverent and sometimes darker humor, follow Dana Gould (@DanaGould), who joked: "When I die, I'd like my remains scattered along the beach. That said, I do not want to be cremated."

See beautiful early sketches and gain insight into the artistic side of *The Simpsons'* origin by following the incredibly gifted David Silverman (@Tubatron), who has posted the original sketches for Homer's heart attack and early character design sketches from *The Tracey Ullman Show*. You can find preliminary ideas for Frank Grimes' character design from a writers' retreat and videos of his vaudevillian band, in which he plays a flaming tuba. We recommend scrolling through Vitti's old tweets, and following John Swartzwelder, whose entire timeline is quotes from his books.

Acknowledgments

Several references helped in research for this book, including AV Club, *Los Angeles Times*, *Entertainment Weekly*, Independent.co.uk, Globeandmail.com, *Simpsons World: Ultimate Simpsons Guide*, Simpsons.wikia, my giant hand, Vox, and years upon years of reruns.

Thank you to our respective parents (Travis Goertz, Victoria Lynn, Tim Prescott, and Suzanne Prescott) who let us watch *The Simpsons* as kids and to the many friends we tricked into helping us write this book, including Bill Morrison, Nick Ciarelli, Casey Boyd, Joe Kwaczala, Sam Wiles, Alison Stevenson, Brandon Beck, Steven Wilber, Joe McAdam, Alex Falcone, and Andrew Hatfield.

Thank you to everyone who has ever worked on *The Simpsons*, but especially Bill Oakley and Josh Weinstein.

Thank you to Julia's husband, Mike Mayfield, whose patience and kindness is unparalleled, especially considering 80 percent of their relationship involves him sitting through deep-cut references from *The Simpsons* that he doesn't understand. Thank you to the wizards at Wikipedia, whose drull and straightforward synopsis of *The Simpsons* themes always bring us joy.

Thank you to our editor Jeff Fedotin, who fixed our typos, and publisher, Triumph Books, who asked us to write about the greatest show in the world.

CPSIA information can be obtained
at www.ICGtesting.com
Printed in the USA
LVHW081106020922
727314LV00010B/247

9 781629 375311